Sustainable Development and Poverty Alleviation in Sub-Saharan Africa

The Case of Botswana

Charles Perrings
Professor of Environmental Economics and Environmental Management
University of York

Foreword by Iftikhar Ahmed

A study prepared for the International Labour Office

SUSTAINABLE DEVELOPMENT AND POVERTY ALLEVIATION IN SUB-SAHARAN AFRICA

ILO STUDIES SERIES

The ILO's work in the field of employment aims to encourage and assist member-states to adopt and implement policies and programmes designed to promote full, productive and freely chosen employment and to reduce poverty.

In response to the pressing challenges of the 1990s, including the rapidly growing interdependence of national economies, increasing reliance on market mechanisms, technological innovation and environmental concerns, the ILO has refocused its work on employment. Specific attention is now devoted to assessing the impact of the above challenges on employment, migratory pressures, unemployment and poverty, examining ways of coping with them and understanding the linkages between macro- and micro-economic policies. Greater emphasis is put on policy-oriented research and technical advisory services. This is to ensure a swift response to requests for assistance, further enhanced through the worldwide network of fourteen ILO multidisciplinary advisory teams.

Through these activities the ILO is helping national authorities and social partners to take advantage of the opportunities created by current global changes, so as to achieve more and better employment. They also provide a basis for continuing dialogue with other international organizations on employment and the social dimensions of growth and development in the world economy.

This publication is an outcome of such work, and is intended to disseminate information that will be of relevance to a variety of countries and to a wide audience.

First published in Great Britain 1996 by
MACMILLAN PRESS LTD
Houndmills, Basingstoke, Hampshire RG21 6XS
and London
Companies and representatives
throughout the world

A catalogue record for this book is available
from the British Library.

ISBN 0–333–64671–1

First published in the United States of America 1996 by
ST. MARTIN'S PRESS, INC.,
Scholarly and Reference Division,
175 Fifth Avenue,
New York, N.Y. 10010

ISBN 0–312–12833–9

Library of Congress Cataloging-in-Publication Data
Perrings, Charles.
Sustainable development and poverty alleviation in sub-Saharan
Africa : The case of Botswana / Charles Perrings.
p. cm.— (Series of ILO studies)
Includes bibliographical references and index.
ISBN 0–312–12833–9 (cloth)
1. Sustainable development—Botswana—Case studies. 2. Poverty-
-Botswana—Case studies. 3. Economic assistance, Domestic-
-Botswana—Case studies. I. Title. II. Series: ILO series.
HC930.Z9E57 1996
338.96883—dc20
95–33988
CIP

© International Labour Organisation 1996

10 9 8 7 6 5 4 3 2 1
05 04 03 02 01 00 99 98 97 96

Printed and bound in Great Britain by
Antony Rowe Ltd, Chippenham, Wiltshire

Contents

Contents

List of Tables

List of Figures

List of Abbreviations

ACP	African, Caribbean and Pacific
ALDEP	Arable Lands Development Programme
ARAP	Accelerated Rainfed Arable Programme
ARB	Agricultural Resources Board
BAMB	Botswana Agricultural Marketing Board
BMC	Botswana Meat Commission
BNCS	Botswana National Conservation Strategy
CSO	Central Statistics Office
DRC	Domestic Resource Cost
DRP	Drought Relief Programme
EEC	European Economic Community
EIA	Environmental Impact Assessment
FAP	Financial Assistance Policy
GCM	Global Circulation Model
GDP	Gross Domestic Product
GNP	Gross National Product
HIES	Household Income and Expenditure Survey
IPCC	Intergovernmental Panel on Climate Change
LBRP	Labour Based Relief Programme
MFDP	Ministry of Finance and Development Planning
NDB	National Development Bank
PDL	Poverty Datum Line
SACU	Southern African Customs Union
SADCC	Southern African Development Coordination Conference
SAM	Social Accounting Matrix
SBF	Small Business Fund
SLOCA	Services to Livestock Owners in Communal Areas
TLGP	Tribal Lands Grazing Policy
UN	United Nations
UNDP	United Nations Development Programme
WMA	Wildlife Management Area
WRI	World Resources Institute

Foreword

Despite frequent debates there is as yet little agreement or under-standing of the concept of sustainable development and the means to translate it into concrete action. The Rio Conference and Agenda 21 adopted by the Conference have paved the way for further analysis and research, particularly as they relate to the problems facing the developing countries. Agenda 21 has set the attainment of sustainable livelihoods and poverty alleviation in developing countries as an important goal of sustainable development.

The study by Charles Perrings of the University of York, United Kingdom, deals with important conceptual and policy issues relating to sustainable livelihoods in Sub-Saharan Africa. What are the factors contributing to the impoverishment of rural households and the degradation of rural environments in this region? The persistently poor performance of the agricultural sector is directly associated with increasing pressure on grazing, arable and forest resources. While this is often ascribed to rapid population growth, other factors – including fiscal, price and incomes policies altering the incentives to private producers – have had a significant role to play.

The study focuses on the rural economy of Botswana and examines the influence of economic policy on rural incomes and decisions of rural resource users. It comes to the conclusion that in Botswana during the last decade, as in much of Sub-Saharan Africa the driving forces behind rural environmental degradation are social and political rather than environmental. While the agricultural sector has been severely affected by drought, the greatest sources of damage have been the restructuring of rural institutions in ways that have weakened social control over access to the resource base. Damage has also been caused by the distortion of the private costs of resource utilization through the use of agricultural subsidies and agricultural income support.

Professor Perrings argues for the elimination of these subsidies; the introduction of a direct targeted system of support to disadvantaged rural households in place of the present agricultural income subsidies; infrastructural development to facilitate rural diversification, partly through the adoption of environmentally-compensating public sector projects (along the lines of the Labour Based Relief Programme); and the development of an environmental data base, together with a natural resource accounting system.

It is hoped that the Botswana study and its policy analysis will be of more general interest to policy-makers throughout Sub-Saharan Africa.

Charles Perrings' study is a sequel to *Environment, Employment and Development* (edited by A. S. Bhalla, ILO, 1992) and *Beyond Rio: The Environmental Crisis and Sustainable Livelihoods in the Third World* (edited by Iftikhar Ahmed and J. Doeleman, Macmillan, 1995), the latter being an ILO contribution to the follow-up of Agenda 21 of the Earth Summit.

IFTIKHAR AHMED
Employment Strategies and Policies Branch
Employment Department
International Labour Office
Geneva

1 Introduction

1.1 THE PROBLEM OF POVERTY AND RESOURCE DEGRADATION

One of the most striking coincidences of the last decade has been that between deepening poverty and accelerating environmental degradation in the arid, semi-arid and sub-humid tropical regions – the drylands – of Sub-Saharan Africa.[1] In a period in which poverty has fallen in many parts of the world, Sub-Saharan Africa has witnessed both declining per capita consumption and an increase in the absolute number of people in poverty (United Nations Development Program, 1990). In the same period, it has seen the progressive degradation of an environment that was already under considerable stress. This coincidence has not, of course, gone unremarked. By the mid-1970s, the existence of a correlation between rural poverty and environmental degradation was already causing alarm. Eckholm (1976) had claimed that environmental degradation was 'a common factor linking virtually every region of acute poverty, virtually every rural homeland abandoned by destitute urban squatters'. Nor was there any illusion about the potential longer-term consequences of the trend. The United Nations Conference on Desertification (1977) estimated that the world could lose one-third of all arable lands by the close of the century as a direct result of environmental degradation, with all that this implied for the welfare of the rural poor. In the countries of the Sudano-Sahelian region, the degradation of dryland environments was judged to have reached crisis proportions. Nor was it significantly less of a problem in Lesotho and the countries straddling the high plateau from Botswana to Kenya. Since the mid 1970s, matters have got steadily worse.

The deepening poverty associated with environmental degradation in Sub-Saharan Africa is reflected in regional trends in per capita consumption. In 1985, average consumption was not only less than it had been in 1975, it was less than it had been in 1965. In nutritional terms, mean daily calorie supply as a percentage of requirements is estimated to have fallen slightly[2] in the whole of Sub-Saharan Africa over this period, while the variance of this measure has increased

1

sharply. Two groups of countries have experienced a significant decline in average nutrition. These are Senegal, Mauritania, Niger, Chad, Sudan, Somalia and Ethiopia in the Sudano-Sahelian region; and the Central African Republic, Zaire, Uganda, Zambia, and Tanzania in East and Central Africa. Of these, the hardest hit have been the Sudano-Sahelian countries. Between 1964–6 and 1984–6, daily per capita calorie supply fell by an average of nearly 20 per cent in Ethiopia, Sudan and Chad.

Nor has the burden been borne evenly within each country. With the exception of Zambia, the countries mentioned above are predominantly rural economies, agriculture accounting for over 70 per cent of the labour force in all but two,[3] and it is in the rural sector that poverty is most highly concentrated. Indeed, the same feature characterizes many of the seemingly less disadvantaged countries of Sub-Saharan Africa, Botswana included. While distributional data are scarce in Sub-Saharan Africa, estimates of the degree of poverty in the period 1977–87 show that the probability that a rural household was in poverty is nearly twice that for urban households, and is as much as 80 per cent in Rwanda, Burundi, the Central African Republic and Malawi.[4]

Other indices of poverty tell a similar story. All of the countries in the two groups noted above recorded zero or negative average annual per capita GNP growth between 1965 and 1988. Moreover, although measures such as life expectancy and infant mortality have not worsened in the period, the rate of improvement in these countries has been much less than elsewhere. Indeed, the populations of the Sudano-Sahelian region remain the most deprived in the world by the UNDP's human development index (United Nations Development Program, 1990).[5] The extreme destitution of famine victims in the refugee camps of Ethiopia and Southern Sudan is only the most acute symptom of a very widespread malaise.

The root causes of the decline in these rural economies are complex, and will be discussed later. They are, at the same time, causes of the collapse of the agricultural sector, the declining productivity associated with the degradation of the natural resource base, the increasing level of dependence on food imports, and the sharp fall in those non-food imports – spare parts, fuels and fertilizers – on which expansion at the intensive margin depends (United Nations, 1986). The proximate causes of the decline of the rural economy are more easy to identify. While there remains some doubt about the extent and reversibility of many of the processes of environmental degradation which lie behind declining agricultural performance, there is a high degree of consensus in the literature that such damage as has occurred is directly due to two things. The first of these is a general increase in the pressure on forest resources, arable and grazing lands. The second is the failure to regulate this pressure to changes in the carrying capacity of the resources due, for example, to drought.

Population growth is commonly alleged to be the immediate source of such pressure, and it is certainly the case that high levels of population growth are associated with increasing levels of pressure on the natural resource base. But it is not helpful to see population growth as an exogenous factor driving essentially short term processes. The strong positive correlation between the rate of population growth, resource degradation, and poverty does not necessarily imply a causal relationship running in one direction only. There is some evidence, for example, that while average fertility in Sub-Saharan Africa has been falling over the period 1965–88, it has been increasing in just those countries where environmental degradation and rural impoverishment has been most marked: Central African Republic, Zaire, Uganda, Zambia, and Tanzania (World Resources Institute, 1990). At the very least this indicates the need for caution in characterizing the nature of feedback effects between environmental degradation and population growth.

What is interesting about the Sub-Saharan African experience is that for various reasons – cultural and institutional rigidities in the societies of Sub-Saharan Africa, plus the effects of government fiscal, price and incomes policies – increasing demand for agricultural products has proportionately increased the pressure on soils, vegetation, and water. Resources have tended to be locked into traditional activities and traditional technologies. The result is livestock densities in pastoral areas that are unsustainably high given the variance in climatic conditions in the arid and semi-arid zones, fallow periods in arable areas that are unsustainably low, and an exponential increase in the demand for construction timber and fuelwood. Overgrazing, over-cultivation and deforestation have, in turn, led to various processes of resource degradation that have been grouped together under the term 'desertification'. They are processes that involve reduced productivity of desirable plants, undesirable alterations in the biomass and the diversity of micro fauna and flora, and accelerated soil deterioration: from bush encroachment at one extreme to the increasing aridity and denudation of soils at the other (Dregne, 1983). It turns out that drylands are particularly vulnerable to such processes, since they tend to be less resilient in the face of stress and shocks than other ecosystems due to the low level of system complexity (United Nations Conference on Desertification, 1977).

The economically interesting question arising out of this is why resource users should have failed to adjust to changes in demand in a way that is consistent with the ecological sustainability of the resource base. This study seeks an answer to this question in the long recognized coincidence of poverty and environmental degradation. Eckholm (1976) ascribed this coincidence to a 'basic dilemma . . . that what is essential to the survival of society often flies in the face of what is essential to the survival of the individual'. This does not question the rationality of individual resource users, but suggests that what is privately rational may not be socially rational. The 'dilemma' implies that the private and social costs and benefits of resource use are different: the incentives confronting individual resource users induces short run behaviour that is inconsistent with the long run interests both of the resource users themselves and of society. This study considers what lies behind the incentives that currently govern resource allocation in the dryland areas of Sub-Saharan Africa, paying particular attention to the institutional and other factors that structure markets in the continent. The aim of the study is both to analyse the incentives confronting resource users in terms of their ecological sustainability, and to identify the necessary conditions for the development of incentives that are compatible with the ecologically sustainable use of resources.

1.2 POVERTY AND INCENTIVES

The common thread running through the arguments of this study is the role of poverty and poverty alleviation. For individual resource users, poverty promotes a myopic approach to the management of resources. The poor tend to discount the future costs of their own behaviour. For governments, the alleviation of both urban and rural poverty is a primary motivation behind many of the policies that have widened the gulf between the private and social cost of resource use, encouraging the overutilisation of natural resources.

This study takes the view that environmental degradation in Sub-Saharan Africa, as in low income countries elsewhere, is the result of the independent decisions of the millions of individual users of environmental resources. Its underlying causes are therefore to be found in the parameters within which those decisions are made: the objectives that motivate decisions, the preferences that lie behind the demand for goods and services and the rate at which individuals discount future costs and benefits of their actions, the property rights that define individual endowments, the set of relative prices that determine the market opportunities associated with those endowments, and the cultural, religious, institutional and legal restrictions on individual behaviour that prescribe the range of admissible actions. If private rational decisions are socially damaging, the problem is to be found somewhere in the decision process, whether it be in the 'technology' of consumption or production, the set of relative prices, or the constraints within which individuals have to act.

The study accordingly has a double focus: the structure of incentives and the responses of resource users to changing incentives. It pays particularly close attention to the market prices which define the private cost of resource use, and to the potential for private costs to diverge from social costs. Since rational individuals, faced with prices that do not reflect the social opportunity cost, will make decisions that are socially suboptimal, it is important to understand why (and with what effect) the private and social costs of environmental resource use diverge. It may be due to ignorance or uncertainty, to the strategic market behaviour of economic agents, to a variety of policy interventions, or it may be due to the incompleteness of markets. In Sub-Saharan Africa, as elsewhere, the incompleteness of markets turns out to be an especially important source of difficulty. Wherever resource users depend on a common environment the activities of one will tend to have effects on all others, but if there is no forum (market) in which to negotiate the value of those (external) effects there is no reason to believe that the outcome of their decisions will be socially optimal.

Some of these external effects are in principle easier to deal with than others. Unidirectional externalities are those in which the hydrological or other cycles of the common environment ensure that the short-run external environmental costs or benefits of resource use are 'one way'. For example, deforestation by the users of an upper watershed inflicts damage on the users of the lower watershed – although as all users are part of the same set of biogeochemical cycles, the term 'unidirectional' should not be taken too literally in this case. Reciprocal externalities are those in which all parties having rights of access to a resource are able to impose costs on each other. The short run external environmental costs or benefits of resource use are the same irrespective of who is responsible (this is the classical problem of the commons). Unidirectional externalities appear to be easier to resolve than the reciprocal externalities that characterize most environmental degradation in the drylands of Sub-Saharan Africa. Either way, it is important to understand the nature of the externalities associated with environmental degradation, and the link between externalities and the range of rights conferred by law or custom on the users of biotic and abiotic resources.

An additional problem is that even if it were possible to eliminate externalities through the creation of markets for all significant environmental effects, this would provide little protection against those for whom it is optimal to degrade the environment under any set of prices. It is in this connection that poverty is argued to be relevant. Part of the problem lies in the fact that the poor have inadequate access to information, and so tend to be unaware of the alternative opportunities available to them in the use they make of resources. Information is not costless and the poor, by definition, are able to command less of it than the rich. More importantly, there is a strong relationship between income and the rate at which people discount the future costs and benefits of present decisions. In meeting their immediate consumption needs, the poor are often compelled to ignore the potential future consequences of their actions. In other words, it is privately rational for them to ignore the future damage they do both to habitats and species (Perrings, 1989a). For similar reasons, poverty turns out to be positively correlated with high rates of population growth, or at least with high rates of fertility – with all that this implies for pressure on environmental resources.

Of course, prices and incomes are not unconnected. There is considerable evidence that a major source of poverty amongst the users of natural resources in many of the least resilient ecosystems has been due to manipulation of the set of prices they face. It has, for example, been observed that one effect of price intervention in agricultural markets in the less developed economies has been the reduction of producer incomes (cf. Warford, 1987; Ghai and Smith, 1987). The same effect has been noted with respect to the pricing decisions of non-governmental monopsonistic and monopolistic agencies operating in the agricultural produce markets (cf. Sen, 1981). A second 'cause' of poverty is the distribution of assets, whether marketed or non-marketed. The very poor also tend to be those with access to few productive assets (natural or produced assets – including human capital), and are frequently the most likely to degrade those assets. That is, those whose asset holdings are inadequate to provide even a subsistence income have no option but to maintain current consumption by realising the value of their holdings, often by accelerating the depreciation (or degradation) of the assets. It is of considerable interest, therefore, that there has been a marked and continuing tendency for the distribution of both assets and income to widen over time in many of the low income countries, reflecting both the erosion of traditional rights of access to the resource base (which has given rise to a long term trend involving widening disparity in the farm and herd sizes of arable and pastoral economies) and increasing human population pressure (cf. Ghai and Radwan (eds), 1983).

1.3 THE STRUCTURE OF THE STUDY

The second and third chapters of the study offer a general review of the driving forces behind environmental degradation in the continent. Chapter 2 addresses the physical and institutional trends that form the context within which the problem of environmental degradation is analysed. Three such trends are considered: climatic change, population growth, and the evolution of institutions. In respect of climatic change the study focuses on the exogenous effects of such change. This is not to deny that the localized feedback effects discussed by Charney (1975) and Hare (1977) exist, but to isolate trends in the productivity and resilience of dryland ecosystems which are beyond the control of local resource users. The evidence turns out to be patchy and incomplete, and most projections are highly conjectural. Nor do the projections of different General Circulation Models (GCMs) always coincide. Nevertheless, there is sufficient agreement to indicate that the current global climatic trends have serious long-run implications for the use of natural resources in these zones. In respect of human population growth, it is argued that feedback effects between resource use, income and population are an important feature of the long run dynamics of the dryland economies, but that there appears to be no simple causal relationship between population growth and environmental degradation. Indeed, the study emphasises the importance of understanding the particular nature of the feedbacks involved. If, for example, there is positive feedback between population growth, income and resource degradation – if an increase in the rate of fertility is as much a result as a cause of resource degradation – it may not be sensible to attempt to control population growth without addressing the factors on which it depends. In respect of property rights in natural resources, and the institutions which regulate the level of activity in areas of common or communal property, we review the evidence on the evolution of property rights and regulatory institutions in Sub-Saharan Africa, and consider the barriers to the emergence of institutions that will enable externalities to be 'internalized' or accommodated.

Against the background of these trends, Chapter 3 identifies a number of key issues in the development of a structure of incentives for the sustainable use of natural and human resources in the drylands of Sub-Saharan Africa. These are risk and uncertainty, price formation and price responsiveness, income determination and the importance of income effects in the decisions made by resource users. What is at issue in respect of risk and innovation, is the observed linkage between risk, savings and technological innovation. The chapter considers the determinants of technology choice in rural Sub-Saharan Africa, and the implications of technological conservatism under high rates of population growth. It addresses the apparent paradox in the extreme risk aversion of resource users revealed by the choice of technology, and the high rate of time preference revealed by the degradation of the asset base.

In respect of the price system, it considers determinants of the set of relative prices confronting resource users, and the responses of resource users to changes in relative prices. The context to this is the argument that government intervention in product and factor markets has deepened the wedge between private and social costs of resource use, and so has exacerbated the misallocation of resources. This argument is reviewed, and the evidence for a systematic bias in government intervention in Sub-Saharan Africa is considered. In addition, the evidence on the relative strengths of income effects in producer responses to changes in relative input and output prices is considered. More particularly, we investigate the connection between income and the rate of discount or the rate of time preference. We pay special attention to the argument that poverty induces both extreme (current) risk aversion, and an unusually myopic view of the future costs of present activities implying that increasing risk aversion and rates of time preference may be positively correlated with increasing levels of resource degradation (Lipton, 1968; Perrings, 1989a).

Chapters 4 to 7 then focus on the evidence offered by Botswana. There are two reasons for the selection of Botswana as a case study. The first relates to those aspects of the Botswana economy which make it representative of the region. The point here is that the rural economy of Botswana is, in a number of very important respects, typical of the dryland economies of much of East, Central and Southern Africa. Patterns of resource use are similar, and many of the social forces that have led to the degradation of environmental resources elsewhere can be observed in Botswana. The structure of the livestock and arable sectors, the nature of institutions and property rights governing access to resources in those sectors, the redistributive mechanisms at work in the rural economy and the pattern of income distribution, the balance between formal and informal sector employment, even the structure and rate of growth of the rural population, are all more or less typical of the region. For this reason an analysis of the link between economic incentives and environmental resource use in Botswana can yield important insights into the problem in other areas of Sub-Saharan Africa.[6]

The second reason for selecting Botswana as a case study paradoxically relates to aspects of the Botswana economy that make it atypical. Botswana is highly unusual among the economies of Sub-Saharan Africa for the fact that it has continued to grow strongly during a period in which, as has already been remarked, Senegal, Mauritania, Niger, Chad, Sudan, Somalia, Ethiopia, the Central African Republic, Zaire, Uganda, Zambia, and Tanzania all recorded zero or negative rates of growth of real per capita GDP. With an average annual rate of growth of real per capita GDP of around 8 per cent since 1966, Botswana's performance is bettered only by a few oil-exporting countries. Even during the years of drought in the 1980s, real GDP grew at an average rate of more than 12 per cent. This performance is in very large part due to the expansion of the minerals sector, and of the diamond subsector in particular. What makes Botswana a valuable case study is not this growth performance, but the fact that it is coming to an end (Harvey, 1992). It is this prospect which has induced the government of Botswana to confront the implications of its dependence on both exhaustible and renewable natural resources, and to address the question of incentives for the sustainable use of natural resources in a way that is atypical in Sub-Saharan Africa, but which has valuable implications for other countries in the region.

It is recognised that if the momentum of the last twenty years is not to be lost, there will have to be a change of direction in terms of the sectoral balance of the economy. The government of Botswana – acutely aware of the fragility of the diamond base – has accordingly placed increasing emphasis on diversification of the economy, and of the rural sector in particular. To this end it has supported two separate lines of inquiry. The first of these is on the structure of incentives and disincentives in the economy. The second is on the sustainable use of the natural resource base. The first line of inquiry has not only generated a number of independent reports on the problem of rural incentives, so creating a database of exceptional quality (cf. McGowan International and Coopers & Lybrand, 1987; Gyekye and Mazonde, 1989; Edwards *et al.*, 1989), it has included a presidential review of the incomes policy that centred on the issue of the price and income effects of changing incentives (Republic of Botswana, 1990a). The second line of inquiry has addressed the problem of the sustainability of natural resource utilization directly. The centrepiece of this line of inquiry has been the preparation of the Botswana National Conservation Strategy (BNCS), completed in 1989 (Republic of Botswana, 1989). The result of these two lines of inquiry is that the linkages between the structure of prices, incomes and unsustainable resource utilization in the rural economy of Botswana is much clearer, as is the scope for addressing the problem. This makes the Botswana experience of particular interest and relevance to other countries in the region now addressing the same problem.

Chapter 4 reviews the recent performance and current trends of the Botswana economy. It pays particular attention to the rural economy, and to the role of the agricultural sector in the rural economy. In recent years the agricultural sector has been unable to absorb the increase in the numbers of people being added to the labour force, leading to the prognosis that Botswana is at risk of acquiring one of the less desirable characteristics of the low-growth economies elsewhere in sub-Saharan Africa – high rural unemployment. The conditions for this are certainly present. The population of Botswana is currently growing at around 3.4 per cent, and is not predicted to slow down with the fall in the rate of economic growth. Indeed, the projections are that Botswana's population could more than double between the 1981 and the 2001 censuses. At the same time, agricultural GDP has been declining. Given the limited prospects for employment creation in the formal sector, in the absence of major improvements in both farm and off-farm productivity, low economic growth and high population growth will widen the employment gap, and depress rural incomes. Chapter 4 describes these trends.

Chapter 5 considers the impact of government policy on the structure of incentives governing resource allocation in the rural economy. Once again it is largely concerned with the agricultural sector. Four areas of policy are considered in detail: policy on output prices, policy on input prices and input subsidies, tax policy, and policy on domestic (particularly) rural credit expansion. The chapter both describes the evolution of policy and its impact on relative prices, and seeks to identify the distributional motives behind policy changes. The dominant fact of the 1980s in Botswana was the collapse in agricultural incomes associated with the drought. It is argued that the need to support agricultural incomes in this period subverted the development objectives of the main agricultural programmes, and turned them into vehicles for the transfer of incomes. The effect of this was to distort relative input prices in a way that encouraged the overutilization of agricultural resources at a time when the resilience of the ecological systems supporting agricultural activity was much reduced.

The next chapter focuses on the distribution of assets and income in the rural economy reflecting the theme of this study. The evidence on income distribution offered by the 1985/86 household income and expenditure survey is reported, along with evidence on transfers that are independent of the agricultural development programmes discussed in Chapter 5. In addition, however, the chapter summarizes the preliminary results obtained from a microeconomic study of the link between income by source and expenditure patterns. There are two questions that are being put to the data in this research. The first concerns the relationship between the distribution of income and the strength and direction of income effects in producer responses to a change in prices. The second concerns the relationship between the structure and flow of rural incomes and rural investment. We offer some preliminary findings on the latter. More particularly, we show that public transfers have a greater impact on investment expenditures at low levels of household income than at higher levels of household income. Since a key problem to be resolved in the diversification of rural economic activity required for sustainable use of the resource base is the unwillingness of the poor to undertake risky investments, this is of considerable interest.

Chapter 7 then considers the implications of the policy reforms currently being implemented by the government of Botswana. Aside from the agricultural sector assessment which has led to a new policy on agriculture, the chapter considers two major initiatives: the presidential commission set up to review policy on prices and incomes, and the development of the Botswana National Conservation Strategy (BNCS). While the first of these has already resulted in the introduction of a new policy on incomes, employment, prices and profits (Republic of Botswana, 1990c), the second has introduced a new way of thinking about environmental problems that is expected to take longer to feed into policy, but is also expected to have more far-reaching effects.

The study concludes with two chapters which draw out the implications of the Botswana case for the general problem of incentives for the sustainable use of human and natural resources in the drylands of Sub-Saharan Africa. It is argued in Chapter 8 that there are both positive and negative lessons to be learned from the Botswana experience. Botswana has gone much further than many countries in the region in designing policies around the goal of sustainable development and diversification of the agricultural sector. It has also invested more heavily in the construction of a conservation strategy that is as sound economically as it is environmentally. Its initiatives in these areas provide positive examples for countries in which a scarcity of public resources has precluded such policy development. At the same time, Botswana has left intact a number of policies and institutions that have been shown to contribute to environmental degradation. Many aspects of the new agricultural policy, for example, will have the effect of locking individuals into unsustainable patterns of resource allocation even more tightly than has been the case in the past. The use of distortionary agricultural subsidies as a means of delivering transfers to the rural poor has not been eliminated in the reforms. One result of this is that many low income rural households (those dependent on wage income in particular) are missed by all except the ad hoc safety nets set up in drought years. Moreover, though the introduction of rights of exclusion over rangeland will go a long way towards preventing the overutilization of the range, other effects of the traditional structure of property rights that inhibit rural diversification have not been addressed. The identification of these unresolved issues provides lessons of another sort. In highlighting areas in which a consensual government has found it hard to move, it points to the politically difficult features of a sustainable development strategy.

The final chapter addresses the least tractable set of problems in the development of a strategy for sustainable development – not just in Botswana, but throughout Sub-Saharan Africa. It is the set of problems surrounding the rate of population growth and the feedback effects between population growth, environmental degradation and poverty. Between 1965–70 and 1985–90, the average annual rate of population growth in all of Africa rose from 2.63 per cent to 3 per cent, and the average annual rate of growth of the labour force rose from 2.2 to 2.5 per cent. Amongst Sub-Saharan African countries, few now have a higher average annual rate of population growth than Botswana, and only Kenya has a higher annual average rate of growth of the labour force. The pressures this places on environmental resources are intense, as are the challenges it poses for an employment generation policy. Chapter 9 explores both the driving forces behind the unsustainably high fertility rates of the region, and the scope for addressing the problem through policy. Its conclusions are controversial, particularly in the present economic climate, but the basis on which those conclusions have been reached should be transparent enough to enable readers to judge for themselves.

2 Secular Trends and Environmental Degradation in Sub-Saharan Africa

The motivation for a study on incentives for the sustainable use of natural and environmental resources lies in the observation that environmental degradation is, to a very large extent, the consequence of the privately rational but socially irrational behaviour of private resource users. As private decisions about the use of environmental resources depend on the incentives facing the decision-maker, they can be changed by changing those incentives. But not all environmental degradation is caused by human behaviour, and not all human behaviour responds quickly to changing incentives. Biogeochemical, population, and institutional changes have such momentum that they would continue to exert an influence on the environment in Sub-Saharan Africa for a considerable period, even if all environmentally harmful incentives were to change overnight. They include global trends in respect of climate (and associated changes in regional hydrological and other biogeochemical cycles), and regional trends in respect of both human population and human institutions. These secular trends constitute the general context within which the link between human behaviour and environmental degradation is explored.

2.1 CLIMATE CHANGE

One of the less tractable aspects of the problem of resource degradation in the rural economies of Sub-Saharan Africa is the role of exogenously determined climate change. It is not at present clear how far climatic shifts have already influenced the sensitivity of the natural environment to the stress imposed by economic activity, and there is a very high level of uncertainty as to the local impacts of projected long term trends.

Nevertheless, there is sufficient consensus in the literature to indicate at least the direction of change in some of the key climatic variables. While the specific predictions of the different GCMs (General Circulation Models) vary, they are agreed that a continuation of emissions of the 'greenhouse gases' – carbon dioxide, nitrous oxide, methane and the chlorofluorocarbons – at present or greater levels will cause an increase in both mean and variance of surface temperatures. Mean temperatures are currently expected to rise at between 0.2 per cent and 0.4 per cent per decade over the next century (Intergovernmental Panel on Climate Change (IPCC), 1990). The lack of resolution in many GCMs makes the problem of predicting regional changes particularly severe, but all are agreed on two things: that mean temperatures will increase in all areas, and that the rate of increase will be greatest in the higher latitudes and least in the tropics. The models do not accommodate cloud effects which could moderate temperature changes, but it is currently conjectured that cloud effects would be unlikely to alter the direction of temperature change. A continuation of greenhouse gas emissions accordingly implies increasing rates of evapotranspiration in all areas, and this effect is argued to be crucial to the impact of climate change on agricultural productivity (Parry, 1990).

At the global level, the evidence on temperature change over the last century is not inconsistent with the broad predictions of the GCMs. Global mean temperatures have increased by between 0.3°C and 0.6°C in this period, which is within the range predicted by the GCMs given the best estimates of change in the level of CO_2 over the same period (IPCC, 1990). It is harder to assess whether changes in precipitation are similarly in line with the GCMs, for the reason that the GCMs do not agree on even the direction of change in precipitation and soil moisture at the regional level. In the case of the Sahel, some models predict an increase in both precipitation and soil moisture due to the northerly penetration of the Intertropical Convergence Zone, while other models predict the opposite. A further possibility is that even if there is an increase in rainfall over the Sahel, higher rates of evaporation (due to higher temperatures) may still make an overall rise in soil aridity likely (Parry, 1990).

The recent history of rainfall patterns in the Sudano-Sahelian region does not appear to support a long-term trend towards increasing precipitation. Not only have there been an unusually large number of rainfall deficit years in the region since the late 1960s, but the duration, intensity and geographical extent of droughts have been exceptional by the standards of other drought periods recorded during the twentieth century (Snijders, 1986, Grouzis, 1990). The results include the collapse of streamflow in a number of significant river systems (both the Senegal and the Niger are affected), the disruption of key lacustral systems (such as Lake Chad), and the general lowering of aquifers. Nevertheless, it is not clear if the duration and intensity of drought in the region reflects a reduction in the mean level of rainfall, or an increase in climatic variability. What is known is that the variability of climate is extremely sensitive to the mean: a small change in mean temperature or precipitation can be associated with a very large increase in climatic extremes. It is in fact likely that the major impact of climate change on agriculture will come not from the changes in mean temperature or precipitation, but from changes in the risks of extreme events (Parry, 1990).

2.1.1 Climate change and ecosystem resilience

The importance of these trends lies in their implications for the level of stress that the ecosystems of the region can withstand without losing resilience. Resilience, as the term is used here, refers to the stability of the organization of an ecosystem, or the propensity of the system to retain its organizational structure following perturbation (Holling, 1973, 1986).[1] It is accordingly a measure of the degree to which ecosystems can withstand the shocks of extreme events and continue to function: that is, it is a measure of the degree to which they can maintain 'productivity' in the face of shocks. Typically, resilience is a decreasing function of the stress to which an ecosystem is subjected. Of the different sources of ecosystem stress, the stress due to economic activity is obviously of prime interest here. But resilience is also a function of environmental conditions. Many dryland ecosystems have a comparatively low initial level of resilience, and so a low level of tolerance to stress. Since an increase in soil aridity due to change in both mean temperature and rainfall may cause such ecosystems to lose resilience, it may also cause them to become less tolerant to stress.

There is accordingly a close link between the resilience of ecological systems and the sustainability of economic activity. If the incidence of extreme events increases with change in average climatic conditions due to global warming, and if the resilience of those ecosystems is simultaneously reduced by that same change in average climatic conditions, it follows that the 'ecologically sustainable' level of economic activity will fall. An economic system will be ecologically sustainable, if and only if the ecological systems on which it depends are resilient. The crucial feature of resilience is the capacity it implies to adapt to the stresses imposed on a system by its interdependence with other systems. Hence the resilience of an ecosystem used in the course of economic activity is the guarantee that it will offer the same options to future generations of resource-users, and that it will not in any sense prescribe those options.

The important point here is that the resilience of ecosystems is itself subject to change. This may be the result of the way in which they are exploited in the course of economic activity, or it may be because of a change in environmental conditions. Much of the remainder of this book will consider the impact of economic activity on the resilience of the dryland ecosystems of Sub-Saharan Africa, but it is important to acknowledge that climate change which is largely exogenous to the region (since it contributes very little to the build-up of greenhouse gases) may independently change the resilience of those same ecosystems. While the available evidence on the impact of climatic factors on the resilience of ecosystems in the region is very sparse, there is little doubt that climatic factors are significant. Indeed, some analysts of vegetation dynamics in the region argue that climatic factors strongly dominate human activity as a source of vegetation change.

2.1.2 Climate change and agriculture in Sub-Saharan Africa

The principal ecosystems of interest in the rural economies of Sub-Saharan Africa are those underpinning agricultural activities. Aside from the indirect effects of greenhouse gas emissions on these ecosystems through climate change, an increase in the concentration of CO_2 is expected to have a number of direct effects on the growth rate of both economic and other plants. Available evidence suggests that increased concentrations of CO_2 will have a significant positive effect on plant growth, through the role of CO_2 in the process of photosynthesis. It has, for example, been estimated that if CO_2 were to double, the photosynthetic rate would rise from between 30 to 100 per cent (Parry, 1990). What is of particular interest for Sub-Saharan Africa is that the increase in the rate of plant growth that this implies would differ from one plant group to another. The major crops in the semi-arid and sub-humid tropical zones of Africa, such as maize, millet and sorghum, would benefit much less than the crops grown in the temperate zones, such as wheat, rice and soya bean.[2] This implies that agriculture could be relatively disadvantaged in the zones in which maize, millet and sorghum are staples.

Current predictions as to the future effects of exogenous climate change in the drylands of Sub-Saharan Africa have rested on a *ceteris paribus* assumption, assuming no change in the basic pattern of resource use. This may be a reasonable assumption with respect to slowly evolving ecosystems, in which the scope for a genotypic evolutionary response to climate change over the sort of time horizon under consideration is very limited. But the same is not necessarily true of human resource users. In their case, the net welfare effects of climate change will depend critically on the flexibility of their responses in respect of institutions, technology and preferences. These are considered in more detail below.

It should also be added that regional patterns of resource use may themselves have climatic effects: not all climate change in the region is necessarily exogenous. The overgrazing of rangeland, the extension of arable activities into marginal lands, and the concentration of populations around water sources all result in a reduction in vegetation. It is now recognised that this may have local climatic effects. It may, for example, increase surface albedo (reflectivity of solar radiation) which causes the air to lose heat radiatively, hence to descend and to lose relative humidity (cf. Charney, 1975, Hare 1977). These are not, however, presently considered to be significant.

2.2 POPULATION GROWTH

Population growth is conventionally treated as exogenous in economic models of human behaviour. Indeed, most models of economic growth are driven by a given rate of population growth. This convention is reflected in the fact that a significant strand in the literature identifies exogenous population growth as a major 'cause' of environmental degradation in the low-income countries, the 'solution' to which is argued to be both institutional reform and institutional control over population levels. This line of argument is worth considering in some detail.

2.2.1 Population growth and resource utilization

The role of human population growth in resource degradation is argued to lie in the connection between population growth and resource use. Taking population growth as a datum, a number of contributions to the literature find that population growth leads to the intensification of subsistence production: the shortening of fallow periods, the increase of stocking densities, increasing rates of timber extraction and so on (Boserup 1965, 1981; Darity, 1980; Pryor and Maurer, 1981). The same trend has been identified in Sub-Saharan Africa (Pingali, Bigot and Binswanger, 1985), and has beca argued to explain the process of environmental degradation (Ruddle and Manshard, 1981). The argument is that population growth implies an expansion of aggregate demand which then forces pastoralists and cultivators to put increasing pressure on a given environment: to intensify the exploitation of land currently in use, to switch land from pastoral to arable uses, and to bring increasingly marginal land into economic use. The cultivation of land that is both less productive and more sensitive to the effects of drought leads, eventually, to the degradation of the resource through both erosion and depletion of soil nutrients. Similarly, the increase in stocking densities on remaining pastoral lands results in overgrazing, which leads to devegetation and erosion of topsoil (Dixon *et al.*, 1989; Pearce *et al.*, 1990). In the absence of technological change, one result of this is argued to be a Malthusian adjustment process in which famine reestablishes a rough equilibrium between the size of the human population and the resource base (Eckholm, 1976; Dregne, 1983).

There are two aspects of this argument to consider. First, the presumption that population increase necessarily implies greater pressure on the environment may be warranted in many cases, but it does not have the status of a universal law. The empirical relation between resource degradation and population expansion is not a monotonic one. Kates, Johnson and Haring (1977), for example, argued that while there was undoubtedly a strong positive correlation between population growth and resource degradation in many instances, localized resource degradation could be a consequence of population decline as well as population growth.[3] It has subsequently been recognized that the proximate causes of resource degradation in Sub-Saharan Africa – overstocking and overcultivation – need bear no systematic relation to population increase (Repetto and Holmes, 1983). As is argued in later chapters of this study, change in the nature of property rights in environmental resources, taken in conjunction with the effectiveness of institutions regulating access to those resources and with the structure of economic incentives, can have devastating implications for the environment, irrespective of demographic trends.

Second, it turns out that the rate of population growth is not independent of the rate of environmental degradation, and that the feedback mechanisms between resource degradation and population growth and are more complex than a Malthusian view would suggest. While average fertility in Sub-Saharan Africa has been falling over the period 1965–88, it has been rising in a number of countries where rural impoverishment associated with the degradation of the resource base has been increasing. It is clear that current population growth rates in the countries of the Sudano-Sahelian region are not consistent with the ecological sustainability of resource use in the region, given the current technology and structure of production. Nor are those population growth rates themselves sustainable. But it is not clear that a Malthusian adjustment in the form of widespread famine will re-establish anything like a stable equilibrium population. The poverty associated with resource degradation contains within it both a tendency towards Malthusian collapse evidenced by rising mortality rates (especially infant mortality rates) in times of famine, and a contradictory tendency towards population expansion. While deepening rural poverty increases the risks of morbidity and mortality among the existing population, it also creates a powerful incentive to expand that population, partly to compensate for the increasing risk of infant mortality, and partly to compensate for the increasing risk of income failure. Children are insurance against the risks that poverty brings.

2.2.2   Population stability and ecosystem resilience

It turns out that the notion of a stable equilibrium population corresponding to a given set of resource endowments and a given pattern of resource use is not helpful. The sustainability of an ecosystem involving both economic and environmental activities does not imply an equilibrium population level, or even an equilibrium growth rate. From a population ecology perspective, the stability of an ecosystem is given by the size and distribution of the population in each species relative to its critical threshold levels (Pielou, 1975). This view recognizes that there may be a range of population sizes over which an ecosystem remains stable, but if any one population in an ecosystem either exceeds or falls below its critical threshold levels the self-organization of the ecosystem as a whole will be radically altered. The system will become unstable. In other words it assumes the complementarity of all species in the ecosystem. This provides a simple, if conservative, index of ecosystem integrity.

From a systems ecology perspective, however, the assumption of the complementarity of all species in an ecosystem is too strong. An ecosystem is not simply the sum of its constituent populations. It is a community of organisms in which the effect of internal interactions between organisms dominates the effect of external events, catastrophes apart. The community is better characterized by the principles of its self-organization than by a catalogue of species populations (Di Castri, 1987). Hence, the size of any given population relative either to other populations or to its own critical thresholds may not be an adequate indicator of the stability of the system. What is required in this approach are indicators of system integrity that are analogous to the diagnostic indicators used to test, for example, human health (Schaeffer *et al.*,1988).

Ecosystems, like economic systems, may be characterized as 'systems of discontinuous change', marked both by successional and disruptive processes (Holling, 1973, 1986). They may be resilient over very large ranges for the species populations in the systems. Nor do they necessarily lose resilience if particular species become extinct. Resilience admits the possibility of multiple equilibrium values for the species populations within the system. Indeed, resilience may be positively correlated with variation in the system populations. Resilience is also, however, an increasing function of the complexity or interconnectedness within an ecosystem: that is, it is an increasing function of the number of constituent populations within an ecosystem. Hence a reduction in the number of species in an ecosystem will cause loss of resilience.

The significance of this for human population growth is that the sustainability of the ecological systems on which human welfare depends does not imply a unique equilibrium level of population, or a unique rate of population growth. What is important for ecological sustainability is that the systems retain their resilience, and this property does not imply a unique balance between species populations. At the same time, however, the resilience of an ecosystem does depend on the level of stress to which it is subjected, and the level of stress is a function of population density. Increasing population may imply increasing levels of stress, and this may in turn imply loss of resilience. The notions of 'carrying' and 'assimilative' capacity common in the literature on environmental degradation in Sub-Saharan Africa are indirect measures of the level of stress that is consistent with a tolerable level of resilience (what level of resilience is tolerable depends on the severity of the 'shocks' expected to occur). Since, for a given technology, human population growth implies an increasing level of stress on the ecosystems exploited under that technology, there is necessarily some point at which the associated loss of ecosystem resilience will become critical. Human population growth will at some point cause the collapse of those ecosystems.

The key points here are, first, that the relationship between population growth in any given environment and the degradation of that environment is not necessarily monotonic. It is mediated by the institutional and economic environments within which resource users operate, and there is no systematic relationship between population growth and either institutional or economic conditions. Population growth is not always and everywhere environmentally damaging. Second, the impact of population growth on resource degradation is highly sensitive to the technology used. Although population growth has frequently been assumed to cause technology change (Boserup, 1965, 1981), population growth in much of rural Sub-Saharan Africa has not had this effect. Why? Once again, the institutional and economic environments within which resource users operate are part of the answer. But a major factor is the risk management strategies that characterize decision-making at very low levels of income. Third, the impact of resource degradation on population growth is more complex than the Malthusian arguments of Eckholm (1976) and Dregne (1983) would suggest. The extreme poverty of resource users in degraded environments is itself a spur to population growth. It is not, therefore, helpful to treat population growth as if it were exogenously determined, or to seek to change the fertility rate amongst resource users without addressing the motivation for large families.

It is important to understand and address the incentives that lie behind population trends, whilst acknowledging that the effect of a change in incentives now will only be realized with a considerable lag. It is certainly not helpful to assume that population trends are simply the product of social ignorance or institutional irresponsibility. The implications of these points for population policy are considered in Chapter 9, which argues that wherever fertility rates exceed the socially optimal rate, population policy should seek to close the gap between the private and social costs of additional births that this implies. This suggests that population policy should consist of much more than direct population 'control'.

2.3 PROPERTY RIGHTS

A third set of factors conventionally taken to be exogenous in economic analyses of resource degradation are the property rights and supporting institutions under which resources are used. It is generally acknowledged that different forms of property rights in resources – open access common property, communal property, private freehold and leasehold property – have different incentive effects for resource users. It is also generally acknowledged that the less complete are property rights, the greater is the propensity for resources to be overutilized. The more environmental services/disservices associated with a given pattern of resource use which are not the subject of well defined rights, the greater is the risk of environmental damage.

Since property rights tend to be least well defined in common and communal property regimes, and since communal property remains the dominant form of property in Sub-Saharan Africa, it is has been argued that Africa is in some sense predisposed to environmental degradation. Specifically, it is assumed that under traditional property rights individual resource users have enjoyed more or less unlimited access to the resource, and have based their decisions with respect to stocking densities or fallow periods on a private cost–benefit calculus that has excluded all costs carried either by other members of the same generation or by future generations. While this structure of property rights is argued to have been efficient when applied to non-scarce resources, for which the external and user costs ignored in the private cost–benefit calculus are insignificant, it is inefficient when applied to scarce resources (Ault and Rutman, 1979).

The problem, in this perspective, is that the 'natural' evolution of property rights in the face of increasing land scarcity towards more well-defined (private) property rights are argued to have been frozen. Traditional land rights are argued to have been preserved more or less intact for political or ideological reasons. South Africa at one extreme, and Tanzania at the other, are claimed to have preserved outmoded systems of communal property rights into the 1980s that led directly to the overexploitation of land in both the South African 'homelands' and the Ujamaa villages of Tanzania. The implication is that the system of communal property rights should be permitted to evolve in a natural way: that is towards a system in which the externalities created by common property are internalized, and individual resource users are encouraged to take full account of the social opportunity costs of their activities (Harrison, 1987).

2.3.1 Traditional property rights

It is beyond the scope of this study to review the historical development of property rights in land in Sub-Saharan Africa, largely because of the very wide range of systems involved. Successive intrusions into Africa have resulted in multi-layered, complex, systems of rights. Nevertheless, in each of these hybrid systems it is possible to identify a substratum of property rights deriving from the customary law of 'traditional' African societies. It is this substratum of traditional rights that is argued to be incompatible with the sustainable development of the resource base under increasing scarcity. All traditional African systems of land rights shared three characteristics: land was 'owned' by the tribe, each member of the tribe had guaranteed access to land in one form or another, but the tribe retained the right to determine the level and pattern of land use (Yudelman 1964). Absolute individual rights of ownership over land and other natural resources were 'unknown' (Caldwell, 1976). Instead, individuals held more or less limited use or usufructuary rights (Herskovits, 1940).

Usufructuaries enjoyed exclusive rights to the produce of their land, but were subject to a number of restrictions regarding its use. They could transfer their usufructs to other members of the tribe or clan, or could pass them on to their heirs. Herskovits called this 'inherited use ownership', which he distinguished from the private property enjoyed by clan or tribe members in assets other than land. The interests of the collectivity were served by the fact that usufructuaries' security of tenure depended on observance of the laws or customs of the tribe or clan with respect to the level of their activity and the technology applied. Land that was not worked in accordance with the laws or customs of the tribe or clan could be reassigned. Subsequent research on customary land law has verified this view (cf. James, 1971), and has confirmed the basic similarities in traditional land rights amongst all 'tribopatriarchal' societies of West Africa (Howard, 1980), and the Horn of Africa (Hoben, 1973). In societies based on hunting, gathering or nomadic pastoralism, individual usufructs typically conferred fewer rights of exclusion. No individual within the group could exclude any other individual from the land or its produce. Nevertheless, the collectivity continued to regulate both the general level of activity and the pattern of land use in systems based on common property (Herskovits, 1940).

The important points here are, first, that traditional tenure systems did permit the limited transfer of usufructuary rights and, second, that the usufructuary rights were collectively controlled to meet social (including environmental) goals. This makes traditional rights rather closer to the modern idea of tradable permits or quota, than to the open access common property model. Many traditional societies prevented usufructs from being sold outside group, but this is effectively true in a number of modern market economies. One only has to think of the restrictions placed on foreign ownership of assets alleged to have national strategic implications. There is no evidence for the inference that traditional systems of property rights in Sub-Saharan Africa were especially insensitive to the environmental constraints they faced because they were based on communal or common property in land. Indeed, all the available evidence suggests just the opposite.

2.3.2   The evolution of property rights in Sub-Saharan Africa

In fact, although it is possible to identify these various elements of traditional land rights it should not be assumed that traditional rights and patterns of resource use have been as static as Ault and Rutman claim. Subsequent work on land rights in Sub-Saharan Africa confirmed that traditional rights have evolved in response to changing institutional, economic and environmental conditions (Feder and Noronha, 1987; Bruce, 1988; Dyson-Hudson, 1984). This is consistent with the historical tendency observed elsewhere for property rights in resources to develop when the gains from so doing become manifestly larger than the costs of change. While there has been a tendency for property rights to some scarce resources to evolve in the general direction of exclusive private property (Behnke, 1990; Dixon, James and Sherman, 1989) this has not been true of all scarce resources. This does not, however, mean that property rights to such resources have been frozen. Property rights comprise a complex collection of rules governing the rights (entitlements) and obligations of resource users, and their evolution in any given set of historical circumstances will reflect the institutional, cultural and intellectual characteristics of the society concerned. It does not follow that any particular structure of rights can be taken to be the logical end-point of evolution. A more satisfactory explanation for the failure of private property in land to develop in many parts of rural Sub-Saharan Africa, despite the scarcity of the resource, is that the introduction of private property in land in Sub-Saharan Africa has offered no advantages over traditional tenure systems either in terms of productivity gains, or in terms of the ability of the resource user to raise credit. The incentive for resource users to opt for private as opposed to some modified form of communal property in Sub-Saharan Africa is not therefore obvious (Migot-Adholla *et al.*, 1991).

Unfortunately, comparatively little empirical work has yet been done on the link between evolving property rights and the management of environmental resources in the region. Two aspects of the evolution of communal property rights are, however, worthy of comment. First, the institutions traditionally charged with the allocation of usufructual rights and with the regulation of the level of activity have either disappeared or been severely weakened, while replacement institutions have failed to exercise the authority vested in them. It might be expected, a priori, that this trend would exacerbate rather than alleviate the problem, and there is now considerable evidence to support that expectation. In pastoral economies, although there is still an incentive to cooperate where land is held communally (cf. Cousins, 1987; Wade, 1987), it remains the case that wherever traditional institutions for regulating the use of communal lands have broken down individual graziers have tended to add stock past the maximum sustainable point (Jamal, 1983). In Botswana, to take a particular example, traditional mechanisms for regulating grazing have degenerated. The *badisa* charged with the care of the rangeland have disappeared and range management decisions have become more individualistic and less coordinated (Abel et al, 1987). At the same time, the Land and Agricultural Resources Boards charged with the allocation of grazing land in the communal areas, the granting of water rights, and the conservation of rangeland have failed to ensure that private stocking decisions are consistent with the sustainable use of the resource. The result is that livestock owners in the communal areas of Botswana currently have virtually uncontrolled grazing rights, and no individual bears the full cost of adding stock beyond the carrying capacity of the range (Arntzen and Veenendaal, 1986). Nor is the example of Botswana unique (Githinji and Perrings, 1993).

2.3.3   Security of tenure and resource degradation

The second feature of evolving property rights is that the security of individual tenure has tended to diminish. People moving on to previously unoccupied land (squatters) typically have no legal entitlement to use of the land, and occupy it only so long as they are permitted to do so by more powerful agencies. Even on lands occupied on the basis of traditional communal property rights, the security of tenure over usufructs has diminished with the weakening of institutions of collective control (Bruce, 1988). From an environmental perspective, this too has adverse incentive effects – albeit of a different kind. The collapse of regulatory institutions opens up the potential for over-exploitation of the resource base by enabling resources users to ignore part of the social opportunity cost of resource use. The collapse of the security of land tenure, on the other hand, tends to increase the rate at which the future costs of resource use are discounted: that is, it lowers the incentive to manage the land on a sustainable basis. Whereas the collapse of regulatory institutions widens the scope for external effects to be ignored in resource use decisions, insecurity of tenure ensures that the future or user effect of resource use are ignored, whether or not markets for those effects exist.

One of the arguments conventionally advanced for promoting private property in dryland environments is precisely that it would increase security of tenure, and so encourage a longer term perspective in land use decisions. This is taken to be a prerequisite for individual resource users to undertake conservation-investments (Dixon, James and Sherman, 1989). It is not obvious that the introduction of private property in land in Sub-Saharan Africa has had this effect, nor is it obvious that private property is the only tenure system consistent with security of tenure. But it is clear that the rate of discount implied by current patterns of resource use in parts of Sub-Saharan Africa is inconsistent with the ecologically sustainable use of the resource base. To the extent that myopia is a function of insecurity of tenure, sustainability does imply the need to revise current tenure systems. The evidence for unsustainably high implicit discount rates in current patterns of resource use lies in the fact that present rates of resource depletion in parts of Sub-Saharan Africa exceed the natural rate of regeneration of the resource base – given existing technologies. Sustainability implies either a reduction in current levels of rural economic activity (whether through a Malthusian adjustment process or some less traumatic means of exiting the rural economy) or technological change. Once again, to the extent that the form of tenure is a factor in the choice of technology, the incentive effects of existing tenure arrangements are relevant. But the evidence to date does not support the notion that privatization in Sub-Saharan Africa has led to productivity-improving investments (Migot-Adholla *et al.*, 1991).

The important point here is that if the sustainability of resource use in the drylands of Sub-Saharan Africa is not to be 'restored' (however temporarily) through a reduction in population, it implies the need for both diversification of the rural economy (Perrings *et al.*, 1988; Pearce,

Barbier and Markandya, 1990) and technological change within the agricultural sector (Conway and Barbier, 1990). This makes it interesting to inquire into the structure of incentives governing the allocation of rural resources, of which the system of property rights is an important component part. It turns out, however, that the incentive effects of property rights per se may be less significant than previously thought, although security of tenure within any given system of property rights may still be important.

3 Environmental Management in Sub-Saharan Africa

3.1 RISK MANAGEMENT AND INNOVATION IN THE RURAL ECONOMY

The main characteristics of closed agrarian economies have historically been a heavy reliance on agricultural or pastoral activities, a very marked technological conservatism, a marginal physical product of all resources at or close to zero, together with zero net savings (Schultz, 1964; Fei and Ranis, 1978). The environmental management strategies in such economies were typically also highly conservative, being designed to minimize the risks associated with the overexploitation of the resource base (Perrings, 1985). All traditional societies have controlled the intensity of land use by regulating the frequency of cultivation or grazing. In nomadic pastoral, hunting or gathering societies the primary means of control over the frequency of land use has been, quite naturally, control over the pattern of mobility. In swidden agriculture primary control of the frequency of land use has taken the form of group regulation of the period of fallow.

Allan (1965) identified a range of what he termed 'land use factors' in agriculture – defined as the relationship between the duration of cultivation on each of the land or soil units used in the classification and the period of subsequent rest required for the restoration of fertility, or as the number of land units required to keep a single unit in cultivation. These land use factors were the basis of collective decisions on the primary means of control – the frequency of cultivation. Very fertile areas – such as the upper Zambezi valley, Buganda or the Oalo lands of Senegal – had a land use factor of less than two, and so permitted semi-permanent cultivation. Three or four years cultivation might be followed by one or two years fallow – what Boserup (1965) called short fallows. A much wider area had a land use factor of between four and eight, permitting what Allan referred to as recurrent cultivation, and Boserup terms bush fallows. A period of between two and six years cultivation had to be followed by anything from six to 30 years fallow. Large areas of the Zaire basin, West Africa, the Guinea savannah, East and Central Africa fell into this category. Finally, the semi-arid zones, including the Kalahari and much of the northern Sahel, had a land use factor of more than ten. These areas permitted only the nomadic form of agriculture Allan termed shifting cultivation.

The most remarkable feature of such land use strategies was that actual fallow/cultivation ratios were almost always significantly greater than the minimum fallow/cultivation ratios implied by the land use factor. The actual population permitted to exploit a given area under cultivation or in fallow was consistently well below the critical carrying capacity of that area (Nash, 1967; Sahlins, 1974), actual levels of activity being linked to the lowest possible rather than the expected carrying capacity. The effect of this was to augment the land required for each member of the group. Indeed, Allan (1965) argued it to be 'axiomatic' that subsistence cultivators would cultivate an area large enough to ensure the food supply in a season of poor yields as part of a risk-minimizing strategy. This is consistent with Leibenstein's (1957) model of the closed agrarian economy, which generated a 'quasi-stable' equilibrium, or a stable equilibrium conditional on the economy concerned being insulated from external influences.

3.1.1 The management of market risks

The opening of the agrarian economies in Sub-Saharan Africa to world product markets changed these characteristics in important ways. Since certain input and output prices were taken from world markets, the relations between the productivity of the resource base and real income, and between savings/investment and environmental conditions were both altered. Capacity utilization was no longer only a function of the distribution of rainfall or temperature, but reflected expectations about input and output prices. There were two sources of uncertainty to be accommodated – the environment and the world market. Indeed, analyses of the succession of famines that have affected the Sudano-Sahelian region in the last three decades have shown that most were induced not by the decline of food availability due to drought, but to the collapse of real income due to changes in food prices (Sen, 1981; Speece, 1989).

There is little evidence that agricultural producers of Sub-Saharan Africa have exploited the potential specialization gains available from international trade. Indeed, the evidence suggests exactly the opposite. Most agricultural producers have done little to change either product mix or technology (cf. Konczacki, 1978), and this has distinguished them from agricultural producers elsewhere. Whereas the introduction of green revolution technologies in Asia resulted in a 27 per cent increase in per capita food production between 1964 and 1986, Africa remained almost untouched. Indeed, per capita agricultural output in Africa has shown a downward trend in this period, a fact that is only partly explained by the less favourable endowments of Sub-Saharan Africa (Conway and Barbier, 1990).

Part of the explanation for the failure of producers to change the technology under which they have exploited an increasingly scarce resource base is to be found in their risk management strategies. It turns out that these strategies are largely driven by income effects, which are considered later in this study. What is important here is that it has long been recognized that risk aversion is a decreasing function of income, and that agricultural producers close to the poverty line tend to adopt highly risk averse strategies (Lipton, 1968). In general, producer strategies for minimizing risk in the rural economy involve two decisions. One concerns the optimal level of activity, the other concerns the balance between production for direct consumption and production for the market (Livingstone, 1981). Neither the market risk nor the direct consumption risk of harvest failure are insurable except through the decisions made by agrarian producers in these two areas.

Producers who are near the minimum subsistence level, and are unable to take a loss below subsistence, tend to adopt what Lipton (1968) has called 'survival algorithms': environmentally conservative practices characterized by the selection of low value but robust crops or livestock suitable for both market production and direct consumption. They tend to avoid high market value but environmentally susceptible crops or livestock that are not directly consumable. Risk minimizing strategies of this sort have biased production and consumption decisions in Sub-Saharan Africa in favour of tried practices and traditional products, and against technological innovation. This is particularly the case where technological change is itself a source of risk, as with 'green revolution' technology (see Schultz, 1964). It follows that the costs of such technological conservatism, in terms not only of the specialization losses of trade but also of the degradation of the natural environment, are implicitly accepted as part of the premium to be paid for the risk of participating in the world market.

A similar set of considerations inform the savings behaviour of agricultural producers. Savings in the open agrarian economy may notionally be made in the form of either financial or real assets; in money, bank deposits, etc., or in natural assets, grain and livestock. Partly because saving in financial assets tends to be limited by the availability of financial institutions, and partly because of the risks attached to saving in financial assets, the safety-oriented survival algorithms employed in Sub-Saharan Africa have favoured saving in real assets. Savings in real assets, particularly grain or livestock, provides both a means of direct consumption in the case of drought and a degree of protection against the volatility of product prices (see for example Speece, 1989). However, it also tends to reinforce the technological conservatism of agricultural producers, since it makes it very difficult to substitute out of existing capital assets.

In terms of its environmental effects, this technological conservatism of agricultural producers has been an important source of stress on the ecological systems of the natural environment. Given a breakdown of controls over the level of activity, the intensification of agriculture within the existing technology has not surprisingly led to diminishing returns due, in large part, to the degradation of the resource base. This is reflected in the fact that as the level of agricultural activity has intensified, so has the sensitivity of output to climatic variation. Even minor variations in rainfall or temperature have been associated with major output losses. That is, the resilience of the ecosystems involved has fallen to the point where normal perturbations in rainfall lead to system failure. Moreover, where expansion has taken place at the extensive margin, it has involved increasingly unsuitable vegetational or topographical conditions, with similar implications for the sensitivity of output to climatic variation (Mosely and Smith, 1989; Barbier, 1988; Pearce, Barbier and Markandya,1988).

3.1.2   Water risks in dryland environments

By comparison with the technological conservatism of private risk management strategies, the collective management of water supply risks in the dryland environments of Sub-Saharan Africa has been highly innovative. A common element in the rural development strategies adopted in all high risk areas of Sub-Saharan Africa in the last three decades has been the attempt to control for fluctuations in the natural supply of water through the provision of dams or, more commonly, wells or boreholes, an immediate consequence of which has been the disassociation of stocking or cultivation levels and the minimum expected level of rainfall.

The results of this are now well documented. It is generally recognized that the most stressed localities of the Sahel and similarly arid zones are water sources. The concentration of livestock in these areas means that whatever average stock levels may be, these particular spots are subject to excessive pressure. Since the number of available water sources tends to diminish with a reduction in rainfall it follows that the problem is exacerbated in dry years. Put another way, rural development programmes which have revolved around the construction of wells have created at least one of the necessary conditions for desertification to occur (Bernus, 1980; Dregne, 1983).

What has changed is that one element in traditional collective risk management, the restriction of stocking levels to the minimum expected carrying capacity of the range, has been discouraged in order to increase aggregate agricultural output. But this has not affected the risk management strategies of individual producers. Hence, herds that have been built up in wet years have not been reduced when the rains have failed, as livestock owners have sought to protect themselves from both the anticipated scarcity of food supplies and expected rises in prices. Where wells provide temporary water sources in the early stages of drought, the decision to destock tends to be deferred for even longer, leading to additional pressure on drought-stressed pastures (Hare, 1977). In addition, water sources have become foci for human as well as livestock concentration, and this has given rise to an increase in the rate of vegetation destruction in the neighbourhood of such sources in a variety of ways. Traffic, cultivation, and above all woodcutting both for arable land and for fuel have all proved to be destructive of the vegetational cover. In the Sahel the 'sedentarization' of nomadic pastoralists around water sources is reported to have resulted in dramatic environmental degradation in the neighbourhood of settlements. More generally, the rate of woodland clearance in these areas far exceeds the natural rate of regeneration, and yet still leaves a current fuelwood 'deficit' (Food and Agriculture Organization (FAO), 1984; Berry, 1984; World Bank, 1986; Markandya, 1991).

The general point here is that the risk management strategies adopted by low income agricultural producers have been built around a technologically conservative pattern of resource use designed to guarantee output in the short run. Risky innovations in terms of both input and output mix have been avoided. Moreover, the lower the private return to agriculture the more risk averse has the behaviour of agricultural producers become. At the same time, however, traditional collective risk management strategies have been largely abandoned as successive governments have promoted an increase in aggregate agricultural output as a major plank of their rural development or food self-sufficiency programmes, and as population growth has stimulated the demand for food. In the absence of collective control agricultural activity has been intensified. This has resulted in stocking densities or cultivation that are well beyond the carrying capacity of the resource base. In these circumstances, sustainable development of the rural economies of Sub-Saharan Africa appears to require either a change in technology, or a change in the regulation of access to the resource base, or some combination of the two. Of course not all technological change is environmentally benign. Indeed, evidence from South Asia suggests that the green revolution technologies adopted in that region have been far from environmentally sustainable (see Alauddin and Tisdell, 1991). Moreover, as is indicated below, many of the technological innovations induced in Botswana have increased the rate of soil loss in range and arable land. The point is, however, that the persistence of traditional technologies without traditional institutional controls on access to natural resources is positively linked with land degradation in much of Sub-Saharan Africa. Consequently something has to give: either institutions or technology. At present, however, most governments lack the political will to address the former, and most incentives militate against the latter.

3.2   PRICE INCENTIVES

Historically, the opening of the agrarian economies of Sub-Saharan Africa to wider markets created at least the potential for gains from trade, but it also introduced both new sources of uncertainty and new constraints on the behaviour of producers. Prices for the main cash and food crops, and for the main animal products produced in Sub-Saharan Africa have historically been extremely volatile. To the extent that independent domestic markets have existed for agricultural products, this volatility has reflected the considerable variance in domestic supply due to fluctuating climatic conditions. But much of the volatility in product prices has reflected conditions that are exogenous to the region. Partly as a result of this, most governments have long invoked measures to stabilize producer prices, usually based on a system of administered prices under monopsonistic marketing arrangements. The economic environment within which agricultural producers have made their decisions has accordingly one or both of two elements: a set of competitive 'parallel' markets in which prices have been driven by local supply conditions, and a set of near-monopsonistic markets dominated by centralized marketing boards, in which prices have been set independently of domestic supply conditions.

One very influential view of the environmental crisis in Sub-Saharan Africa is that it is predominantly an agricultural crisis, and that it is driven by the contradictory signals coming out of these marketing arrangements (Pearce, Barbier and Markandya, 1988). Certainly, considerable attention has recently been paid to the microeconomic decisions of resource users in Sub-Saharan Africa, and to the role of economic incentives in such decisions. The main finding in these studies is that the existing system of administered prices in African agricultural markets has both driven a wedge between the private and social opportunity cost of the use of the resource base, and reduced rural incomes.

It is widely believed that administered prices have driven the cost of tradable inputs below their social opportunity cost, thereby encouraging their overutilization. For example, destumping subsidies in agriculture, and stumpage fees or royalties in forestry have encouraged deforestation at excessive rates both in terms of rates of felling in timber concessions and the clearance of ever more marginal land for agricultural purposes (Berry, 1984; World Bank, 1986; Repetto, 1989; Warford, 1987; Perrings *et al.*, 1988) with significant implications for the subsequent rate of soil loss (Younis, 1985). Subsidies designed to promote cash cropping as a means of increasing export revenue have been argued to contribute to leaching, soil acidification, and loss of soil nutrients, and to the reduction in the resilience of key ecosystems (Grainger, 1990). The result is that the price system has been unable to guide the allocation of resources in a socially efficient way. Resource users have faced a positive incentive to misallocate resources.

The second effect reflects the control of output prices under monopsonistic marketing arrangements. The marketing boards set up in many countries in Sub-Saharan Africa to handle purchase, grading and marketing of a variety of agricultural products, are argued to have depressed producer prices below world prices (taken to define the social opportunity cost of the resource). The significance of this, at the risk of oversimplification, is generally taken to be the fact that it has reduced producer income and so discouraged investment in land conservation (cf. Warford, 1987; Ghai and Smith, 1987). It has already been argued that the impoverishment of resource users encourages an extreme degree of (current) risk aversion which inhibits technological innovation. It turns out that impoverishment also encourages a myopic approach to the intertemporal allocation of agricultural resources, since the future costs of resource use must be subordinated to the need for immediate survival. In addition, it ensures that the income effects of changing relative prices will tend to offset the substitution effects so dampening the response of agricultural producers to relative price changes (Perrings, 1989b).

The main conclusion of the literature on the incentive effects of the existing agricultural price system in Sub-Saharan Africa in the 1980s was that the liberalization of agricultural markets is a necessary condition for the conservation of the resource base (Bond, 1983; Cleaver, 1985, 1988; Repetto, 1986, 1989; Warford, 1989; Barbier, 1988, 1989). Indeed, liberalization of the agricultural sector became a key component of the conditionality attached to structural adjustment lending by both the World Bank and the International Monetary Fund (Johnson, 1989). The near-unanimity of this conclusion is compelling, but care needs to be taken in interpreting it. The literature is not nearly as convincing on the consequences of price reform as it is of the need for it.

3.2.1   Price liberalization

The liberalization of agricultural markets has implications for both the level and stability of prices. It is expected that average producer prices will rise, and although little attention is paid to the stability issue in the literature, it must also be expected that producer prices will become more variable. If we take the issue of price stability first, even though this is seldom addressed explicitly in these analyses, it is implied that monopsonistic marketing arrangements have imposed welfare losses that significantly outweigh any welfare gains from stabilization. This may be true given the level of administered producer prices, but it leaves open the possibility that stabilization close to the expected value of world prices for tradables would be preferred to the kind of price volatility experienced in many world agricultural markets. Indeed, this may be particularly important wherever the cause of famine is the failure of real purchasing power rather than food availability decline. All that can be said at present is that the price stability implications of the liberalization of agricultural markets in Sub-Saharan Africa have yet to be analyzed satisfactorily.

The implications of liberalization for the price level are easier to identify. In most cases, the average price of food crops has been held well below the expected world price in the interests of controlling consumer costs, and so urban wages (Markandya, 1991). There has been an anti-agricultural bias in policy reflected in the distortion of tradable input and output prices due to the monopsonistic pricing of outputs, monopolistic pricing of inputs, and the income-depressing effects of taxes and tariffs. Indeed, one of the dominant motivations for liberalization is the belief that it will result in an increase in producer prices. This, it is claimed, will lead to the expansion of agricultural supply, and will provide both the incentives and resources to conserve the agricultural resource base.

In the short run, it seems clear that the liberalization of agricultural markets should result in a rise in producer prices. But it is not nearly as clear what the long run effects will be. The long-term trend for real non-oil commodity prices has been a declining one. In respect of agricultural products, the index of world prices of non-food agricultural products has declined much more sharply than that for foods. But, as Figure 3.1 shows, both have fallen dramatically. Removing the wedge between administered and market prices may not therefore be sufficient to ensure a sustained increase in the real income of agricultural producers. The efficiency arguments in favour of liberalization remain, but it cannot be assumed that it will necessarily have a positive impact on long run producer prices.

3.2.2 Incentive effects

To date, evidence on the impact of agricultural price liberalization on the allocation of resources in the agricultural sector has been very mixed. A number of countries have introduced the principle of export parity pricing for major cash crops – but there has been no continent-wide trend towards this objective (Mosley and Smith, 1989). Indeed, in most countries agriculture continues to be 'penalized' by the protection of the industrial sector, either directly or through the overvaluation of the exchange rate. But where price regimes have been liberalized, the supply responsiveness of farmers has been muted. The short-run price elasticity of supply of individual cash crops has been shown to be positive and sometimes high, but findings on long-run supply elasticities are mixed. One survey found that the long-run supply

Figure 3.1   Real agricultural commodity prices, 1950–1986 (1979–1980 = 100)

Key:

-■- Non-food products   -□- Food products

Sources: World Bank (1987); World Resources Institute (1990).

elasticities of all crops tested was positive (and generally identical to the short-run supply elasticity) (Gammage, 1990)[1]. However, other studies have found generally low, and in some cases even negative long-run elasticities (Green, 1989; Rao, 1989; Perrings, 1989b).

While no attempt has been made to disentangle the income and substitution effects of the changes in relative prices that have followed liberalization, a number of explanations have been offered for the lack of a sharper response. The first is that price responsiveness is more tightly constrained by institutional factors in Sub-Saharan Africa than elsewhere (Delgado and Mellor, 1984; Lipton, 1987; Junankar, 1989).

Certainly, most of the evidence on own- and cross-price elasticities of supply and demand that is used to support the use of economic incentives in agriculture is drawn from non African data (Markandya, 1991). A second is that since a substantial proportion of goods and services are not traded, farmers are less sensitive to price changes than elsewhere (Ghai and Smith, 1987; Beynon, 1989). A third is that constraints on the supply of basic natural resources limits the capacity of those who do participate in the market to respond to price incentives. Raising the return on productive assets will not help if people do not have access to those assets. In many parts of Sub-Saharan Africa, for example, it has been argued that poorer farmers cannot increase productivity at the extensive margin simply because they do not have access to land (Feder and Norohna, 1987). Moreover, even where farmers do have access to productive assets, the lack of physical and financial infrastructure may limit their capacity to respond to the incentives offered by changing real returns on those assets (Beynon, 1989; Addison and Demery, 1989).

3.2.3 The problem of non-traded resources

It is not easy to distinguish between the various effects of price liberalization in practice. The 'anti-agricultural bias' in the system of administered prices implies that average agricultural income is below the level that would obtain under the same distribution of the agricultural product at socially efficient prices – which are no less than export and import parity prices in the case of tradables, and are equal to marginal social cost of resource use in the case of non-tradables. In other words, an anti-agricultural bias implies non-neutral intervention in respect of both input and output prices. Price liberalization in the case of the markets for tradables may be a necessary condition for the alignment of private and social costs, but it is not a sufficient condition. If non-tradable inputs are priced below their marginal social cost, and if there are no other restrictions on the use of such resources, then price liberalization may increase rather than decrease the level of environmental stress.

A particular feature of the price structure of agriculture in much of Sub-Saharan Africa has been the implicit subsidy on agricultural land offered by traditional (common or communal) land tenure systems. Land has been almost universally priced below its marginal social cost, and in most cases has been 'free'. Yet the cost of arable and range land to the user is not at issue in the liberalization of agricultural markets.

The general implication of this is that an increase in rural incomes will not, by itself, address the gap between the private and social costs of environmental resources.

To be more specific about this last point, there are three elements in the cost of committing an environmental resource to some economic use: (a) current and future direct costs of use including the costs of extraction or harvest of potentially depletable resources, the site costs of resource-using processes, and the costs of waste disposal; (b) current external costs of use, comprising intersectoral external costs due to the interdependence of activities reliant on a common environment (damage done to third parties which is not compensated within the existing structure of property rights, such as the cost to 'downstream' activities of the loss of watershed protection from deforestation); and (c) future indirect external costs of use, comprising 'user costs' or future opportunities foregone from committing a resource to a current use (costs imposed on future generations of committing a resource in a way that deprives future users of the benefit of its use, such as the loss to future generations everywhere caused by the extinction of a species in one location now). Price liberalization in respect of the markets for tradable input and outputs in agriculture leaves the last two of these untouched.

At present there is a strong presumption in the literature that market prices are superior environmental indicators than either administered prices, or market prices net of taxes. This implies that government intervention is systematically biased against the ecological sustainability of resource use. While it is possible to determine a systematic bias in the administered prices of tradables, since these have tended to be well below the market prices which give the lower bound of the social opportunity cost of resource use, it is not possible to identify any systematic bias in respect of other forms of government intervention. It is certainly the case that many macroeconomic policies which do impact on resource prices and interest rates tend to be targeted at short- or medium-term objectives. Nevertheless, the presumption of a systematic bias in government intervention seems untenable.

3.3 INCOME AND ASSET DISTRIBUTION

One factor that recurs again and again in the analysis of both causes and effects of environmental degradation in Sub-Saharan Africa is the level and distribution of income and assets. While rural poverty is very clearly an effect of rural resource degradation, it is also a cause. Following the famines of the Sahel and the Horn of Africa in the 1970s, Sen (1981) made the point that the basic cause of famine was not food availability decline due to drought, nor was it the economic dislocation caused by war. It was the collapse of the purchasing power of agricultural producers: what he called the failure of trade, direct, and transfer entitlements. While something similar can be said of the recurrence of famine in these areas, it is now clear that food availability decline is a large part of the problem. However, it is food availability decline due not to drought, but to the degradation of the resource base. The resilience of the ecological systems on which agriculture depends has been reduced to the point where even modest fluctuations in rainfall and temperature have severe effects on output, and this is the direct result of land use practices that are largely driven by poverty. Poverty distorts attitudes to risk and innovation, just as it distorts savings and investment decisions, and the weight given to the future effects of current activity. Poverty also dominates the responses of resource users to changes in relative agricultural input and output prices, in taxes and transfers. It generates a 'vicious circle' of responses in which the options available to successive generations are steadily eroded. It is in this sense that the sustainability of resource use implies the need to address the poverty of current generations (cf. World Commission of Environment and Development, 1987).

3.3.1 Rural poverty in Sub-Saharan Africa

As was remarked earlier, the evidence for the increasing impoverishment of people in many of the dryland regions of Sub-Saharan Africa is overwhelming. This is reflected both in the number of people judged to be in need by some absolute measure, and in the distribution of assets and income. Measures of the depth of absolute poverty include the proportion of the population judged to be in need of emergency relief, or to have access to goods or services judged to be basic needs, such as drinking water or sanitation services. By both sorts of measures, absolute poverty is increasing in parts of rural Sub-Saharan Africa. The first measure tends to focus on short term poverty, the second to capture trends. But the two measures often coincide. In the Sudan, to take one example, the percentage of the population judged to be in need of emergency relief in 1990 is higher and the percentage of the population without access to safe drinking water is lower than in 1980 (World Resources Institute (WRI), 1990).

At the same time, there has been a marked and continuing tendency for the distribution of both assets and income to widen over time. In part, this reflects the erosion of traditional rights of access to the resource base, which has given rise to a long-term trend involving widening disparity in the farm and herd sizes of arable and pastoral economies (Ghai and Radwan (eds), 1983). Nor has this trend been interrupted by the decolonization process. Colclough and Fallon (1983), for example, have reported that the distribution of cattle ownership in Botswana has become increasingly skewed following independence.[2] A study of agriculture in Northern Hausaland in the mid-1970s found that although land was communally owned, 50 per cent of the farmers worked only 22 per cent of the available land (Norman, 1977). Moreover, it would seem that the Gini coefficient for land distribution in the 'traditional' agricultural sectors of most African countries in the same period lay between 0.42 and 0.55 (Ghai and Radwan (eds), 1983): which is very different from the egalitarian distribution expected by Ault and Rutman (1979) under the archetypal traditional tenure system. It turns out that gender is an important factor in this trend. Female headed households typically have access to a much smaller asset base, whether in terms of land or livestock, than male headed households, and it is not coincidental that relative poverty in the sense of relative deprivation is reckoned to bear most heavily on women (UNDP, 1990).

3.3.2   Poverty and the rate of discount

The main problem with poverty in the context of the intertemporal allocation of environmental resources is the effect it has on the individual resource user's rate of time preference. This has two main implications. First, those in poverty will tend to discount the future costs of current activities at a much higher rate than others. The higher the discount rate, the less relevant are the very important user costs of environmental resources. Second, since the rate of discount determines the optimal rate of extraction of potentially exhaustible resources, those in poverty will tend to deplete such resources at a much higher rate than others. It can be shown that if the price of a natural resource is constant over time, it will be optimal to deplete that resource so long as the discount rate exceeds its natural rate of regeneration. And if the price is not constant, it will be optimal to deplete the resource so long as the discount rate exceeds its natural rate of regeneration plus the rate of change in its price. The so-called Hotelling rule for exhaustible resources is a special case of this (see Dasgupta and Heal, 1979; Clark, 1976).

Poverty in the sense in which it is used here is 'subjective poverty'. That is, it is defined by the household's perception of what constitutes a minimum acceptable level of consumption. Such perceptions vary both from household to household, and within households over time. An exogenous shock which necessitates a downward revision of consumption levels will be accepted with a lag which depends on the speed of adjustment of consumption expectations. For those at the subjective poverty point this implies some period of dissaving. Indeed, the zero savings level of income for any household may accordingly be regarded as the 'subjective' poverty point for that household, while dissaving may be taken to indicate that the household is in 'subjective' poverty (Drewnowski, 1977).

The recorded dissaving that has occurred in many Sub-Saharan African countries during the last decade is consistent with this view (see World Bank, 1990). What is more important from an environmental point of view is that there has been additional dissaving in terms of real assets that is not accounted for in the standard system of accounts. Because the natural resource base is not valued, neither the flow of environmental services nor the degradation/depreciation of the resource base is recorded in the accounts, and there is no available measure of such dissaving (Perrings *et al.*, 1989; Markandya and Perrings, 1991). Nevertheless, the depletion of ground water, soil nutrients or vegetation in order to maintain current consumption represents dissaving just as much as the drawing down of financial assets for the same purpose. Moreover, the lower the initial level of consumption, and the longer the history of poverty, the more that dissaving involves degrading the basic agricultural assets.

4 Botswana: Economy and Environment

4.1 STRUCTURE AND TRENDS

4.1.1 Output

The development of the Botswana economy since the country gained independence in 1966 has been impressive by most indicators: social as well as economic (see Appendix 1). One major study of the country ascribes this to a combination of sound economic management, unusually effective negotiating skills and leadership, a deeply entrenched commitment to consensual governance and a fair amount of luck (Harvey and Lewis, 1990). Whatever the relative importance of each of these factors, the net result has been higher average growth rates than in any other non-oil exporting country. Despite strong growth in both the manufacturing and service sectors, the economy is dominated to an unusual degree by natural resource-based activities. The sectoral composition of GDP, recorded in Table 4.1, shows that in terms of output this translates as a high level of dependence on the mining sector. In 1988/9 mining accounted for some 50 per cent of GDP (at current prices), around 90 per cent of exports, and around 60 per cent of tax revenue.

Of the non-resource based sectors in the economy, the most rapidly growing sectors have been wholesale and retail trade (commerce), financial services, government and manufacturing, although only the last is considered to be a 'leading sector' with the potential for sustained growth. It should be added, though, that the share of government in GDP is still expanding. This is partly due to the increasingly prominent role of government in developing infrastructure and capacity in the economy. Indeed, development expenditures accounted for a steadily increasing share of public expenditure during the 1980s, reaching just over 49 per cent in 1989/90. This share is estimated to have declined in 1990/91, and in the longer term it may be expected that government will play a diminishing role in the economy.

Table 4.1 GDP by sector: 1979/80–1988/89 (P million, 1979/80 prices)

	1979/80	1980/81	1981/82	1982/83	1983/84	1984/85	1985/86	1986/87	1987/88	1988/89
Agriculture	83.3	75	71.8	60.1	50.9	46.8	53.2	51	59.7	59.7
Mining	210.7	260.7	222.4	393.6	533.9	560.2	573.2	662.4	692.1	806.7
Manufacturing	29.2	37	45.8	42.4	44	35.8	45.4	49.7	52.2	55.1
Electricity, water	15	15.3	15.9	15.7	19.5	23.5	31.4	34.8	36.6	38.6
Construction	36.4	32	37.2	26.2	38.7	35.6	30.3	34.1	40.3	52.5
Commerce	157	163.8	150.7	162.1	182.2	205.7	236.8	251.7	273.4	319.2
Transport	13.6	14.8	18.1	23.8	23.1	28.6	39.3	37	40.9	43.8
Financial	57.6	49.7	55.6	58.9	65.2	82.2	96.6	100.1	116.2	128.7
Government	100.6	114.2	123.8	136.1	150.5	172.5	186.2	202.3	238.3	261.4
Services	20.9	25.6	29.2	35	34.9	42.9	48.8	54.3	63	65.8
Dummy*	-14.8	-16.7	-17	-19.9	-22.4	-22.3	-33	-36.4	-42.3	-48.5
Total GDP	709.5	771.4	753.5	934	1120.5	1211.5	1308.2	1441	1570.4	1783

Note: * Dummy sector is a correction for imputed bank service charges.

Source: Republic of Botswana, *Statistical Bulletin*, 15, 3, September 1990.

Nevertheless, for the foreseeable future, the development of the Botswana economy is expected to be strongly influenced by public expenditure (Jefferis, 1991). The relative growth performance of the sectors expected to play a leading role in the economy in the future, including government, is illustrated in Figure 4.1.

4.1.2 Employment

In terms of employment, the agricultural sector plays a dominant – if residual – role. Although agriculture accounts for less than 4 per cent of formal sector employment, the formal sector accounts for only about 25 per cent of total employment, and the vast majority of those in informal employment are engaged in agriculture. Indeed, traditional agriculture offers what may be termed employment of the last resort. A reasonable estimate is that formal and informal sector agriculture taken together account for something like 75 per cent all employment within Botswana. The structure of employment is described in Table 4.2.

It should be noted that employment data in Botswana refer to formal sector employment only. In Table 4.2, the size of the labour force has been estimated on the basis of population projections of the age cohorts normally assumed to be economically active. The table is

Figure 4.1   Sectoral GDP at constant 1979/80 prices

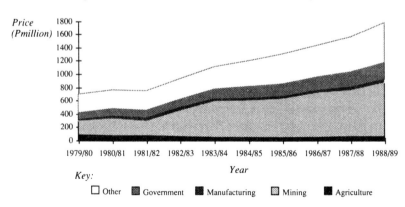

Source: Republic of Botswana, *Statistical Bulletin*, 15, 3, September 1990.

Table 4.2   Employment by sector (1000 employees), Botswana, 1980–1989

Sector	1980	1981	1982	1983	1984	1985	1986	1987	1988	1989
Total formal	438.1	454.5	471.4	488.8	506.7	525	544.8	564.6	584.9	606.6
Agriculture	4.3	4.8	4.2	4.5	4.5	5.4	4.9	5.6	6.5	6.6
Mining	7.2	7.3	7.1	7.2	7.5	7.3	7.5	7	7.5	7.6
Manufacturing	5.6	6.4	7.2	9.8	9.5	9.9	12.2	14.7	16.4	18.1
Elect, water	1.5	1.6	2.2	1.9	2	1.9	2	2.2	2.3	2.2
Construction	13.4	15.2	13.6	9.6	11.1	11.5	13.7	16.9	22.2	23.9
Commerce	10.4	15.3	16.6	15.3	18.1	18.3	20.9	25.7	28.8	28.6
Transport	3.4	3.9	3.7	3.9	5.5	5.7	5.1	6.7	7.9	7.3
Financial	4.3	4.9	5.7	6	6.2	6.8	7.4	9.8	11.2	11.6
Services	3.7	5.4	5.5	5.1	5.1	5.8	5.7	8.7	9	9.7
Government	29.5	32.6	34.3	37.3	39.6	45.6	50.7	52.8	58	60.7
Total formal empl	83.4	97.4	100.1	100.6	110	116	130.1	150.2	169.8	176.3
Informal empl[1]	354.7	357.1	371.3	388.2	396.7	409	414.7	414.4	415.1	430.3
Labour force	438.1	454.5	471.4	488.8	506.7	525	544.8	564.6	584.9	606.6
SA mines	21.3	20.3	18.4	18.7	18.9	20.1	21	20.1	19.3	17.9

Note: 1. This includes the unemployed.

Source: Republic of Botswana, *Labour Statistics 1989 – Part 1*, Gaborone, CSO.

derived from the 1981 census, and will be subject to revision in the light of the 1991 census. Informal sector employment has then been determined as a residual: the difference between the estimated labour force and formal sector employment. Because informal sector employment is a residual it represents an upper bound estimate of employment in traditional agriculture. The figure given for informal sector employment includes, for example, both off-farm informal rural employment as well as open and disguised unemployment. It also includes the informal activities of Batswana who have migrated from the rural areas to either larger rural villages or towns – a process which has been underway for some time (see Republic of Botswana, 1982). Nevertheless, it serves to indicate the critical importance of the agricultural sector for the majority of the population (see Figure 4.2). Indeed, it is clear that the exhaustible and renewable resource based sectors in Botswana exhibit very large differences not only in performance, but also in function.

Figure 4.2   Employment by sector, Botswana, 1980–1989

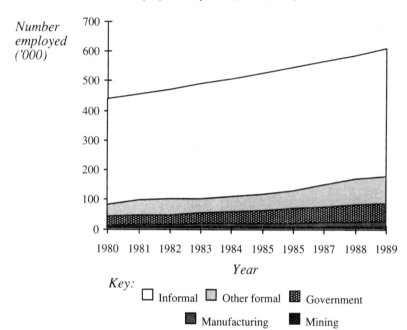

Key:
□ Informal   ▨ Other formal   ▦ Government
■ Manufacturing   ■ Mining

Source: Republic of Botswana (1990b), *Labour Statistics 1989 – Part 1*, CSO, Gaborone.

The difference in performance is most striking. Whereas mining GDP grew at an average annual rate of 16 per cent between 1979/80 and 1988/89, agricultural GDP contracted at an average annual rate of 4 per cent over the same period. The difference in function may be less obvious. At the risk of caricaturing the different roles, mineral revenues may be said to have provided the resources for the development of a dynamic modern sector, whilst traditional agriculture may be said to have provided a safety net for those unable to participate in that development. Not only does traditional agriculture directly provide for the consumption needs of the majority of economically inactive Botswana, it is also the vehicle through which the government of Botswana has chosen to provide income support to those who are economically active but either unemployed or underemployed.

Figure 4.3 shows labour absorption in both informal sector activities, and in the leading sectors in the modern economy. The

Figure 4.3 Formal sector employment gap ('000s)

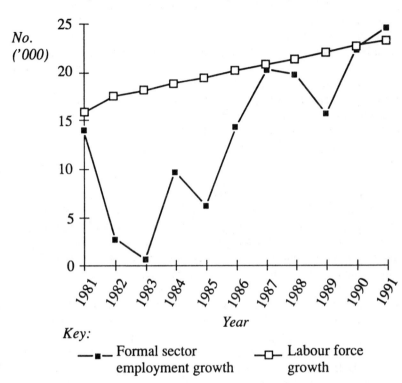

Key:

—■— Formal sector employment growth   —□— Labour force growth

Note: Labour force growth is calculated from the projected growth in the population aged 15–64 from the medium variant of the national de facto projections (the projections which exclude nationals abroad). The numbers are greater than the growth registered in the labour force surveys available for some of this period.

Sources: Republic of Botswana (1987) *Population Projections 1981–2011*, Gaborone, CSO. Republic of Botswana, *Labour Statistics* (various years), Gaborone, CSO.

most striking feature of the recent record is that during the period of very rapid growth in the value of mining output, employment in the mining sector has been more or less constant. Employment in the manufacturing sector has increased sharply, but from a very small base. Employment in government has also increased sharply, but is not expected to provide a continuing source of new jobs in the future. At the same time Botswana has a high and accelerating rate of population growth. Between 1971 and 1981 the rate was 3.3 per cent per annum. It is currently between 3.4 and 3.6 per cent and the fertility rate appears to be rising.[1] The future rate of population growth is expected to lie somewhere between 2.4 per cent and 3.8 per cent per annum. The former hardly seems likely, but even if the rate were closer to 2.4 than to 3.8 per cent, it would still put considerable extra pressure on natural resources. Realistically, the population can be expected to double between the 1981 and 2001 censuses.

As was remarked in Chapter 2, the effects of population growth are not necessarily negative. An expansion in the size of the domestic market may, for example, offer important long run benefits to the Botswana economy. But at the present rate of population growth, the number of new entrants to the labour force considerably exceeds the number of new formal sector jobs. In the short run, the most realistic prognosis is that continued population growth will lead to an increasing demand for an already stretched set of rural resources, as the excess of new entrants over vacancies in the formal sector finds employment in the rural economy. The evidence for increasing pressure on scarce rural resources is already highly visible, including increased average use of water in the rural economy, the concentration of livestock and smallstock around many of the south-eastern settlements, the depletion of wood around the larger settlements, and the depletion and pollution of water reserves available to the larger villages in south-eastern Botswana (cf. VIAK, 1985). Population growth has ensured that resources which were once non-scarce, are now scarce. At the same time, however, the same resources are still open to all, and for the most part are unpriced. The Botswana rural economy has been forced to switch from expansion at the extensive margin to expansion at the intensive margin, without the benefit of markets to assist with the reallocation of resources that this involves.

Two things, therefore, have motivated Botswana's recent reappraisal of both sectors. The first is the prospect that the mining sector will no longer be able to function as the engine of economic growth. There are no new diamond mines in prospect, and the Sua Pan soda ash project aside (which has had an impact on GDP from 1992), there are few other obvious large scale mineral prospects. To underscore the dependence of the economy on the mining sector, it is worth noting that between 1988/9 and 1989/90 the rate of growth of GDP fell from 13.6 to 5.7 per cent, due solely to a turnaround from 17 per cent growth to 3 per cent contraction in the mining sector. Indeed, in 1991/92 the government ran a budget deficit for the first time since the recession of 1982/83. The second thing which has motivated the reappraisal of the agricultural sector is the continuing high rate of population growth which requires extremely high rates of formal sector employment growth if the formal sector employment gap is to be closed (see Figure 4.3). The combination of these two things has compelled the government of Botswana to reassess the role of agriculture in the economy, and to pay serious attention to the sustainability of the patterns of resource utilization that have driven the economy in the post-independence period.

Given the size of the formal sector employment gap, much has been expected from the agricultural sector. To date, however, it has failed to meet expectations. It was, for example, projected that the rate of growth of agriculture would average 6.5 per cent over the period of the sixth national development plan (1985–1991) – amongst the highest growth rates projected for any sector. The goals set out by the national development plan for the agricultural sector made the point explicitly that agricultural growth was required to compensate for the fall-off in mineral sector growth. At the same time it was recognized that agricultural growth depended on the sustainability of agricultural resources. Indeed, the plan emphasized 'the need to safeguard the long term future of the livestock industry by conserving the rangeland that is Botswana's most valuable agricultural resource' (Republic of Botswana, 1985, p. 168). It turns out that per capita agricultural growth has been negative almost throughout the plan period (see Figure 4.4), and that successive reports have recorded persistent deterioration of the natural resource base. The important point here is that the conjunction of trends in the economy has made it crucial to understand not only what it is that determines the degradation of natural resources, but what scope there is for reversing the process without the benefit of growing mineral revenues.

4.2 THE RURAL ECONOMY

The climate of Botswana is characterized by long periods of high pressure and low humidity, high summer temperatures, and highly variable rainfall. The northern and eastern parts of the country tend to be significantly wetter than the western parts, the long run seasonal average varying between 564 mm in Lobatse to 305 mm in Tsabong. Rainfall records reveal a 15 to 20 year rainfall cycle, with rainfall being below the mean for six out of ten years. Figure 4.5 records rainfall in

Figure 4.4   Real GDP per capita: agriculture (left axis) and total GDP per capita (right axis), Pula

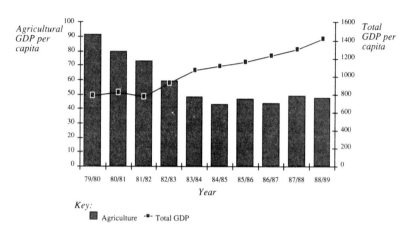

Key:
■ Agriculture   -■- Total GDP

Source: Republic of Botswana, *Statistical Bulletin*, 15, 3, September 1990.

selected centres as a percentage of the long run seasonal average for the last decade. It has, for the most part, been a period of drought, and this has had a major effect on the development of the rural economy. Rainfall is strongly seasonal, mostly falling during the summer months. Because the rain tends to fall in showers exceeding 10 mm, the hydrological cycle is dominated by quick flows – surface run-off. Yet surface water is generally scarce, due to the fact that during the period of the rains evaporation and evapo-transpiration rates are extremely high. The main sources of surface water are the Okavango and Chobe river systems, with few other rivers and none of the pans holding surface water on a perennial basis. While data on groundwater sources has been significantly improved in recent years little is yet known about groundwater reserves in much of the country.

    Most soils are characterized by low organic content, and low levels of nutrients. They are, in particular, deficient in both nitrogen and phosphorus. They tend to be sandy, of unstable surface structure and poor surface sealing. Once again there is a marked difference between the eastern and western parts of the country: the soils of the eastern *hardveld* being more capable of sustaining arable production than the soils of the western *sandveld*. In general, the vegetation of the country

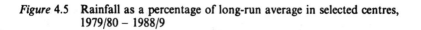

Figure 4.5   Rainfall as a percentage of long-run average in selected centres, 1979/80 – 1988/9

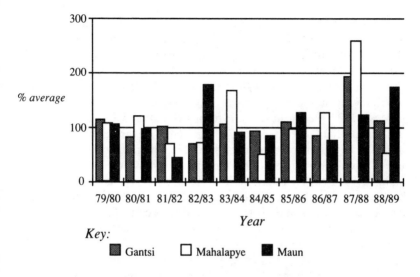

Source: Republic of Botswana, *Statistical Bulletin*, 15, 3, September 1990.

may be characterised as savannah, varying from semi-scrub arid savannah in the west to tree and scrub savannah in the east. The Okavango and Chobe areas are characterized by aquatic grassland and dry deciduous or riparian forest. This combination of climatic and soil conditions makes Botswana in general better suited to animal husbandry than to arable agriculture. Indeed, arable agriculture is largely restricted to the hardveld where some 85 per cent of the population is concentrated. Even in these areas, however, arable agriculture is extremely risky, as is evidenced by the wide variability in the ratio of area planted to area harvested described in section 4.2.2.

4.2.1   The livestock sector

Livestock accounts for the greater part of the agricultural sector in Botswana, on average some 80 per cent of agricultural GDP. The sector is divided into traditional and commercial subsectors. We are concerned with the former. The main emphasis in the subsector is on cattle of which some 85 per cent are held in the traditional subsector.

One effect of the drought and recent policy changes has been a dramatic increase in the number of goats, and of these more than 97 per cent are held in the traditional subsector. Although both dairy and beef cattle are kept in Botswana, the beef sector is predominant. Most agricultural exports are made up of meat products, hides and skins.[2] In the past, output has been subject to a near monopsony held by the Botswana Meat Commission (BMC). More recently, however, the proportion of animals slaughtered outside the BMC – by municipal abattoirs or home slaughters – has increased. In 1984 the BMC processed 87 per cent of all recorded cattle kills. By 1989 the proportion had dropped to 72 per cent. Nevertheless, the BMC remains the major force in the beef market, and the incentive effects of BMC price policy are an important part of the story.

Since 1986 external conditions have been generally favourable for beef producers.[3] In the fifteen years after independence the national herd increased substantially from around 1.4m cattle to just under 3.0m, partly in response to strong external market for beef. Net sales of the BMC increased from P9m in 1967 to P44.5m in 1976 and to P96m in 1983, much of the product going to the EEC under a series of agreements based on the Lomé convention. A rebate of 90 per cent of the EEC 'variable levy' on beef import quotas was granted to the ACP group of countries under Lomé I and has been repeatedly renewed. The same countries were exempted from the EEC's Common External Tariff of 20 per cent and were given quota. In Botswana's case this stands at 19,000 kg per annum, although it has never yet been filled.

The present characteristics of the livestock sector reflect a pattern of extensive rather than intensive growth. This has been the product both of a historically low ratio of population to land and a structure of property rights under which all Batswana have enjoyed more or less unrestricted access to rangeland. The average herd size in the traditional sector was 37 in 1989, compared with 920 in the commercial subsector in the same year, and more than half of all traditional farms had less than 20 cattle. Productivity in the sector is low and declining, partly reflecting the negative effects of a long period of adverse climatic conditions, and partly reflecting the impact of environmental degradation due to overgrazing. The immediate effect of the drought was a reduction in the size of the national herd. Between 1982 and 1987 it fell from 2.98m to 2.26m. This reflected increasing off take rates after 1980, but this notwithstanding the number of cattle slaughtered by the BMC at its Lobatse and Maun abattoirs has fallen steadily over the last decade (see Table 4.3).

Table 4.3 Livestock production, 1980–1989

		Year									
		1980	1981	1982	1983	1984	1985	1986	1987	1988	1989
Cattle	total (000)	2910	2967	2979	2818	2685	2459	2332	2264	2408	2543
	offtake rate	7.9	8.1	8.1	10.2	9.6	12.8	9.4	8.4	8.3	9.5
	BMC index of no. killed	100	143	168	156	158	136	123	90	75	77
	BMC index of av. value	100	121	120	125	125	135	148	167	232	306
Goats	total (000)	638	621	636	783	889	1138	1332	1470	1691	1897
	offtake rate	7.8	7.1	8.5	7.0	7.6	6.5	6.9	7.7	9.8	12.0
	BMC index of no. killed	100	22	108	1336	2659	5421	7392	9944	8322	10320
	BMC index of av. value	100	103	119	155	174	181	193	208	216	242
Sheep	total (000)	149	140	140	165	167	200	229	240	259	286
	offtake rate	18.1	8.9	8.2	12.1	12.8	13.1	5.7	7.1	9.7	11.7
	BMC index of no. killed	100	18	133	1708	4023	5067	5114	6251	6104	6790
	BMC index of av. value	100	69	132	169	193	201	228	254	268	277

Sources: Republic of Botswana, *1989 Botswana Agricultural Statistics*, Gaborone, CSO; Republic of Botswana, *Statistical Bulletins, 1982–1990*, Gaborone, CSO.

Aside from the drought of the 1980s, three trends have turned out to be important contributory factors to the decline in physical productivity in the subsector. The first was the change in the spatial distribution of the national herd as a result both of the increase in the size of average holdings in the 1960s and 1970s, and of the introduction of the Tribal Lands Grazing Policy – which saw the establishment of large leasehold ranches in the sandvelt. Cattle spread further and further into the western and northern sandvelt where they not only had to compete for grazing with wildlife, but also to depend on increasingly fragile ecosystems with much lower and more variable carrying capacity (Cooke, 1985). A second significant trend was the increase in grazing pressure in the eastern parts of the country as a consequence of both the proliferation of boreholes to tap groundwater supplies and the expansion of small farmer herds, with effects to be described momentarily. The third important trend has been a change in the ratio of cattle to sheep and goats shown in Figure 4.6.

Figure 4.6   Livestock population, 1980–9 ('000)

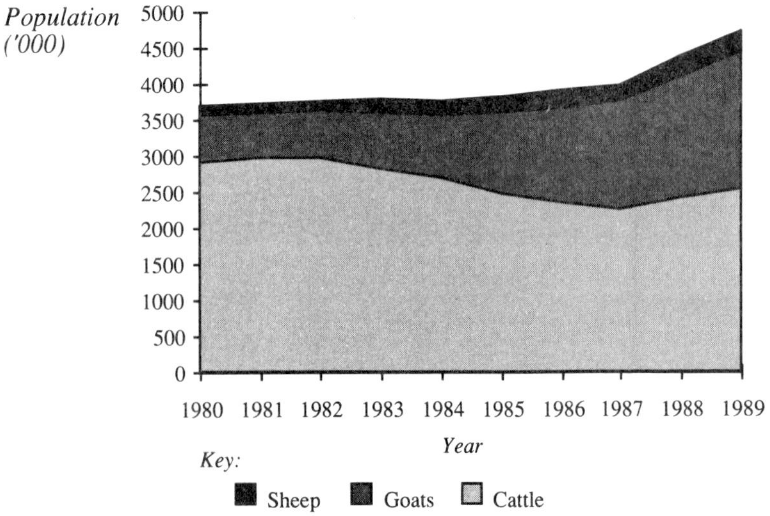

Sources: Republic of Botswana (1990b) *1989 Botswana Agricultural Statistics* (Gaborone: CSO); Republic of Botswana, *Statistical Bulletins, 1982–1990* (Gaborone: CSO).

Indeed, the most striking development in the livestock sub sector during the drought years has been the combination of climatological and price incentives to expand holdings of goats. The net effect of an increase in grazing pressure due to expanded goat holdings, at the same time as the drought has caused a reduction in carrying capacity, has been lower overall levels of productivity. It is not a coincidence that grazing and not water availability has been perceived by farmers to be the binding constraint on herd expansion for some years now (Arntzen and Veenendaal, 1986).

Rangeland degradation is now severe in a number of areas due to the combined effects of soil erosion, depletion of soil nutrients, increasing soil aridity, undesirable alteration in biomass and the diversity of fauna and flora. In the wetter eastern areas this is evidenced by the steady reduction in useable rangeland due to the increase in woody plants, the associated decrease in grass biomass and ground cover, the loss of soil organic matter, and widespread erosion (Abel *et al.*, 1987). In the drier areas it is evidenced by more widespread devegetation leading to reduction in organic and moisture content and erosion. Indeed, in parts of Kgalagadi and Ghanzi, areas of rangeland have been reduced to near-deserts (Arntzen and Veenendaal, 1986). While this is due in part to rainfall deficiency – the rainfall experience of the last decade is shown for selected centres in Figure 4.5 – the consensus is that it reflects persistent overgrazing of a sort that has been observed in many of the drylands of Sub-Saharan Africa.

Despite the reduction in cattle during the drought years indicated in figure 4.6, Arntzen and Veenendaal (1986) argue that range degradation due to overstocking increased sharply in these years. There are two reasons advanced for this. The first relates to a widely documented feature of traditional 'opportunistic' range management strategies. These strategies are marked by strong herd growth on communal pastures during the wet phase of the rainfall cycle, but no matching tendency to destocking in the dry phase. This is alleged to have led to livestock densities in excess of the carrying capacity of the range over long periods of time (cf. Dixon, James and Sherman, 1989; Pearce, Barbier and Markandya, 1990). Recently, this view has been questioned in the range management and ecological literature. Several studies have claimed that traditional opportunistic range management techniques are not only more productive than techniques based on equilibrium range succession models (Behnke, 1985; Westoby *et al.*, 1989; Abel, 1990; Scoones, 1990), but do not lead to 'unacceptable' rates of range degradation (Biot, 1990; Abel, 1990). The issues this literature raises are considered later in this study. What is important here is that the delay in destocking at the onset of the drought exacerbated the level of overgrazing caused by a fall in the carrying capacity of the range. A second reason relates to the change in herd composition. Even though the numbers of cattle fell, the overall number of livestock increased as pastoralists substituted goats for cattle.

The importance of the declining physical productivity observed in the livestock subsector is that it imposes costs not just on the immediate users of the resource – the livestock owners – but on other members of society not party to their stocking decisions. The soils, vegetation and water supplies that are used for animal husbandry are also used for mining, tourism, fisheries, forestry, arable agriculture or domestic consumption. Aside from the reduction in returns to all livestock owners, the overstocking of rangeland has already led to the nitrate pollution of a number of aquifers and to changes in the availability and quality of water elsewhere in the economy through increased run-off and sedimentation leading to lower rates of recharge of groundwater, reduction in surface water for wildlife, silting of dams, output losses in dam and river fisheries, and pollution of drinking water. Moreover, the lower returns to agriculture have encouraged rural–urban migration giving rise to the consequential cost of providing urban infrastructure and services. The overgrazing of rangeland involves much more on the debit side than the cost to future users of rehabilitating the range, or relocating themselves. We argue that the reasons for overgrazing are to be found in the structure of incentives created in large part by government policy, and these are considered in detail in Chapter 5. This change in the composition of the national herd together with the concentration of cattle holdings in traditional grazing areas represents a privately rational response to the exigencies of the drought, given the incentives facing producers. At the same time it has resulted in severe degradation of the resource base in the communal areas, especially around water sources, and this has had adverse effects on productivity.

4.2.2   Arable agriculture

The potential arable area of Botswana is estimated to be 1.36 million ha., 20 per cent of which is currently cultivated. Once again, the sector can be divided into traditional and commercial subsectors. Most of the area cultivated comprises what are generally referred to as traditional 'subsistence' rainfed farms where yields are low (under 100 kg per planted hectare on average for the two main cereals grown in the country, sorghum and maize) and highly sensitive to intraseasonal and interseasonal variation in rainfall. Commercial farms are larger. They comprise less than half of one percent of the total number of farms, but produce 37 per cent of total sorghum and maize. Yields are higher (around 800 kg per hectare for sorghum and up to 1400 kg per hectare for maize), but are also sensitive to variation in rainfall.

Two types of farming predominate in the traditional subsector: 'subsistence' dryland crop farms; and 'subsistence' or 'semi-subsistence' mixed dryland crop and livestock farms. Commercial farming is also of two types: commercial dryland crop farming, and medium and large scale commercial irrigated farming. The first group comprises a small number of farmers in the Pandamatenga area. The second covers an area of less than 2,000 hectares in total in the Tuli Block, Maun and near Selebwe Phikwe. The water sources for these farms are the Okavango and Limpopo Rivers, and groundwater supplies.

The description of traditional farms as 'subsistence' is rather misleading for two reasons. The first of these is that few such farms are entirely disengaged from the market, and even fewer produce enough for the farming household to be said to be self sufficient in food. Farming households are reliant on food purchases to satisfy their subsistence needs. To be sure, many traditional farms produce little marketable surplus, much of the surplus grain from this sector coming from the 21 per cent of farmers who have holdings of between 6 and 15 hectares. Thus, resource allocation decisions in the traditional 'subsistence' sector are not as independent of market conditions as the term might imply.

As in the livestock subsector, the market for cereals is dominated by a monopsonistic parastatal: in this case the Botswana Agricultural Marketing Board (BAMB). Certainly, not all grain is marketed, but the proportion is an increasing one. A 1987 estimate by Love, Babikanyisa and Mrema (1989) put the proportion of the sorghum crop sold to the BAMB at 27.5 per cent. In 1982, the first year of the drought, it had been only 8 per cent. There are a number of factors at work here, but one at least has been the government's price policy with respect to cereals. In 1982 the BAMB was granted a monopsony in the purchase of sorghum, whether domestically produced or imported, but was required to set a preplanting price for sorghum each year based on the import parity price plus a regional allowance for notional transport costs to different production areas. From 1984, a premium of 10 per cent above the corresponding maize import parity price was added. The regional pricing policy dates from 1982/3 and the 10 per cent premium from 1984. The pattern of BAMB prices which has emerged is recorded in Table 4.4.

As in the livestock sector again, the drought has been associated both with a decline in average productivity, and the substitution of traditional drought resistant crops for the higher yielding but more drought sensitive maize. These trends are illustrated in Figures 4.7 and 4.8, and in Table 4.5. Figure 4.7 indicates changes in the level of output of the three major crops, maize, sorghum and millet, and a catch all category of other crops (mostly beans and pulses, sunflower and groundnuts). The high correlation between aggregate levels of output and rainfall is obvious, as one would expect in a rainfed system. The progressive substitution of sorghum for maize reflects both changes in farmer expectations of rainfall, and changes in the relative prices of the two crops.

The pattern of yields during the 1980s can only be described as extraordinary, whether measured by the yield per hectare harvested or by the ratio of the area harvested to the area planted. In 1983 this last ratio fell below 35 per cent for every major crop produced in Botswana, and much lower for some. Only 15 per cent of lands planted in beans and pulses, for example, were harvested. This indicates the total failure of up to 85 per cent of crops planted in that year. In 1984, while an effort was made to harvest a slightly higher proportion of the area planted, total output was even lower – just over 13 per cent of the 1981 figure.

Two indices of productivity are included here. First, Table 4.5 shows the average yields per hectare planted of the three major crops without distinguishing between type of farm (traditional or commercial) between 1979/80 and 1988/89. To get a sense of the degree to which these figures differ from those in traditional sector alone, note that the average productivity of land shown recorded for 1989 is around 40 per cent greater than that in the traditional subsector, and nearly 70 per cent greater than that recorded in the bottom 50 per cent of traditional farms.

The second index is offered in part explanation of the first, and is the ratio of land harvested to land planted, shown in Figure 4.8. Despite the close correlation between this ratio and the mean level of rainfall, it is argued later in this study that changes in this ratio are not independent of the incentives confronting farmers. Both indices show a sharp fall in the average productivity of arable land during the dry

Table 4.4 Producer prices paid by BAMB (P per metric tonne)

	Year									
	1980/81	*1981/82*	*1982/83*	*1983/84*	*1984/85*	*1985/86*	*1986/87*	*1987/88*	*1988/89*	*1989/90*
Sorghum	135	149	175	208	271	281	290	309	309	329
Maize	130	143	163	22	268	276	294	282	282	323

Sources: Republic of Botswana, *Statistical Bulletin*, 15, 3, September 1990. Bank of Botswana, *Annual Report 1985*, Gaborone, Bank of Botswana.

Table 4.5 Yields per hectare planted, 1979/80 to 1988/89 (metric tonnes)

	Year									
	1980	*1981*	*1982*	*1983*	*1984*	*1985*	*1986*	*1987*	*1988*	*1989*
Sorghum	0.2	0.2	0.04	0.04	0.05	0.12	0.1	0.09	0.34	0.2
Maize	0.15	0.25	0.2	0.15	0.01	0.03	0.08	0.07	0.14	0.23
Millet	0.18	0.1	0.03	0.03	0.04	0.11	0.07	0.03	0.28	0.1
Total	0.17	0.2	0.09	0.07	0.04	0.09	0.09	0.08	0.29	0.19

Source: Republic of Botswana (1980–1989), *Botswana Agricultural Statistics*, Gaborone, CSO.

Figure 4.7   Total crop production, 1980–89 ('000 metric tonnes)

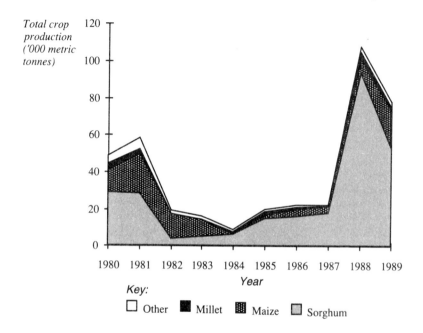

Source: Republic of Botswana, *1989 Botswana Agricultural Statistics*, Gaborone, CSO.

years of the 1980s, and point up the differences between the two major crops, sorghum and maize. Although the ratio of area harvested to area planted of both crops fell at much the same rate during the early part of the dry cycle, the persistence of drought affected maize more strongly than it did sorghum.

While much of the decline in the physical productivity of land resulted from water deficiency due to drought, it is clear that, as in the livestock sector, the degradation of an environment under increasing stress has also had a role to play. Evidence in Botswana suggests that erosion has tended to increase with the area ploughed, and to fall with the quality of the crop cover (van der Poel, 1980; Arntzen and Veenendaal, 1986). If the area ploughed increases during drought conditions as it did in the mid-1980s, there is an increased risk of degradation due to the direct depletion of soil nutrients, the loss of topsoil due to erosion, and the threat to the regenerative power of soil

Figure 4.8   Ratio of area harvested to area planted, sorghum and maize

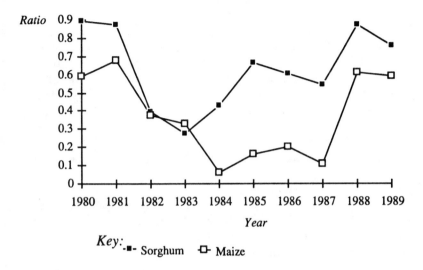

Source: Republic of Botswana, *1989 Botswana Agricultural Statistics*, Gaborone, CSO.

life through desiccation (cf. Reber and Borkott, 1983). It is not possible to be precise about the environmental costs of arable activity in this period, but it is possible to make some indicative remarks. The clearing of land for ploughing probably has a smaller effect than the felling of trees for fencing timber or to deny a habitat for predatory birds such as the quelea. Some indication of the relative importance of tree-felling for fencing timber, and fuelwood is given by the fact that per capita demand for fuelwood is estimated to be 0.5 tonnes per annum, while that for fencing timber is between 2 and 2.5 tonnes per annum (Perrings *et al.*, 1989). Moreover, the damage inflicted on the rangeland surrounding arable areas as a result of tree-felling varies from one zone to another according to the topography of the land. Where land is sloping, evidence from a range of countries in Africa and elsewhere suggests that erosion prompted by devegetation can be extremely severe (Eckholm, 1976), and while Botswana does not have the mountainous topography of many of the worst affected countries, gully erosion in many of the hillier areas is pronounced (Arntzen and Veenendaal, 1986).

4.2.3   Off-farm economic activity

The main economic activities in the rural economy of Botswana are livestock and arable farming. Most other economic activities are adaptations of the hunting and gathering that is a traditional part of the Kalahari economy, and so fall under the general rubric of 'traditional' economic activities. There are, however, two sets of commercial non-farm activities of increasing importance in the rural economy – forestry and tourism – and these are discussed below. The non-farm traditional activities vary in importance, but are of most significance in the remote areas. In north-western and western Botswana (Kgalagadi, Ghanzi and Ngamiland districts) hunting remains the main subsistence activity of the population, and wildlife is regarded as a common property resource in much the same way as rangeland is elsewhere in the country. Arntzen and Veenendaal (1986) estimate that between ten and 20 thousand people still hunt for subsistence but there exist no estimates of the implicit value of subsistence hunting to the economy.

In the absence of external influences, subsistence hunting tends to be self-regulating to sustainable levels. Given wildlife densities in these areas the sustainable level of subsistence tends to be very low. The major external influences in Botswana are the expansion of livestock into the northern and western parts of the country as a result of the TGLP and the westward movement of cattle posts supported by boreholes. Both have resulted in (a) increasing competition for grazing from the livestock, and (b) increasing restrictions on the migration of wildlife. Migratory species that depend on similar flora to cattle include hartebeeste, wildebeeste, eland and springbok. During the wet season they tend to concentrate in the central-southern Kalahari, or on the Makgadigadi Pans. In drier periods, particularly during drought years, they move towards a variety of water sources – but particularly towards the lake Xau and the lower Boteti. This movement brings them into direct competition with the livestock being grazed around the more reliable water sources. This has been limited by the construction of veterinary cordon fences designed to regulate cattle movement, and to limit the dangers of contagious bovine diseases due to the movement of other species. But the resultant deaths of migratory species denied access to water imposes costs on the subsistence hunters who prey on those species.

Gathering – the direct harvesting of natural or veld products – is also a major source of income in the more remote parts of Botswana. Like subsistence hunting, though, there is a paucity of data on the volume and value of products obtained in this way. The most significant by a wide margin is wood for fuel and construction. Other important veld products are a variety of roots, tubers, fruit, edible leaves and fungi (for consumption), shoots (for infusions), grasses (for thatching), Mokola palm leaves (for basket weaving), grapple tubers (for their medicinal qualities) and mophane worms (delicacies for consumption). Although the value of commercial transactions involving these products is small, reasonably well developed markets exist for the last three. The others are still largely produced for the direct use of the households concerned, except that markets for thatching grass now exist around larger settlements where it has become scarce. In terms of market value, mophane worm, which had an estimated market value of production in 1986 of P300,000 to P400,000, dominates 'gathered' veld products other than wood. Grapple production was estimated in the same year to be around P50,000, and basket weaving to be around P100,000 (Arntzen and Veenendaal, 1986).

Fisheries are as yet very poorly developed in Botswana. The 10,000 square kilometers of the Okavango delta are characterized by a floodplain-riverine system that provides an exceptionally prolific breeding ground for a number of commercially useable fish species. Within the Chobe system, Lake Liambesi and the Linyati swamps have similar potential. At present the resource is underutilized, although government policy is to stimulate the industry with a view to generating both income and employment for the poorer sections of the rural population although it remains low on the policy agenda. The main mechanism for stimulating fish production has been the Financial Assistance Policy (FAP). One third of all small grants made under the FAP going to remote area fishing households for the purchase of improved equipment. Additional financial assistance is available under the AE 10 grant programme for cooperative activities. There are now estimated to be around 850 commercial fishing households in the Okavango, of whom half have benefitted directly or indirectly from one or other of the grant schemes. Between 1982 and 1986, commercial fishing output in the northern Okavango is estimated to have risen from zero to over 100 tonnes. There are also between three and four thousand households fishing for 'subsistence' purposes. The potential growth of the Okavango fisheries is generally assumed to be considerable. Most fishing households still use top-set gill nets from traditional Mokoro boats, and sell fish only in the dried state (Merron, 1988). As yet no attempt has been made to market fish frozen rather than dried.

While overgrazing is already endemic, fish stocks have yet to be seriously utilized, far less to be seriously threatened. It is recognized that since the resource is collectively owned, there exists at least the potential for overfishing. Except for rivers like the Boteti, the location of the fisheries and the difficulty of access provide enough natural protection that overfishing would not be a problem in the foreseeable future. The scope for massive depletion of fish stocks through seining is argued to be minimal, and the recharging of the Okavango stocks in the annual flood is claimed to protect against the disturbing of the balance between species as a result of intensive fishing of one or two particular species. Equally, unless fishing techniques change dramatically, commercial fishing would appear to impose no negative externalities on the utilization of other wildlife in either the Okavango (where there is some fishing activity) or Chobe (where there is not). At present the externalities tend to run the other way, with fish stocks negatively affected by water pollution associated with the spraying programme designed to control the trypanosomiasis vector – the tsetse fly.

Botswana's timber resources are utilized under a variety of regimes in a wide range of activities. Most timber felled is used for construction or fuelwood by farmers in the communal areas in non-commercial operations. There is open access to the resource, so no charge is made to the users. In particular areas, where this has led to the depletion of the resource (around the larger villages and towns), there has developed a market for both fuelwood and construction timber. However the timber felled is still largely in the public domain. The only significant exceptions to this are the royalties paid by the four commercial companies that have secured licenses to utilize the hardwood forest reserves in Kasane and Chobe. Most depletion of timber reserves is due to traditional activities, and is concentrated in specific areas and relates to specific species. This has led to the denudation of certain species in large areas around the main sources of demand in south eastern Botswana. In South East District the natural rate of growth of these species is no longer capable of meeting local demand, and Kgatleng, Southern and Kweneng Districts are approaching the same position. Indeed, to ease the pressure on fuelwood supplies both Kgatleng and Kweneng have introduced by-laws preventing the export of fuelwood to other districts. Elsewhere fuelwood supplies have been depleted only in the immediate vicinity of villages or cattleposts, and supplies remain plentiful at greater distances. Where bush fences are used in preference to wire fences, similar species and similar parts of the tree are required for both fencing and fuelwood and this has exacerbated the problem of depletion.

The two commercial activities of interest are forestry and tourism. The utilization of the hardwood forest reserves at Kasane and Chobe constitutes the only commercial forestry activity in Botswana, and is regulated by the licenses under which the concession companies operate. Like agriculture, the commercial forestry sector does not service the domestic market, up to 90 per cent of output being exported. The sector is currently of minor economic importance either in terms of the value of output or in terms of employment, though it is argued to have considerably greater potential (cf. Muggeridge, 1988; Millar, 1987).

Tourism is also accorded a low level of priority at present, but it is rapidly emerging as one of the more sustainable avenues for the exploitation of the natural resource base of Botswana. Currently, 17 per cent of the country is set aside as national parks, game reserves, and educational reserves. The flora and fauna in these areas are the basis for an industry that is expected to make an increasing contribution to foreign exchange earnings, rural income and employment. It is assumed that current utilization of these resources lies 'below the ecological and economic optimum, leaving considerable potential to expand commercial utilization' (Republic of Botswana, 1985, p. 251). Data on the net contribution of that part of the tourist industry which is founded on the national parks do not exist, but it is clear that there has been very rapid development of selected areas of Chobe and the Okavango. Taking the number of air passengers passing through Maun (the entrypoint to the Okavango swamps) as a proxy for the expansion of tourist traffic in the region suggests that tourism has expanded sharply since 1985 (see Figure 4.9). In that year the industry was estimated to account for less than 5 per cent of GDP, although it was the fourth largest source of foreign exchange (Fowkes, 1985). In NDP6, it was estimated that formal sector employment generated by tourist activities was little more than 3000 (Republic of Botswana, 1985, Table 11.3). To this point, tourism has been a more or less incidental beneficiary of infrastructural developments such as the construction of the international Sir Seretse Khama airport, and the sealing of the Kasane road. However, the industry will be the principal beneficiary of the sealing of the Maun road currently underway. The

Figure 4.9   Air passenger traffic: Maun (left axis) and total (right axis) ('000)

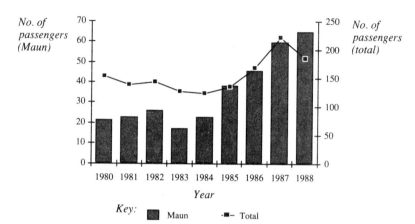

Source: Republic of Botswana, *Statistical Bulletin*, 15, 3, September 1990.

industry is largely in private hands, although a parastatal, the Botswana Development Corporation (BDC), has an active tourist division with a number of holdings. To this point it has refrained from taking a prominent role in the development of the Okavango/Chobe area.

The key environmental questions associated with the development of the tourist industry relate to the management of the wildlife that is the raison-d'être of the industry, and the ecological systems on which that wildlife depends. Those ecological systems are currently being exploited in different ways by hunting, agriculture and mining as well as by tourism. The point has already been made that the tendency for agriculture to expand at the extensive rather than the intensive margin has brought a conflict of interest between those whose livelihood depends on the exploitation of wildlife as a resource. Moreover, it is widely recognized that this is likely to increase rather than decrease in the future. At the core of such conflict are the externalities that arise out of the private use of a common environment. The privately rational decisions of one class of user imposes costs on other classes of user that cannot, given the nature of the resource and the existing institutions, be resolved through transactions between them. The result is that the welfare of all users, now and in the future, is at risk.

4.3 CONCLUDING REMARKS

This Chapter began by identifying the trends in the economy that make the sustainable growth of the rural economy a high priority for the future of Botswana. These are the decline in the expected rate of growth of mining GDP, and the continuing high rate of population growth. Current expectations are that the manufacturing sector will continue to grow at a faster rate than the rate of population growth, as will financial services, commerce and – for the time being at least – government. However, it is likely that for some time yet the number of new jobs created in the formal sector will fall below the number of new entrants to the labour force. Growth in mineral revenues has, in the past, provided a cushion against this formal sector employment gap – despite the negative effects of drought on rural income. But the prospects for the future are less optimistic. The government has now revised downwards its earlier optimistic expectations for agricultural growth, and is identifying manufacturing and services (including tourism) as the most likely sources of new growth in the future (Republic of Botswana, 1990b). Given the size of informal sector employment relative to formal sector employment, however, it is important that the agricultural sector should grow at positive rates. In this respect, the experience of the drought years is discomforting. This study suggests that while the dominant influence on output and productivity in the agricultural sector has undoubtedly been the low levels of rainfall experienced, this is not the only source of the problem. It is argued that a structure of incentives which encourages the overutilization of the resource base has much to do with the decline in output.

5 Economic Policy and Economic Incentives

The short review of the structure and trends of the Botswana offered in Chapter 4 indicates a pattern of development that has been dominated by a centralized decision-making process involving a combination of central government/private sector partnerships and parastatals. The best example of central government/private sector partnership is the collaboration between the government of Botswana and De Beers, through Debswana, in the exploitation of the country's diamond wealth. Government involvement in economic activity has, however, by no means been limited to the mining industry. Indeed, the effect of the parastatals has been pervasive in the rural sector discussed above. The near monopsonies enjoyed by the BMC and the BAMB have given the government an extraordinary influence on the resource allocation decisions of independent farmers. Botswana is not at all unusual in this respect. Similar systems of administered prices in the markets for animal products and cereals are to be found in many countries in Sub-Saharan Africa. But rapidly expanding mineral revenues during the past two decades have enabled the government to undertake a range of 'development' expenditures in and transfers to the agricultural sector that has given it a degree of influence on farmer decisions that is unusual by any standards.

The principal objectives of agricultural policy under NDP6 were stated to be: to assist those in the agricultural sector to enjoy adequate and secure incomes through the provision of 'incentives'; to create sufficient employment to meet the formal sector employment gap; to encourage self-sufficiency in domestic food grain production; and to maintain agricultural land for future generations. The microeconomic policies developed to satisfy these objectives (apart from the usual support services involving extension, research and infrastructure) included the pricing policies implemented by the Botswana Meat Commission (BMC) and the Botswana Agricultural Marketing Board (BAMB); the Tribal Lands Grazing Policy (TLGP) designed to change certain aspects of the structure of property rights over grazing lands and to encourage longer term investment in the livestock sector; two programmes designed to provide assistance to small and medium crop farms, the Arable Lands Development Programme (ALDEP) and the Accelerated Rainfed Arable Production programme (ARAP); and an agricultural credit policy operated through the National Development Bank (NDB) and the Financial Assistance Policy (FAP). These programmes are summarised in Table 5.1.

The evolution of the government's microeconomic policies for the agricultural sector through the 1980s took place in the context of drought conditions. The conditions had a strongly negative effect on rural incomes, and there is evidence that many of the development goals of the policies were subverted by the need to provide relief to rural households at a time of acute need. The agricultural development programmes were notionally separate from drought relief, but it is not just coincidence that they have expanded dramatically during the drought – although the number of households affected varied considerably between the programmes. Of the arable programmes ALDEP affected a comparatively small number of households – an average of 5500 per year since 1982. ARAP on the other hand touched

Table 5.1   Principal features of the major agriculture programmes

Programme	Target group	Objectives	Key measures
1. ALDEP	Smallholders with < 40ha	Promoting self-sufficiency	Subsidies on draught power, water supply, fencing
2. ARAP	Medium-sized farms	Encourage planting during drought	Subsidies on ploughing weeding, destumping, row planting, water supply, fertiliser, fencing
3. FAP	Commercial farms	Promotion of employment	Grant of P1000p.a. for 5 years for each unskilled job created
4. DRP	Drought affected farms	Prevention of malnutrition	Feeding programmes, Cash-based labour relief programmes

Abbreviations:
ALDEP   Arable Lands Development Programme
ARAP   Accelerated Rainfed Arable Production
FAP   Financial Assistance Programme
DRP   Drought Relief Programme

Source: Love, Babikanyisa and Mrema (1989).

a majority of rural households. In 1987/8, for example, over 96,000 draft power grants were made under the programme at a cost to the Government of Botswana of over P22 million. Of the pastoral programmes, the cattle purchase scheme affected a comparatively few rural households, whereas the feed and vaccine programme offered very widespread benefits.

This chapter considers the impact of this set of policies on the incentives faced by independent resource users in Botswana. More particularly, it considers whether there exists a link between the incentive structure and productivity trends in agriculture (controlling for climate); and if so, which policies may be identified as the source of the trend. While there are insufficient data to address these questions systematically, it is possible to draw a number of reasonably strong inferences from the available evidence. Rural income maintenance and rural income distribution became a major – if not *the* major – goal of microeconomic policy in the agricultural sector. The drought reduced not only the levels of money income deriving from the sale of livestock and crops, but also the in-kind income that is a major feature of the traditional sector, and many of the policy initiatives of the period were geared to provide assistance to the people affected. By using what had been intended as vehicles for agricultural development to deliver relief to the rural sector, however, the government ended up distorting the set of relative input and output prices in ways that placed future productivity at risk by encouraging the overutilization of the natural resource base.

5.1 THE LIVESTOCK SECTOR

5.1.1 Property rights

We have already stated that the current incentive structure encourages the stocking and farm management decisions that have led to rangeland degradation in a number of areas of Botswana. In terms of the government's microeconomic policies there are four aspects of the incentive structure that are important contributory factors: the system of property rights, producer prices, taxes and subsidies.

Property in land in Botswana falls into one of four categories. The most widespread form of land tenure is communal or 'tribal' land. This accounts for 70 per cent of the total. Individual Batswana enjoy use rights over this land, but do not have legal title to the land itself. Most communal land is allocated to grazing. Individual Batswana have automatic rights of access to the range, but these are not exclusive rights. That is, access to the range is open to all Batswana. Unlike grazing rights, cultivation rights are allocated to individual users, and these rights do carry the right to exclude other users. Communal land cannot be bought and sold. Nor can it be used as collateral for purposes of raising credit. Following communal land, the next most common form of tenure is State land, comprising all National Parks, wildlife and educational reserves, and accounting for 23 per cent of the total. The last two categories of land are freehold land, comprising 5 per cent of the total in the Tuli and Lobatse Blocks in the east and Ghanzi in the west, and leasehold land which accounts for the rest, including both the TGLP ranches and the Pandamatenga farms.

Corresponding to these categories of property in land, there are three types of livestock farm in Botswana: freehold commercial ranches; leasehold ranches established under the TGLP; and traditional farms based on communal grazing. Almost all problems of overgrazing are associated with the 85 per cent of cattle and more than 97 per cent of sheep and goats held on traditional farms and cattle posts. The virtually uncontrolled grazing rights enjoyed by farmers in the communal areas have ensured that no individual farmer bears the full cost of adding stock beyond the carrying capacity of the range. It is well recognized that where access to a communal resource is not controlled, individuals may, in their own self interest, ignore the user cost of the resource. This is the 'tragedy of the commons' argument due to Hardin (1968). Although this argument ignores the incentive to cooperate where land is held communally, the point was made in Chapter 2 that there is a good deal of empirical evidence that wherever traditional institutions for regulating the use of communal lands have broken down, individual herdsmen have tended to overstock.

The evidence for overstocking in Botswana is clear enough. There is not much evidence on the way in which traditional institutions regulated the use of the resource in the past, but it has already been remarked that the position of *badisa*, who had a range management function, has certainly fallen into disuse (Abel *et al.*, 1987). In principle the allocation of grazing land in the communal areas (and the authorisation of boreholes) is the responsibility of the Land Boards. Conservation matters are the responsibility of the Agricultural Resources Board (ARB) working through District Conservation Committees. Moreover, these bodies are empowered to reduce stocking levels if these threaten the range. But neither the Land Boards nor the

Conservation Committees have yet applied the legal sanctions available to them. The particular problem faced in Botswana accordingly appears to be a combination of the lack of institutional restrictions on access to communal rangeland, combined with positive incentives to expand livestock holdings.

In these circumstances it might be expected that the increasing scarcity of the resource would lead either to the development of market-like allocative mechanisms or to the creation of regulatory institutions, or to a combination of these things. What is happening in Botswana is that an indirect market for grazing land is developing around boreholes, but that the institutional control over the number of boreholes remains very weak. More particularly, licenses to drill boreholes for purposes of providing a water source for livestock are granted by the Land Boards to associations of graziers called 'syndicates'. Although the syndicates do not have rights of exclusion with respect to the range around a borehole, they do have rights of exclusion with respect to the water. The result of this is that a market is developing around the sale of water to herdsmen. It is, however, a very imperfect market, since authority to drill boreholes necessarily grants monopoly rights to the syndicate. The Land Boards accordingly have some capacity to influence the general level of grazing pressure through the number of boreholes they authorize. As yet, however, they have not made use of this power, and it is argued that boreholes continue to be sanctioned that are 'too close' to neighbouring holes to prevent overgrazing.

There is a close relation between overgrazing in at least some communal grazing lands and the leasehold ranches set up under the Tribal Lands Grazing Programme. The original TGLP had a number of goals including the expansion of commercial rangeland (through the establishment of new leasehold ranches), relief to the overcrowded communal areas (by diversion of stock to the ranches), and improvements in the management of livestock and natural resources in the communal areas (through the introduction of communal grazing cells with responsibility for both range and herd management). Since there has been little evidence of improved resource management either on ranches or in the communal grazing cells (Sweet, 1987), the emphasis subsequently switched to the improvement of integrated land use planning at district level and trials with community based range management in all districts (as part of the Livestock Development and Range Improvement Project, Livestock 3). What is important to the discussion here is that TGLP leaseholders have retained rights of access to the communal grazing areas, with the result that they are encouraged to base their stocking decisions on the carrying capacity of both the leasehold land and the communal range. These 'dual grazing rights' have, if anything intensified the pressure on the communal range to which leaseholders have access.

5.1.2 Pricing structures

The point has already been made that producer prices for livestock are determined by the BMC. Producer prices for cattle are a function of prices received by the BMC in its two major export markets, the EEC and South Africa. More particularly, the price paid to producers is based on the export parity price less the cost of slaughter. This implies that exchange rate policies may be expected to have a significant impact on producer prices, and this is the case. Exchange rates are considered in section 5.3 below. Historically, producer prices have been allowed to fluctuate on a seasonal basis, partly to encourage a more even offtake and partly to compensate producers who may have been prevented by the BMC quota system from selling cattle in peak condition. Producer prices for smallstock are a function of excess domestic demand, and a range of policies discussed below. The evolution of the best available proxy for relative livestock prices, the BMC average value of livestock, is indicated in Figure 5.1.

Figure 5.1   Cattle: index of real average value (1980 = 100, left axis) and offtake (percentage, right axis)

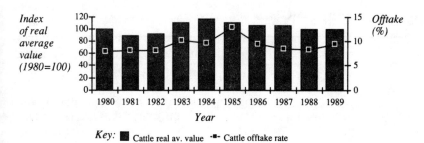

Key: ■ Cattle real av. value   -■- Cattle offtake rate

Sources: Republic of Botswana, *1989 Botswana Agricultural Statistics*; Republic of Botswana, *Statistical Bulletins*, 1982–1990.

The BMC strategy during the early years of the drought has been argued to have been to use price increases as a means of encouraging offtake (Fidzani,1985). What Table 5.2 indicates, however, is that average values for cattle changed very little during the early years of the drought. In part this reflects a particular feature of BMC pricing policy, and that is the tendency to 'overprice' higher grades of cattle relative to sales returns from each by up to 30 per cent, and to 'underprice' lower grades of cattle correspondingly (McGowan International and Coopers & Lybrand, 1987). It may be noted in passing that since the former tend to derive from commercial ranches and the latter from the traditional sector, this has significant distributional implications. In the present context, however, it indicates one reason why cattle prices did not increase sharply during the early years of the drought.

The relation between producer prices and offtake rates is a complex one, and the data do not exist to examine this systematically. It is not at all clear whether producer prices have a stronger effect on stocking decisions or offtake rates. What is clear is that income effects complicate the picture. A 1987 report on incentives in the sector concluded that the long-run price elasticity of supply might be expected to be positive: that higher producer prices would result in higher offtake rates if only after a period of restocking, but that this might not be so where cattle owners had access to alternative sources of income (McGowan International and Coopers & Lybrand, 1987). There is a weak positive correlation between the real average producer prices and offtake rates in the period of the drought consistent with evidence from elsewhere (cf. World Bank, 1987).

Table 5.2   BMC index of average value of livestock purchases

	Year									
	1980	*1981*	*1982*	*1983*	*1984*	*1985*	*1986*	*1987*	*1988*	*1989*
Cattle	100	121	120	125	125	135	148	167	232	306
Goats	100	103	119	155	174	181	193	208	216	242
Sheep	100	69	132	169	193	201	228	254	268	277

Sources: Republic of Botswana, *1989 Botswana Agricultural Statistics*; Republic of Botswana, *Statistical Bulletins*, 1982–1990.

Moreover, the substitution away from cattle that occurred during the first half of the 1980s reflect movements in relative prices of livestock, implying positive elasticities of substitution between goats and cattle in the traditional sector. However, the relationship between rates of offtake and average real producer prices for goats turns out to have been negative for much of the drought. This is illustrated in Figure 5.2 below which shows that an increase in offtake rates for goats after 1985 (and an increase in stocking levels) was associated with falling real average producer prices. Part of the explanation for this may lie in the fact that goats are associated with traditional farms in which supply responses tend both to be weaker than in the commercial farms, and more subject to income effects. For example, it has been observed in respect of cattle supply from the traditional sector that factors other than producer prices tend to dominate the intraseasonal supply of animals: traditional producers supplying most animals during the periods when the prices paid by the BMC are at a minimum (McGowan International and Coopers & Lybrand, 1987).

5.1.3 Subsidies and taxes

Part of the problem in any discussion of the price elasticity of supply in these markets in fact lies in the difficulty of isolating price effects from the changes in other aspects of the incentive structure that may have

Figure 5.2   Goats: index of real average value (1980 = 100, left axis) and offtake (percentage, right axis)

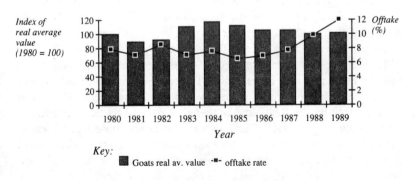

Key:
■ Goats real av. value -■- offtake rate

Sources: Republic of Botswana, *1989 Botswana Agricultural Statistics*; Republic of Botswana, *Statistical Bulletins*, 1982–1990.

been occurring at the same time. In the livestock sector, the pricing policies of the BMC took place in the context of a number of government initiatives to support the agricultural sector, which almost certainly had the effect of increasing rather than reducing stocking levels. These initiatives included a cattle purchase scheme designed to support farmers offering cull cattle for sale; a subsidy on the hiring of draught cattle; a scheme entitled Services to Livestock Owners in Communal Areas (SLOCA) which involved matching grants for cattle owners; and, most importantly, a sheep and goat development project which was directly designed to encourage small farmers to increase their holdings of goats. In addition, the owners of both small and large cattle herds benefit from extensive veterinary subsidies, as well as a substantial veterinary infrastructure (the veterinary cordon fences).

The net effect of these subsidies has been to increase the level of grazing pressure by encouraging traditional farmers to expand their herds. The draught cattle hiring subsidy, SLOCA and the sheep and goat development project have all provided direct incentives to increase stocking levels in the communal areas by reducing the cost of acquiring livestock. At the same time, the cattle purchase scheme for cull cattle, while overtly designed to increase offtake rates during the drought, can be seen to have reduced the costs to the farmer of overstocking, so encouraging larger than optimal herd sizes. In addition to these positive incentives to increase the level of grazing pressure in the communal lands, the second and third Livestock Development Projects contain subsidized credit provisions for potential ranchers on leasehold land. Given dual grazing rights, however, this too translates as a subsidy on the acquisition of cattle in the communal areas.

The method chosen to recoup the cost of subsidies also turns out to encourage herd expansion, and to discourage offtake. In 1988 it was estimated that the value of these various subsidies amounted to some P200 per animal slaughtered (Rohrbach, 1988). To offset this, the BMC is liable for a turnover tax of 40 per cent, which yielded about half the estimated cost of subsidies. The same tax is estimated to have reduced effective producer prices by around 20 per cent. The tax is payable only by the BMC and is therefore carried by those producers who supply to the BMC. This has had two important effects. First, it has led to the diversion of livestock sales into the private market (noted in Chapter 4) both in Botswana and, increasingly, in South Africa. Second, since the BMC producer price is the reference point for the domestic livestock market it has depressed producer prices across the board. The net result is a disincentive to increase rates of offtake.

A second aspect of the tax system which has the same effect are the tax incentives available for investment in cattle. These not only offer a direct incentive to expand the size of the herd independent of the condition of the range, they also divert investment from other productive activities. The fact that cattle are a traditional store of wealth means that there is a strong predisposition to invest in such an asset. This predisposition is clearly reinforced by the current structure of incentives. Regardless of the costs imposed by overstocking on future generations, cattle remain a very attractive asset for Batswana. They are self-reproducing wealth requiring comparatively little labour, or no labour at all if let out under the *mafisa* system. Ownership of cattle automatically attracts a very wide range of subsidies on inputs including rent-free grazing land. Cattle constitute a hedge against inflation, they are convertible to cash in times of need but are privileged currency in some very important transactions (e.g. *bogadi* or 'bride price'). They also entitle the owner to a very generous set of tax write-offs against other income. On top of this they confer status and prestige. No other asset is currently as accessible or offers a wider set of benefits to the owner.

5.2   THE ARABLE SECTOR

5.2.1   The pricing structure

In arable agriculture, as in the livestock sector, government policy is directed by the National Food Strategy, which was originally founded on the goal of assuring food self-sufficiency. This strategy requires a very significant increase in the output of food crops. It is administered by the Ministry of Agriculture which operates either directly or through the Botswana Agricultural Marketing Board (BAMB). Producer prices for grains and cereals purchased by BAMB are based on the landed costs of imports from South Africa marked up by a factor sufficient to cover transport costs within Botswana. Because of a policy decision to give preference to sorghum over maize due to its greater drought resistance, however, historical price relativities between crops in Botswana have not matched those in South Africa.

Indices of nominal prices and purchases of major crops sold to the BAMB between 1979/80 and 1988/89 are shown in Table 5.3. There exists no price series for agricultural input costs that may be used to calculate the real (income) change in producer prices. The cost of living

Table 5.3 Indices of producer prices and crop purchases, BAMB, 1982/3– 1989/90 (1982/3 = 100)

		1983/4	*1984/5*	*1985/6*	*1986/7*	*1987/8*	*1988/9*	*1989/90*
Sorghum	Purchases	89	154	1254	1566	2486	18641	9195
	Price	119	155	161	166	177	177	188
Maize	Purchases	42	3	14	19	42	69	205
	Price	137	165	169	180	173	173	198
Pulses	Purchases	19	3	22	15	3	1068	251
	Price	118	136	149	160	178	178	178
Sunflower	Purchases	23	1	11	11	2	3	5
	Price	100	102	111	137	151	151	183
Groundnuts	Purchases	28	12	67	22	15	63	32
	Price	103	114	115	115	117	117	113

Note: 1. Producer prices are for grade 1 quality except for pulses, which are for 'fair/average' quality.
2. Prices are fixed for the whole season, April through March.

Source: Republic of Botswana, *Statistical Bulletins*, 1987–1990, CSO, Gaborone.

index is not a very good proxy for farm input costs, since the effect of the various subsidies and grants offered under the Accelerated Rainfed Arable Programme (ARAP), the Arable Lands Development Programme (ALDEP), and the drought relief programmes has been to hold increases in farm input costs for the traditional producers below general consumer costs. Nevertheless, using the cost of living index, Figure 5.3 illustrates the relationship between output and real producer prices for the two major crops, maize and sorghum. Since the prices are regionally determined – by the South African market – they are influenced by the same climatic changes as affected Botswana producers and increase with the reduction in aggregate supply associated with the drought.

What is interesting is that, despite the downward trend in real producer prices after 1984/5, crop sales to BAMB increased steadily. Output and sales of sorghum both increased more rapidly than maize. While this has been ascribed to the change in relative prices of the two crops due to the sorghum premium, one report on the agricultural sector makes the point (a) that the trend predates the introduction of the premium on sorghum, and (b) that it is not possible to isolate the effects of price from such factors as relative seed availability (Arup-

Figure 5.3   Sorghum and maize: indices of purchases (left axis) and real
producer prices (right axis) 1982/3 = 100

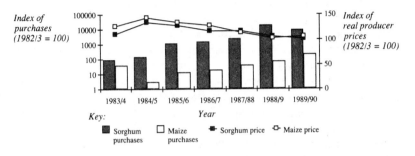

Sources: Republic of Botswana, *Statistical Bulletins*, 1984–1990; Bank of
Botswana, *Annual Reports* 1985–1990, Gaborone, Bank of Botswana.

Atkins, 1988). It remains the case, though, that sorghum was
increasingly being produced on a commercial basis during the latter
half of the 1980s. Between 1983 and 1985 total output of the crop
collapsed to around 15 per cent of what it had been in 1981, but by
1989 total output had increased to 96 thousand metric tons. The
proportion deriving from commercial farms had risen from 20 to 34 per
cent, and the proportion of total output marketed through BAMB had
gone up from 24 to 54 per cent. In other words, a dominant trend
during this period was towards the commercialization of the crop, and
this trend appears to have been driven by factors other than the trend
in real producer prices.

The difficulty in discussing the price elasticity of supply in this case is
analogous to the livestock case. Without an adequate measure of the
value of a range of input subsidies to producers it is not possible to
calculate real (income) producer prices. If these were increasing over
the period, the supply responses of producers would be more
understandable. To get a sense of the significance of the set of
subsidies, the following section considers the effects of the 'development' programmes on production decisions.

5.2.2   Taxes and subsidies

The vehicle for the set of subsidies to arable agriculture offered by the
government are the Arable Lands Development Programme (ALDEP),

the Accelerated Rainfed Arable Production programme (ARAP), the Financial Assistance Programme (FAP) and the Drought Relief Programme (DRP). Although these programmes are designated as development programmes, it is hard not to conclude that their primary purpose was to be the vehicle for transfers to the agricultural sector.

The stated aims of ALDEP are both to raise rural incomes and to increase the country's self-sufficiency in food production. The target group consists of the majority of middle and poorer farmers, defined as those with less than 40 head of cattle. The mechanism by which the programme is intended to achieve its goals include the expansion of the average area ploughed per farm to 10 hectares (presently around 5 or lower), and improvements in the use of draft power. ARAP, on the other hand, offers what is expected to be temporary assistance to farmers to assist them in coping with the results of drought through a mix of grants and subsidies. It is less geared towards enhancing farming capital than ALDEP. Neither programme addresses the problem of land improvement (except in so far as destumping and ploughing are thought to constitute improvements). Nor do they address the problem of the efficiency of water use.

Specific subsidies offered under both programmes include the following:

- seed for open-pollinated sorghum and millet is distributed free (hybrid sorghum and maize are not covered;
- destumping subsidies are offered to arable farmers (of between P30 and P50 per hectare cleared) up to a maximum of 10 hectares;
- subsidies are available for wire fencing;
- fertilizer is provided free of charge at a rate of 4 bags per hectare for each of the first 3 hectares ploughed;
- water development grants cover the cost of tanks, boreholes, and water reticulation.

In addition, ALDEP offers subsidies on the acquisition of draft power (donkeys or oxen) to farmers with no cattle, while ARAP offers a subsidy equal to the full cost of ploughing up to 10 hectares, plus additional subsidies for row planting and weeding. Over and above the subsidies offered under these two programmes, loans at subsidized interest rates and investment grants are available to crop farmers by the National Development Bank (NDB). The Financial Assistance Policy (FAP) offers similar benefits in the case of irrigation projects. These are discussed in section 5.3.

While it has been claimed that both programmes have resulted in an increase in current output, it is clear that the costs of each have been far from trivial. Arup-Atkins (1988) estimated that ALDEP and ARAP together may have increased grain production in 1987/88 by around 50 per cent: a very substantial amount. However, they also estimate that this was at a cost significantly greater than the benefits. Their estimate of the marginal cost of maize production under ARAP in that year was three times the border price for the crop. While the Arup Atkins calculation focussed on present costs and benefits of the programme only (see Table 5.4), it is not at all clear that the position would improve if future flows of costs and benefits are taken into account. What is clear is that the programmes raised the domestic resource cost of grain production in Botswana above (the lower bound of) its opportunity cost: the border price of grain. The programmes are, in this sense, inefficient. Part of the explanation for this undoubtedly lies in the impact of the drought on productivity, but it seems clear that efficiency and productivity gains are less important in the programmes than income transfers. Love, Babikanyisa and Mrema (1989) calculate that the cost of the programmes per tonne of grain marketed through BAMB rose from 14 per cent of the average market price for sorghum and maize in 1981/2 to 870 per cent in 1985/6. The productivity gains would have to have been very substantial indeed to warrant such expenditures.

Of more interest from the point of view of the sustainability of resource use are the longer-term costs and benefits of the programmes. To the extent that both programmes involve a considerable amount

Table 5.4   Estimated cost of the agricultural development and relief
programmes, 1981/2–1987/8 (Pm)

	Year						
	1981/2	*1982/3*	*1983/4*	*1984/5*	*1985/6*	*1986/7*	*1987/8*
ALDEP	668	774	735	4756	3151	2322	4251
ARAP					11273	21910	34792
DRP	260	3	1617	7062	3582	4771	1882
FAP			31	8	349	2355	1292
Total	928	777	2388	11726	18355	31358	42217

Source: Arup-Atkins (1988).

of extension work it may be expected that they would have some longer-term benefits. But there are also longer-term environmental costs. Perrings *et al.* (1988) note that the full cost of ploughing subsidy along with the free distribution of seed provides an incentive for mixed farmers confronting a binding constraint in respect of the availability of graze to plant an area in food crops well in excess of the expected harvested area. The costs of ploughing and planting up to 10 hectares are close to zero under the programme, while the short-run benefits of untended and unharvested crops are considerably greater than zero. They argue that since crop residues may be utilized for fodder, and since the fencing of arable fields allows the exclusion of unwanted stock, the food crop incentives may be working in an unexpected way to promote private grazing.

Leaving this effect to one side, it should be noted that the incentives offered under the programmes are not contingent on one another. Hence the programmes have encouraged the clearance of land for ploughing (but contain no mechanism to ensure that it is ploughed). Similarly, they have encouraged the expansion of the area ploughed (but contain no mechanism to ensure that it is subsequently planted or tended). The denudation of land in drought conditions has very well known implications for soil erosion, and this imposes costs on all future users of the resource.

An additional point is that while the destumping subsidies undoubtedly contribute to the devegetation of arable lands, the fencing package may be more significant for grazing lands. The promotion of wire over traditional bush fencing qualitatively and quantitatively changes the timber demands of fencing. Wire fencing requires posts that can only be obtained from larger trees, and require regular replacement (due to the effect of termites). The fencing of arable lands is essential to the improvement of yields in the absence of any controls on grazing, but the fencing programme may have unexpected costs in terms of the quality of rangeland through the elimination of tree cover, and the encouragement of bush encroachment.

5.3 OTHER INCENTIVE EFFECTS OF POLICY

5.3.1 Agricultural credit

One of the most striking characteristics of the financial system in Botswana over the last decade has been a low rate of growth of domestic credit combined with high and persistent levels of excess liquidity. Associated with this, real interest rates have been either very low or negative. Indeed since 1985 the prime rate has been negative except for one year, deposit rates have been uniformly negative, and lending rates have been negative for many classes of borrower. The significance of these characteristics is that domestic credit has been rationed by the financial institutions on the basis of risk assessments and collateral requirements that have effectively excluded the traditional agricultural sector. Figure 5.4 shows the percentage share of total commercial bank lending to three sectors between 1983 and 1988: agriculture, wholesale and retail trade, and households. The pattern is a striking one. Whereas loans to consumers formed a steadily increasing share of bank lending, loans to the agricultural sector as steadily declined – from 8.8 per cent of bank lending in 1983 to just 4 per cent in 1988. In nominal terms, the value of commercial bank lending to all

Figure 5.4   Share of bank lending to agriculture, commerce and households, 1981–1989

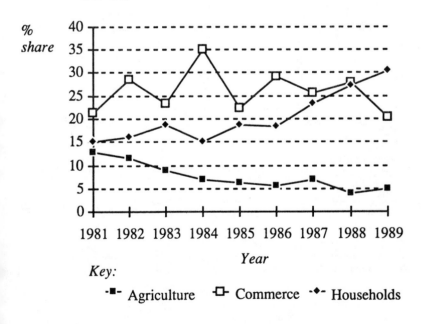

Source: Bank of Botswana, *Review of Economic Developments*, February 1989.

sectors of the economy increased at an annual average rate of around 14 per cent between 1980 and 1987, but lending to the agricultural sector (mainly the commercial subsector) remained more or less constant (see Table 5.5).

Because the commercial banks have been to all intents and purposes inaccessible to the traditional agricultural sector, the government of Botswana has underwritten alternative sources of credit. Since 1980 the credit requirements of 'traditional' agriculture have been met, at least in principle, by the National Development Bank operating either on its own account or as the conduit for finance being made available by government through the FAP and ALDEP. In 1986 all small loans (< P20000) were transferred to a separate facility, the Small Borrowers Fund (SBF), which the NDB administered for the government, but for which it had no financial responsibility. The interest rate charged under the fund was set at 10 per cent, the same as the commercial banks' prime rate in that year. All risks of default were carried directly by the government. As Table 5.5 shows, NDB agricultural lending through all facilities increased sharply between 1980 and 1987 – from P5.5m to P42.4m.

In 1989 a World Bank report on financial policies in Botswana drew attention to a number of undesirable effects associated with the interest rate regime and the way in which agricultural credit had been handled (World Bank, 1989). In respect of the system of agricultural credit, the report observed that the extraordinary high default rate on NDB and SBF agricultural loans, the low level of loan supervision, and the use of subsidized interest rates meant that agricultural lending was to all intents and purposes just another vehicle for rural transfers. In 1988,

Table 5.5   Agricultural lending by the NDB and commercial banks, 1980–1987 (Pm)

Year								
	1980	*1981*	*1982*	*1983*	*1984*	*1985*	*1986*	*1987*
Commercial banks	16.7	17.7	16.2	15.0	16.4	16.1	15.8	19.9
NDB	5.5	10.3	17.3	19.0	25.0	37.2	40.4	42.4
Total	22.2	28.0	33.5	34.0	41.4	53.3	56.2	62.3

Source: World Bank (1989).

64 per cent of the NDB and 80 per cent of the SBF portfolios were in arrears, and in that year the government made P24m available to write off principal and interest areas on certain categories of NDB agricultural loans.

The report argued that the use of financial institutions as a means of transferring funds to the rural population was both inequitable and inefficient. Loans did not, typically, go to those most in need (especially female-headed rural households), while the use of subsidized credit encouraged an inefficient allocation of rural resources. It pointed out that the real problem lay not with the cost of credit, but with its availability. That is, it was the unwillingness of the commercial banks to entertain loan applications from farmers based in the communal areas at any rate of interest that was the problem, and not the rate of interest itself.

The link between agricultural property rights, the availability of rural credit, rural interest rates and the specific credit facilities of the NDB and the SBF may be complicated, but it has had a clearly defined negative effect on the use of environmental resources in Botswana. By subsidizing the cost of agricultural inputs and agricultural capital (especially livestock), and by ignoring the risks associated with agricultural activity in Botswana, the system of agricultural credit that developed during the 1980s encouraged the overutilization of the agricultural resource base: range and arable land in particular. In 1990 the Bank of Botswana determined to raise the level of interest rates to counter the trend towards higher levels of consumer borrowing. Using the Bank's call deposit rate as the lever, it has forced the commercial banks to raise their prime rates, and both lending and deposit rates have now followed suit. This represents one step in the direction of a sustainable agricultural credit policy.

5.3.2 Exchange rates

The exchange rate is one of the most important instruments available to the government of Botswana to promote the diversification of the economy, and to establish an environment conducive to economic growth. As a consequence of Botswana's close trading relationship with South Africa (just under 80 per cent of imports come from the common customs area so that the rand is heavily weighted in the currency basket against which the pula's value is determined) there has been a significant depreciation of the real effective exchange rate of the pula against the major currencies. The problem for policy is to determine how far this movement should be modified, given that the strong incentives towards diversification associated with a depreciating currency have costs in terms of the need to maintain a balance between restrictive monetary, public expenditure and incomes policies and inflation.

The exchange rate is of interest because of its direct and indirect effects on the incentive structure in the rural economy. The direct effects have already been mentioned. The Botswana Agricultural Marketing Board (BAMB) uses import parity prices for maize and sorghum as the basis for setting producer prices for these crops in Botswana. The Botswana Meat Commission (BMC) similarly uses border prices to set producer prices in the livestock sector. It is important to note in this context, that whereas there is a direct link between border prices and the prices of agricultural output in both the arable and livestock sectors, traditional agriculture is characterized by minimal use of imported intermediate inputs. The higher the value of the pula, the lower are import parity prices and hence producer prices in agriculture. But higher values of the pula do not reduce farm costs in the same way.

Figure 5.5 illustrates the general movement of exchange rates since 1982. The main features of this are a sharp depreciation against Special Drawing Right (SDR) currencies between 1983 and 1985 followed by a gradual depreciation between 1987 and 1989; and, symmetrically, a

Figure 5.5   Exchange rate indices (March 1984 = 100)

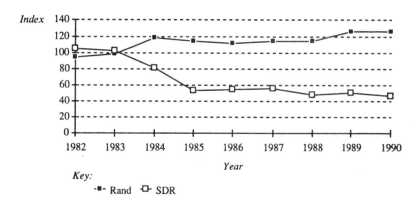

Source: Republic of Botswana, *Statistical Bulletin*, 15,3, September 1990.

sharp appreciation against the rand between 1983 and 1984 followed by a long period of stability ended by a 5 per cent revaluation against the rand in June 1989.

The implications of these features are considered briefly below. However it is important to be aware that in a general equilibrium system it is not always possible to identify the comparative static effects of changes in policy with respect to one or other economic variable. Although the exchange rate with the rand is critically important to the determination of producer prices in Botswana, those prices also reflect a range of demand and supply conditions that may themselves influence exchange rate policy. Exchange rate movements do not take place in isolation.

For the livestock sector, the opposing trends with respect to the rand on the one side and the SDR currencies on the other, and the difficulty in controlling for quality, make it hard to trace the direct links between exchange rate changes and producer price series. Between 1983 and 1985, for example, producer prices did rise, but by less than might have been expected given the extent of the depreciation against sterling in this period. The effects of the drought on the quality of livestock is undoubtedly part of the explanation for this. On the other hand, the sharp increases in price per kilogram between 1987 and 1989 are much greater than might have been expected given the depreciation of the pula against the SDR currencies in the same period. The effect of the exceptional rains of 1987 on the quality of livestock are probably part of the explanation for this. For the arable sector, the relationship between producer prices and exchange rates are also unexpected in terms of exchange rate movements: the two periods during which the pula has appreciated against the rand, 1982–1984 and 1989, both being associated with an increase not a decrease in the producer price of grain. The reason for this lies both in the fact that these were periods in which adverse climatic conditions affected aggregate output. Between 1982 and 1984, average aggregate output of sorghum was less than 20 per cent of the 1980–1981 level.

Despite the difficulty of tracing direct links between exchange rate policy and agricultural incentives, the broader implications of the policy option being pursued by the government of Botswana are clear. The use of a depreciating exchange rate against the SDR currencies to promote the diversification of the economy provides an incentive to expand SDR currency-denominated exports from the livestock sector by increasing the domestic purchasing power of livestock earnings. It follows, however, that this incentive effect holds only so long as

Botswana retains access to the EEC markets under the Lomé convention. Appreciation against the rand, on the other hand, decreases the domestic purchasing power of earnings from the production of grain, although arable producers might be expected to benefit from the lower cost of imported consumer goods. The net effect of exchange rate policy, as of so many other economic policies, is to stimulate livestock production.

6 Income and Asset Distribution

In the introduction to this study it was noted that a common thread running through its arguments would be the role of poverty as a determinant both of the structure of incentives, and of the responses of resource users to incentives. This chapter draws together the available evidence on the distribution of income and assets in Botswana, and provides a preliminary analysis of the impact of this distribution on producer responses. It should be said that the data do not exist to address the question of income effects in producer responses to relative price changes in a systematic way, and much of the following is indicative only. One recent study considers the question of the relationship between the structure and flow of rural income and expenditure pattern, but it is based on cross-sectional survey rather than time series data, and so does not address the impact of secular trends. Nevertheless, some of the preliminary results of this study are reported. The chapter is organised as follows. Section 6.1 reviews the distribution of income and assets in Botswana using the 1985/86 household income and expenditure survey data as a baseline, and paying particular attention to rural income levels and income distribution. Section 6.2 then considers the impact of the direct income support offered by the government as a consequence of the decline in rural incomes during the drought. This is income support which is independent of the various microeconomic agricultural sector policies discussed in Chapter 5. Finally, section 6.3 discusses the impact of income changes on resource allocation decisions, using the preliminary results from the study referred to above.

6.1 THE DISTRIBUTION OF INCOME

6.1.1 The 1985/86 household income and expenditure survey

The 1985 household income and expenditure survey (Republic of Botswana, 1988) was conducted at a time when rural incomes were experiencing the results of three years of drought. Despite the impact of the rural sector 'development programmes' discussed in Chapter 5, the net effect of this was to depress rural incomes and to exaggerate the inequality of income. Even making allowances for this, however, the survey revealed an unexpectedly unequal distribution of income, and an unexpected degree of rural poverty. The general characteristics of the distribution revealed by the 1985/86 Household Income and Expenditure Survey (HIES) include an overall distribution which is highly skewed, together with significant differences in the mean and variance of both urban and rural household income, and of male- and female-headed household income. Inclusion of income in kind significantly modifies the distribution. These characteristics are explored in detail below.

Taking urban and rural households together, the HIES revealed mean monthly cash household income in Botswana to have been P234.09; P313.15 for male headed households and P141.23 for female headed households. Some 45 per cent of all households were headed by females. Distribution of this income was highly skewed, the Gini ratio on cash income (calculated on a population rather than a household basis) being 0.703. Inclusion of income in kind raised the national mean total income to P306.12; P395.12 for male headed households and P201.59 for female headed households. At the same time it made the distribution of income more even, the Gini ratio for total income falling to 0.556. Nevertheless, even allowing for income in kind, just under one third of all households in Botswana had a monthly total income of less than P100 (US$55 at then current rates of exchange).

Considering urban and rural households separately reveals some of the most important characteristics of the social structure of Botswana. The mean monthly cash income among urban households was P505.30 contrasting with P136.38 for rural households. In the case of urban households the mean income of female-headed households, P255.82, was just 37 per cent of the mean income of male-headed households. In the case or rural household, the mean income of female-headed households, P104.55, was 63 per cent of that of male-headed households. Taking account of in kind income, the mean total income of urban households was P546.82, and of rural households P219.41. Urban female-headed households received on average P286.73, or 39 per cent of male-headed household income. Rural female-headed households, on the other hand, received an average of P174.34, or 60 per cent of male-headed household income. The distribution of rural cash income was very unequally distributed compared to the distribution of urban cash income: the Gini ratios being 0.674 and 0.563 respectively. But the addition of in kind income reverses this pattern: the Gini ratios for total income being 0.477 for the rural population and 0.536 for the urban population. This is not surprising given that the rural economy is dominated by traditional 'semi subsistence' agriculture.

The very sharp differences between urban and rural household income are in large part explained by demographic and social factors. Females head a greater proportion of rural than urban households. But, more importantly, a much higher proportion of the rural population was economically inactive (at least in terms of standard definitions): 41.7 per cent of the urban population being under 15 or over 65 as compared with 56 per cent of the rural population. Indeed 50 per cent of the rural population was under the age of 15. This reflects the fact that many Batswana households are split between urban and rural components, the latter comprising both older and younger members of the household. Although separate urban and rural households were identified for purposes of the HIES, the two sets of 'households' are not discrete entities, but are closely linked by income transfers and by the movement of members of the household between one location and another – both seasonally and over the life cycle.

The main characteristics of the rural distribution of income are shown in Table 6.1: the most striking characteristic being that for substantially more than one half of the rural population, over 60 per cent of their total income was in kind – whether from own production, earnings or transfers. Note that the column headed ' < 50' in the Table describes the income of a group of households for which 'business profits' (farming revenue less farming expenditures) were negative during the month of the survey. Since total income has been defined as the sum of business profits, earned income and transfers, the ratio of income in kind to total income for this category is inflated. The implications of the low level of market engagement this implies is considered in section 6.1.2 below.

A second very striking characteristic of the distribution is the importance of transfers in rural income. The point was made in Chapter 5 that many agricultural development expenditures under ALDEP, ARAP and the agricultural credit programmes of the NDB were effectively little more than income transfers. Since these are subsumed in business receipts and expenses they do not show up in the HIES results. However, other transfers were recorded, and these are summarized in Table 6.2. Once again, the position of those households

Table 6.1 Rural income distribution

Income range	<50	50–100	100–150	150–200	200–250	250–300	300–500	>500	Total
Percentage weights	15.6	21.5	18.0	11.7	9.5	4.9	8.5	10.4	100.0
Cash income	−19.59	27.20	45.36	89.37	117.65	159.60	236.00	770.94	140.29
Income-in-kind	27.25	48.11	77.29	85.95	105.35	116.49	149.41	159.44	83.46
Total income	7.66	75.31	122.65	175.31	223.01	276.08	385.41	930.38	223.75
Income-in-kind as percentage of total income	355.74	63.88	63.02	49.03	47.24	42.19	38.77	17.14	37.30

Note: Food transfers include food gifts, food aid and school meals. Other transfers include goods received, non-food gifts and non-food aid.

Source: Republic of Botswana (1988), *Household Income and Expenditure Survey 1985/86*, Gaborone, CSO.

Table 6.2 Transfers in rural income

Income range	< 50	50–100	100–150	150–200	200–250	250–300	300–500	> 500	Total
Value (Pula)									
Cash gifts	5.08	12.45	22.01	38.3	44.41	55.42	72.94	112.17	36.65
Food transfers	7.01	11.65	21.62	21.18	21.84	21.82	26.31	24.48	17.88
Other transfers	5.19	10.98	21.99	24.57	27.03	24.71	34.39	34.15	20.24
Total transfers	17.28	35.08	65.62	84.05	93.28	101.95	133.64	170.8	74.77
Percentage of all income									
Cash gifts	66.3	16.5	17.9	21.8	19.9	20.1	18.9	12.1	16.4
Food transfers	91.5	15.5	17.6	12.1	9.8	7.9	6.8	2.6	8.0
Other transfers	67.8	14.6	17.9	14.0	12.1	9.0	8.9	3.7	9.0
Total transfers	225.6	46.6	53.5	47.9	41.8	36.9	34.7	18.4	33.4

Note: Food transfers include food gifts, food aid and school meals. Other transfers include goods received, non-food gifts and non-food aid.

Source: Republic of Botswana (1988), *Household Income and Expenditure Survey 1985/86*, Gaborone, CSO.

which made negative business profits (the column headed < 50) is exceptional, and should be interpreted in the light of the definition of income used in the survey. On average, however, one third of all rural income derived from transfers other than those hidden in the rural development programmes, and one half of all transfer income was in the form of cash gifts.

For the most part these represent private transfers between the urban and rural components of the more generally defined Botswana household. The first thing to note about them is that the total value of transfer income is a monotonically increasing function of monthly income. The total value of transfers was greatest for the richest households and least for the poorest households. In part this reflects a problem in the targeting of drought relief. For example, more food aid was given to households with a monthly income greater than P500 than to any other category of household. But it also reflects the fact that higher income rural households have access to the resources of higher income urban households – both within the urban areas of Botswana and elsewhere. Indeed, since the average value of cash gifts received was more than five times the average value of cash given, receipts from outside Botswana would appear to be significant.[1]

An additional point to note about transfers concerns their impact on the distribution of total income. Against expectation, the proportion of total income accounted for by transfers was lower for those households with an income less than P100 (37 per cent of households), than for those with an income between P100 and P200 (30 per cent of households). While the proportion of total income accounted for by transfers decreases at levels of income above P200, it remains substantial. Indeed, if account is taken of the distributional effects of transfers under the agricultural development programmes, it is probable that transfers have had a generally disequalizing effect within the rural population.

6.1.2   Market engagement, income and asset distribution

The question of the degree of market engagement of farmers in the traditional sector has been raised elsewhere in this study, and the point has been made that the term 'subsistence' agriculture may be misleading to the extent that it implies that traditional farmers are insensitive to price incentives. Nevertheless, the very high proportion of total income accounted for by income in-kind does indicate a comparatively low dependence on the market, and this requires some explanation. In the Introduction it was argued that farmers in dryland environments in Sub-Saharan Africa typically adopt highly conservative risk management strategies biased in favour of tried practices and traditional products, and against technological innovation. Given this strategy, the principal choices to be made on a seasonal basis concern (a) the level of activity, and (b) the balance between production for direct consumption and production for the market (Livingstone, 1981). The degree of market engagement recorded in the HIES indicates one outcome of this decision process.

The best evidence the HIES provides on the second choice is the data offered on the consumption of 'own production'. Tables 6.1 and 6.2 show (a) that amongst lower income households more than sixty per cent of income generated by the household was in kind rather than cash, and (b) that a significant proportion of this was not own production, but transfers. If we consider food consumption alone, the average proportion of total food consumption accounted for by own production was 39 per cent. An additional 19 per cent was accounted for by transfers or wages in lieu, and the balance was purchased on the market. While food consumption accounted for a greater proportion of total consumption in poorer households than in richer households (as one would expect), the proportion of food consumption accounted for by own food production increased with household income. Higher income rural households tended to have less recourse to the market to satisfy their food requirements than lower income households (see Figure 6.1).

Since the choice between production for direct consumption and production for the market depends on the marginal net benefits of the two options, this suggests that the marginal costs of own production were higher for poorer households than for richer households. This follows from the fact that, given household demand for food and its market price, the proportion of household demand satisfied from own production of these commodities will be a decreasing function of own-production costs. If the marginal cost of own production at the equilibrium level of consumption is below the market price, the household will satisfy all of its consumption requirements from own production. Conversely, if the marginal cost of own production exceeds the market price at the equilibrium level of consumption, the household will use own production to satisfy only that portion of its requirements for which the marginal costs of own production are below the market price.

Figure 6.1   Proportion of rural food consumption by income and source

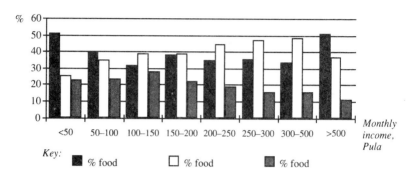

Key: ■ % food   □ % food   ▨ % food

Source: Republic of Botswana (1988), *Household Income and Expenditure Survey 1985/86*, Gaborone, CSO.

This point is illustrated in Figure 6.2 which shows two sets of marginal and average cost curves, one without subsidies and the other (indexed '*T*') with subsidies. The effect of the subsidies is to reduce the private costs of production. *P* denotes the market price of the commodity, and D denotes the household's demand curve. Without subsidies, a household deciding whether to satisfy its consumption needs through own-production or market purchases will consume *OB* units of the commodity, of which *OA* units will be own-production, and AB will be purchased. With subsidies, on the other hand, the household will choose to consume *OC* units, all of which will be own-production. This is of considerable interest, given that the new agricultural policy continues to rely on input subsidies as a means of delivering assistance to 'semi subsistence' farmers precisely because of their low level of market engagement. If inputs are subsidized enough, households will choose to supply at least some of their output to the market, *OE* in Figure 6.1, but at the cost of severe overutilization of the resource base. Few hard data on relative (economic) production costs in traditional agriculture exist, but indirect evidence may be obtained from data on two factors known to have a significant impact on agricultural production costs: access to productive assets, and the productivity of such assets. Three classes of assets are important in this respect in Botswana: livestock, draft power, and land. Since access to grazing land is a common right, it is not possible to estimate the private costs of range use, although it is known that these costs rise with the

Figure 6.2 Impact of subsidies on production for direct consumption

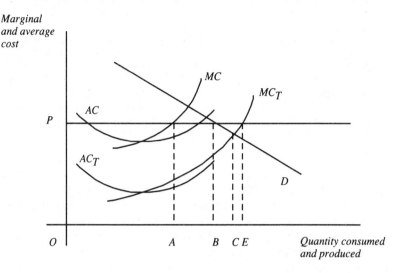

degradation of the range. But there do exist data on the distribution of livestock holdings. In the case of the arable sector, there also exist data on the distribution of land holdings. Moreover, the HIES provides information on the ownership of at least some of these assets by the distribution of income (although it does not indicate the size of average holdings in each income category).

Table 6.3 reports HIES data on the proportion of rural households owning or having access to four classes of asset by income group. As already mentioned, the Table says nothing about the average size of holdings of each class of asset. But it does indicate a comparatively even distribution of access rights for all assets (except vehicles for which donkeys are substitutes at lower levels of household income) among households with a monthly total income in excess of P100. Two things are significant about this in the present context. The first is the high proportion of low income (<P100) rural households without access to draft power of any sort (donkeys, cattle or vehicles). This was a major motivation for the draft power facility in ARAP, introduced in the year of the survey. It is also an explanation for the higher marginal cost of own production faced by these households, and hence for their greater relative dependence on market purchases of food.

Table 6.3   Proportion of households owning or having access to rural assets

Income (Pula)	< 100	100–200	200–300	300–500	500–1000	1000–2000	> 2000	Total
Vehicles	1.2	5.2	15.8	16	32.4	56.8	57.8	5.9
Cattle	51.9	69.0	61.1	72.1	51.8	44.6	69.1	56.2
Goats	61.5	73.9	55.6	63.0	51.1	51.9	100.0	62.8
Donkeys	30.0	34.5	24.2	28.2	19.9	17.2	42.2	29.7

Source: Republic of Botswana (1988), *Household Income and Expenditure Survey 1985/86* (Gaborone: CSO).

Secondly, given the high degree of equality of access to productive assets among households with incomes greater than P100, if the positive correlation between the proportion of food consumption from own production and household income does reflect falling costs, this is further indirect evidence that the agricultural development expenditures under ARAP and ALDEP may have increased rather than decreased rural inequality.

These remarks are indicative only of course, but they are consistent with the available data. Analysis of arable farm enterprise budgets in Botswana during the drought years (Edwards *et al.*, 1989) has shown that the range of subsidies available to traditional farmers so far reduced private costs that the domestic resource cost (DRC) ratio calculated on the basis of border prices was negative for all crops except millet. What is being suggested here is that the subsidies and the distortions in private cost were greater for higher income households, and this is explored further in section 6.3.

6.2   RURAL POVERTY AND SUPPORT FOR THE DESTITUTE

In 1989 the government of Botswana drew up a new poverty datum line (PDL) to replace the PDL in use since the mid-1970s (Republic of Botswana, 1991). The new PDL was then applied to the HIES data to generate measures of the extent, variation and depth of poverty at that time. To judge variation the HIES data were divided into six regions: two urban and four rural. The four rural regions comprised: (a) the rural south east, including South East, Kgatleng and the eastern parts of Kweneng and Ngwaketse Districts; (b) the rural north east, including North East and Central Districts; (c) the rural north west, including Chobe and Ngamiland Districts; and the rural southwest, including Ghanzi, Kgalagadi and the western parts of Kweneng and Ngwaketse Districts. The results are shown in Table 6.4.

Without considering the basis on which the PDL was constructed, the results of the exercise are remarkable. The difference between urban and rural areas is striking, 64 per cent of all rural households being judged to be in poverty compared with 30 per cent of urban households (and compared with 45 per cent of all rural households in the 1974/75 Rural Income Distribution Survey). So too is the difference within the rural areas, the range extending from 56 per cent in the south east to 83 per cent in the north west. Moreover, the average income shortfall of households judged to be in poverty, shown in the rightmost column of Table 6.4, varied between 29 per cent in the south east and an extraordinarily high 45 per cent in the north west.

Even allowing for the fact that 1985/86 was a drought year, it has to be questioned as to whether there is any value in a PDL that places such a high proportion of the total population in poverty, especially when it may be used as a reference point in establishing key variables such as minimum wage rates. Nonetheless, the exercise did underline the point that the distribution of rural income and the welfare of a significant part of the rural population had declined since 1974/75. We

Table 6.4   Rural poverty, 1985/86

	Total households	Households in poverty	Proportion of households in poverty	Proportion of households in poverty weighted by the poverty gap ratio
South east	68318	38115	0.56	0.29
North east	64101	43585	0.68	0.34
North west	16959	14001	0.83	0.45
South west	14113	9055	0.64	0.37
Rural	163491	104756	0.64	0.33
Urban	58897	17474	0.3	0.17
Rural/urban	2.78	5.99	2.13	1.94

Note: The poverty gap ratio is (PDL - income)/(PDL)

Source: Republic of Botswana, *A Poverty Datum Line for Botswana*, Gaborone, CSO, 1991.

have already considered some of the ways in which the government of Botswana had sought to address this problem. In this section it considers policy measures that were independent of the agricultural development programmes.

Botswana has no formal system of social security under which those without adequate means of support by reason of age, unemployment or disability are automatically assured of government assistance. Assistance is generally given on an ad hoc basis. Leaving aside the transfers under ALDEP and ARAP, the main targeted support for rural incomes during the drought years were the food distribution and labour-based relief programmes. These programmes were explicitly designed to alleviate the rural poverty that followed harvest failures between 1982 and 1985. They provided direct support to the rural poor in both cash or kind. It is estimated that during the drought approximately 60 per cent of the rural population benefited from one or both of these programmes.

The most widespread form of rural relief was the direct feeding programme, which took the form of both school meals and food rations. The labour-based relief programme, provided income support in the form of wages for public sector projects (road and dam construction, bush clearance etc.). It supported an average of 42,000 people between 1982 and 1989. In 1985/6, the year of the HIES, the average value of LBRP support was P173, which accrued to approximately one quarter of all rural households. Both food aid and the labour-based relief programme were conceived as temporary measures to deal with the problem of drought-induced rural poverty. The only regular programmes of assistance for those impoverished due to the fact that they are not employed and have no access to other means of support are the destitute programmes administered by the City Councils in urban areas and by the District Councils in the rural areas. Under these programmes core support is given to those declared to be destitute in the form of rations to the value of P30.00 per month. This is the same throughout the country, and does not vary with either the size of the destitute family or with the cost of the items included in the rations. In addition to rations, destitutes are entitled to a number of benefits including: housing where they have no other shelter; school uniforms and meals for their children; paupers burials; free medical attention and prescription drugs; and free blankets and clothing if they have none of their own. In addition, councils attempt to trace the relatives of needy families, and bear the cost of repatriating the individual destitute or destitute family if those relatives are found.

Evidence presented to the presidential commission on the incomes policy indicated that the destitute problem was then growing rapidly. The total number of registered destitutes had doubled in the four years between 1984 and 1988, and in 1989 stood at around 7000 – about the same number as were then employed in the mining sector. Moreover, this number excluded those declared to be temporarily destitute because of the drought, although by 1989 it was evident that most recruits to the ranks of the permanently destitute came from the rolls of the temporarily destitute. While the majority of registered destitutes were in the rural areas (see Figure 6.3), the most rapid rate of growth in destitutes was taking place in the urban areas.

The growing problem of rural destitution is closely linked with the growing number of rural households without access or with reduced access to agricultural assets, and in particular livestock. Between 1985 and 1989, the successive agricultural surveys showed that the proportion of traditional farms having no cattle was steadily increasing. While this may have been in part due to the incentive effects of ARAP, there is little doubt that a growing number of rural

Figure 6.3   Registered destitutes: rural Botswana

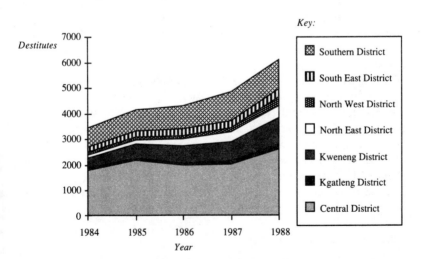

Note: The totals for the rural areas are much larger.
Source: Republic of Botswana (1990), *Report of the Presidential Commission on the Review of the Incomes Policy* (Gaborone: Government Printer).

households are poor not only in terms of income but also in terms of assets. Insufficient work has been done on the system of transfers to determine the extent to which it has created poverty traps – implying incentive effects that discourage rural households in poverty from earning additional income – and this remains an important topic for further research. However, some work has been done on the impact of transfers on expenditure patterns, and this is reported in section 6.3.

6.3   THE INCENTIVE EFFECTS OF PUBLIC TRANSFERS

As in other semi-arid areas, investment decisions in rural Botswana reflect a general risk management strategy based on diversification of income source. It is a characteristic feature of rural communities in such areas that cash income derives from a number of different sources: sale of goods and services, wages and transfers being the main categories. This section reports preliminary results generated by research on the investment decisions of rural households in Botswana. The research tests the general hypothesis that savings and investment expenditure are not independent of the source of income. It therefore questions a standard assumption of economic theory (based on the notion that money is fungible) that the source of income is not relevant to either consumption or investment decisions. This is an assumption which has tended to persist in microeconomic analysis despite long experience of contrary evidence at the macroeconomic level, of which tied aid would be the best example.

Unlike earlier work in the area, the household is defined to include all members drawing on or contributing to the income pool available to the resident household. This is intended to capture the part played by non-resident members both in terms of their direct impact on the intrahousehold distribution of income through private transfers, and on household investment decisions. The research is based on a small sample of households drawn from four villages in Central and North Eastern Districts. The sample was surveyed at monthly intervals over one year in 1989/90.

6.3.1   Sample characteristics

The demographic distribution of the sample is described in Figure 6.4: the two distributions shown being for the household resident in the village/lands/cattleposts (HHTOT) and for the household inclusive of

Figure 6.4   Demographic distribution of households

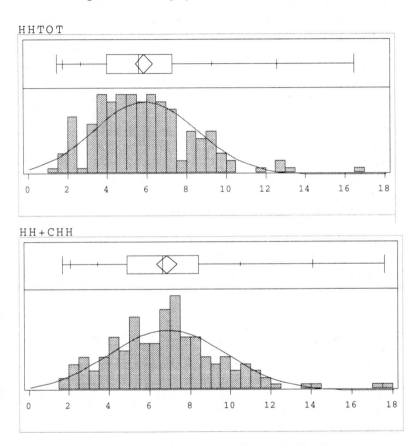

Source: Perrings *et al.* (1990) *Income and Employment Generation in Rural Botswana: Second Report* (Gaborone: University of Botswana).

cooperating members resident elsewhere (HH + CHH). The human resource base of the broadly defined household is somewhat greater than that of the conventionally defined household. Whereas the mean size of the resident household was 5.9, the mean size of the broadly resident household plus cooperating members was 6.8. The mean dependency ratio of the sample (defined as the ratio of household members aged under 15 and over 64 to the total household size) is 0.46, and this ratio was found to vary inversely with mean cash income.

Cash 'income' was defined to be equivalent to gross cash revenue (gross monthly household cash receipts from all sources). Hence while the distribution of income does say something about equity in the sample villages, it also conveys information on both the degree of market engagement and the scale of economic activity, and the results should be interpreted in the light of this. The definition ensures that households are treated identically irrespective of the type of economic activity in which they are engaged. Thus, wage earning activities are dealt with in the same way as business activities – including farming. As might be expected, the sample was characterised by a very wide dispersion of income under this definition. The mean monthly income was P318.98, with standard deviation of 556.19. Median income was only P129.70, while the bottom quartile had a cash income less than or equal to P82.60.

The sources of cash income were grouped into the following five categories: income from the sale of goods and services (*ISALE*); property income deriving from rent, interest, hire or lease of property (*IRENT*); wage or salary income (*IWAGE*); public transfers (*ITRANS*); and private transfers (*IGIFT*). The mean level of gross income, and its distribution between these categories were as follows for the whole sample and for each quartile:

	ITOTAL	ISALE	IRENT	IWAGE	ITRAN	IGIFT
All	318.98	0.41	0.02	0.22	0.14	0.27
Q 1	50.85	0.39	0.00	0.09	0.15	0.38
Q 2	99.83	0.32	0.02	0.30	0.13	0.36
Q 3	204.06	0.35	0.01	0.23	0.21	0.28
Q 4	931.95	0.60	0.04	0.25	0.05	0.06

As in the HIES, the survey showed income to be highly correlated with a number of demographic and locational characteristics including gender of household head (shown in Figure 6.5 in which quantile plots and means diamonds have been superimposed on the data), geographical location, and the dependency ratio. So, for example, households in Shoshong (the westernmost village sampled in Central District) which had the lowest mean income in the whole sample was characterized by the highest dependency ratio, and the highest proportion of female-headed households.

The most striking feature of the distribution is that over 40 per cent of mean monthly cash income in the study area derived from transfers (public and private). This is not unusually high by Botswana standards.

Figure 6.5   Income distribution by gender of household head

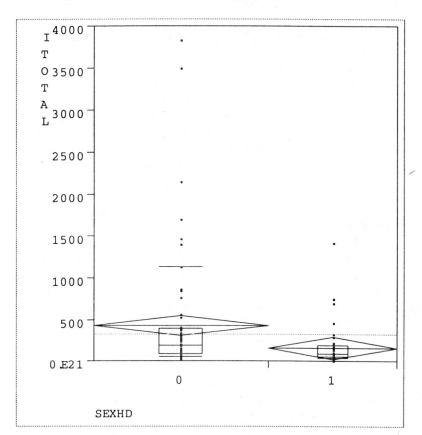

Note: The width of the diamond in this case is proportional to the size of the
sample. The line across the diamond indicates the mean, and the
vertical distance spanned by the diamond indicates the 95 per cent
confidence interval. The upper and lower lines indicate the 90 and 10
per cent quantiles respectively. Males are indexed '0' and females '1'.

Indeed, it is similar to the Figure reported in the HIES. What is
especially significant is the distribution of transfer income by income
level. While the share of total income accounted for by private transfers
is a monotonically decreasing function of mean income, the share of
public transfers is not. Public transfers account for only 5 per cent of

the income of the top quartile, but they also comprise a significantly smaller share of income in the bottom two quartiles (15 per cent and 13 per cent respectively) than the third quartile (21 per cent). This feature reflects on the targeting of public transfers, which we have already discussed.

For purposes of preliminary analysis, expenditures were amalgamated into four broad groups: consumption expenditure comprising food, drink and tobacco, clothing, household goods, utilities, fuels, transport and communications and other expenditure (ECONS); expenditure on capital assets including buildings and construction, land, farm goods, stocks for resale, machinery and tools plus expenditure on human capital – health and education (*ECAP*); payments to other factors, including wages, rents, interest and hire charges, taxes and transfers (*EPAY*); and savings (*ESAVE*). The last is a balancing item set equal to the difference between income and expenditure.

The distribution of mean expenditure shares on each category by income quartile is reported below. The *ETOTAL* column is the sum of expenditure on capital and consumption goods together with payments to other factors. The difference between *ITOTAL* and *ETOTAL* is *ESAVE*. Expenditure shares were obtained by evaluating average shares at the sample mean value of total income, both for the whole sample and for each quartile.

The main concern of the research is with savings and investment decisions. Hence it concentrates on the expenditure categories *ESAVE* and *ECAP*. What is of interest here is (a) how far the propensity to save or invest is affected by the source of income, and (b) to what extent is the pattern of investment determined by income type. Over the whole sample the strongest correlation was found between expenditure on capital assets and income from the sale of goods and services. This follows from the definitions used in the analysis, and merely implies a direct relationship between business expenditures and receipts. However, expenditure on capital assets was also positively correlated with public transfers and property income, but was negatively correlated with private transfer and wage income. Savings were negatively correlated with other expenditure categories as expected, but were positively correlated with public transfer income, with wage income, and with income from the sale of goods and services. Payments to other factors – the category that includes expenditures on wages, rents, taxes and transfers – was positively correlated with all income sources except for private transfer income.

	ITOTAL	ETOTAL	ECONS	ECAP	EPAY	ESAV
All	318.98	262.36	0.62	0.20	0.05	0.15
Q 1	50.85	56.07	0.97	0.20	0.03	−0.14
Q 2	99.83	85.94	0.68	0.18	0.04	0.15
Q 3	204.06	119.36	0.44	0.13	0.03	0.41
Q 4	931.95	798.36	0.40	0.32	0.11	0.18

6.3.2 Savings, investment and public cash transfers

Public cash transfers includes all cash benefits to households deriving from public sector programmes. That is, it includes all cash grants or allowances under the agricultural development programmes as well as welfare payments. To explore the conditioning effect on savings and investment of the four income categories identified, including public transfers, and of gender of the head of household and location, a model was estimated specifying 3rd degree polynomial forms for regressors measured by interval values (income sources). The results for the whole sample and for each quartile are reported in Appendices 3 and 4. This section considers the conditioning effect of public sector cash transfers only.

To make it easy to see the significance of transfers at each income level, consider the leverage plots in figures 6.6 and 6.7. Figure 6.6 shows the statistical significance of the effect of transfer income on the share of the categories *ESAVE* and *ECAP* in total cash expenditure at the level of the whole sample. Figure 6.7 shows the same thing for the bottom income quartile.[2] What the first of these figures indicates is that public transfer income is a statistically significant explanator of savings and investment behaviour at the 5 per cent level for the whole sample. But it is not highly significant. It turns out, though, that when the sample is broken down by income quartile, the share of total income accounted for by public transfers affects the propensity of low-income households to save and invest much more markedly than it does higher-income households.

This finding is rather remarkable, since it is contrary to the relationship one would expect to find at very low income levels. Generally, the perception of income and expenditure patterns amongst the poor is that transfer income boosts consumption expenditure, and that the propensity to save is very low. But this is not what is shown here. For all income quartiles the slope of the line of fit on the share of savings and capital expenditure due to transfer income is positive, but only in the case of the first income quartile is it statistically significant.

Figure 6.6   Leverage plots: public transfer income on savings and capital expenditure shares (whole sample)

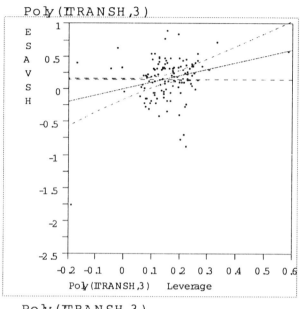

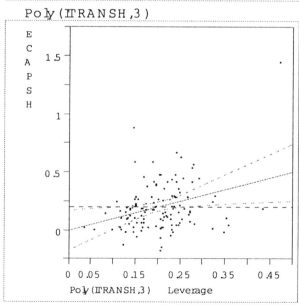

Figure 6.7   Leverage plots: public transfer income on savings and capital
expenditure shares (quartile 1)

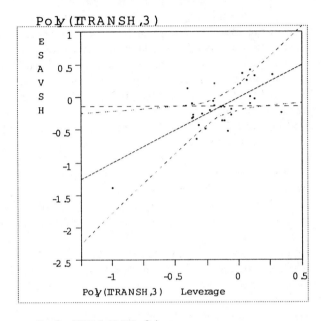

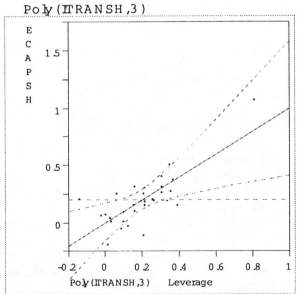

Both savings and investment in total cash expenditure for the poor are significantly influenced by public sector transfers.

The figure also shows, however, a significant difference between savings and capital expenditure. In respect of the former, 81 per cent of the variation in the share of savings in total cash expenditure in the bottom income quartile was shown to be explained by the shares of the four main income sources and the locational and gender variables. And four of the six conditioning factors were significant: public transfer income ($F = 4.29$), private transfer income ($F = 2.45$), income from sale of goods and services ($F = 2.04$) and location ($F = 2.43$). The gender of the household head was shown to be irrelevant, as was both property and wage income. The results are much more striking in respect of the share of capital expenditure in total expenditure. Eighty per cent of the variation in the share of investment in total cash expenditure in the bottom income quartile was shown to be explained by the shares of the four main income sources and the locational and gender variables, with only one of the six conditioning factors significant: public transfer income (F = 6.54). Once again, the gender of the household head was shown to be irrelevant, as were all sources of earned income. Location and private transfers were slightly more important than the remaining conditioning factors, but neither were significant.

For all higher levels of income the relationship between savings and investment are much weaker. The implication is that public transfers over the sample area are less effective in inducing a change in either savings or investment behaviour in the upper income quartiles than in the lower. However, since the bulk of public sector transfers in this area accrue to the third income quartile, making up over 21 per cent of the income of that group, and since most transfers to this income category are intended to stimulate investment in agricultural activity, this indicates a real problem in the targetting of transfers.

In terms of the general concerns of this study, these results suggest that even though (category) income elasticity of demand for (category) goods has yet to be estimated, income effects in household responses to changes in the structure of price incentives are likely to be of increasing importance as the level of household income falls. Transfers will in general have greater allocative effects as the income level of the recipient households fall. Chapter 3 emphasized the fact that agricultural producers close to the poverty line tend to adopt highly risk averse strategies. They adopt survival strategies based on environmentally conservative practices characterized by the selection of low value but robust crops or livestock that may be directly consumed. This implies a very strong bias against technological or product innovation, particularly where this involves heightened risk or uncertainty. Similarly, savings tend to take the form of retained real assets – grain stocks, livestock, or the means of producing such assets – and this reinforces the technological conservatism of agricultural producers. The findings reported here offer at least indicative support for the power of transfer income to encourage expenditure on non-traditional assets, and while the results are preliminary their implications for policy are worth serious consideration.

7 Policy Reform

Faced with the evidence that the set of policies which evolved during the drought years have had a range of undesirable allocative effects, particularly in respect of the use made of scarce environmental resources in the agricultural sector, the seventh national development plan (NDP7) presages significant changes in policy. NDP6 had anticipated that the agricultural sector would grow at an average rate of 6.5 per cent over the plan period. Mineral revenues were to be used 'to support the themes of rural development and employment creation', and agricultural growth was expected to compensate for the fall-off in mineral sector growth. The agricultural development programmes reflected these goals, at least in concept. It turns out, as has been indicated in earlier chapters, that agricultural output has contributed a declining not an increasing proportion of GDP. Indeed, agricultural GDP has been declining in absolute terms, being lower in 1988/89 than it had been 1982/83. It turns out also that the agricultural development programmes were used as much as vehicles for drought relief as instruments for improving the asset base, and that they involved incentive effects which were inconsistent with their stated objectives.

The two goals of NDP7 are the achievement of sustainable development through the diversification of the economy, and the promotion of social justice (implying greater equity in the distribution of income). It is proposed to move towards these goals by raising the productivity of the poor and by reducing their dependence on the government. That is, it is proposed to increase the earned household income, and to reduce the share of transfers in total household income. Two policy changes are involved here. The first involves a significant increase in the weight given to diversification of the rural economy away from agriculture. The second involves the reappraisal of the system of incentives and, specifically, of the distortionary role of transfers delivered via the price system.

The two policy changes stem both from a more realistic set of expectations of the agricultural sector, and greater sensitivity to the fact that incentives developed to promote agricultural growth may, perversely, have prejudiced the prospects of further growth by encouraging the degradation of the agricultural resource base. Long-term agricultural growth is not now expected to exceed 0.5 per cent.

Hence, while the government will continue to support agricultural development, it no longer expects that the agricultural sector will have the dynamism to lead the economy. The macro outline for NDP7 (Republic of Botswana, 1990b) summarised the policy changes associated with this in the following terms:

> The reappraisal of agricultural strategy, crystallized in the Agricultural Sector Assessment, has emphasized the importance of rural industrialization and agricultural diversification as major contributions to rural development in Botswana. The strategy for industrial development in the Districts will be to build out from the existing industrial base, and create linkages into the rural areas, emphasizing development in major villages and the use of local natural resources and agricultural surpluses. (Republic of Botswana, 1990b, p. 27)

> By the end of the 1980s, it had become evident that there was large-scale dependency on the Drought and Recovery Programmes in the west of the country. Government will take measures early in NDP7 to promote food and economic security in all regions so that drought relief, when required, is only made available to those suffering reduced incomes as a direct result of drought. A main element of such household security policies is the recognition that household income, and not the household's agricultural production, is the primary determinant of whether household members get enough to eat. The diversification of rural sources of earned income to off-farm production will be emphasized through the promotion of activities which are specifically suited to the ecology and economy of different areas of Botswana. (Republic of Botswana, 1990b, p. 27)

The problem of targeting identified above is also part of the motivation for the change in policy on incentives. The key points in the new approach are the separation of income support from intervention designed to correct for the divergence between private market signals and the social opportunity cost of resource use, and the evaluation of intervention in terms of its incentive effects:

> The private sector responds to market signals, which from time to time are distorted and inappropriate. In such circumstances, where market signals can lead to socially undesirable outcomes, it may be necessary and appropriate for Government to intervene. One of Government's most important roles in the economy is to ensure that

the price signals received by the economic actors reflect real costs to the nation. . . . Government can intervene in the economy to correct inappropriate market signals in a variety of ways, including imposing taxes and other fees and charges, providing subsidies and establishing regulations. . . . They should be targeted, not broad, in scope, and should be viewed in terms of their economic incentive effects. . . . Subsidies should not be directed towards consumption, but rather towards promoting efficient, sustainable production. (Republic of Botswana, 1990b, pp. 23–4)

Very low material living standards, often involving malnourishment, medical problems, lack of education and lack of productive assets represent definite barriers for participation in productive activities. In such cases, productive powers may be released by programmes aiming explicitly at removing the barriers to participation. An emphasis throughout NDP7 will be to identify the most disadvantaged groups in order to improve the targeting of assistance to those living in poverty. (Republic of Botswana, 1990b, p. 27)

Aside from the Agricultural Sector Assessment referred to above, two key initiatives lie behind these policy shifts. The first was the development of a national conservation strategy. The second was the review of existing policy on prices and incomes. This chapter considers these two initiatives in detail, and the importance of the recommendations they contain for the development of a set of incentives that will be more consistent with the ecologically sustainable use of the natural resource base in the country.

7.1 REVIEW OF PRICE AND INCOME POLICY

In 1989 the President of Botswana appointed a commission to review the incomes policy which had then been in effect since 1976. The commission reported its results in March 1990 (Republic of Botswana, 1990a), and in September 1990 the government published a white paper (Republic of Botswana, 1990c) indicating which of the commission's recommendations had been accepted, accepted subject to amendment or rejected. The commission reported on a variety of issues associated with the incomes policy including education and training, public, parastatal and private sector salary structures, minimum wages, rents, prices and profits. This section concentrates on the commission's deliberations on the rural economy in three areas: price control, subsidies and income support; industrial licensing and rural diversification; and minimum wage policy.

7.1.1 Price control, subsidies and income support

Existing price policy in 1989 was governed by the goal of protecting consumer interests wherever there was insufficient competition to control traders profit margins, and wherever widely consumed commodities such as paraffin, blankets, clothing and basic foodstuffs were involved. The main components of price policy were, by implication, the promotion of competition and the regulation of profit margins where competition was inadequate to protect consumers. The main instrument of price control where competition was judged to be inadequate was the *Control of Goods (Trading Margins) Regulations (1975)*, which authorized the Ministry of Commerce and Industry to control consumer prices in such cases through the regulation of profit margins.

The commission found that the existing policy had been interpreted in a much more restrictive way than originally intended. It had been implicitly assumed that the 'normal mechanism of competition' was absent not just in some special cases, but for practically every good sold in Botswana. The regulations had therefore been used to restrict the wholesale and retail mark-ups on almost all commodities traded. Moreover, margins had been established with a view to achieving a particular distributional outcome. Under the regulations permissible mark-ups varied widely from one category of good to another depending on their importance in satisfying the basic consumption needs of low-income households. Permitted wholesale mark-ups for maize, wheat, sorghum, tea, candles, bottled gas, milk or milk powder, and matches, for example, were lower (7.5 per cent) than for all other goods (10 per cent). Similarly, permitted retail mark-ups for the same 'essential' consumer goods were set at 10 per cent, while allowable mark-ups for other goods were anything up to 50 per cent.

The commission accepted the validity of what it took to be general principles underlying the treatment of prices in the original incomes policy: that product prices should not be regulated by government except where there existed evidence of monopolistic exploitation of consumers, or where government had itself granted a monopoly. And it observed that in most industries, and in most areas, the primary conditions for the competitive pricing of goods and services did exist in

Botswana. It accordingly recommended that price controls be lifted on all commodities at the wholesale level, and that prices be directly controlled at the retail level only where there existed hard evidence of monopoly exploitation. Wherever possible, it argued that prices should be regulated indirectly by encouraging competition. Indeed, it was argued that the first responsibility of government was to create the conditions for competitive pricing including the free and unrestricted entry and exit of firms into the market, the promotion of consumer awareness of market conditions, and the provision of adequate infrastructure.

The last was argued to be especially important in rural Botswana, where prices were strongly influenced by transport costs. It was observed that an improvement in transport infrastructure since the incomes policy was first drawn up had significantly reduced both the costs of retailing in remote areas and the level of retail activity. More generally, since rural vehicle usage and fleet size had increased at a faster rate than could have been explained by changes in rural incomes alone, indicating positive externalities to the new road network, the commission argued that transport infrastructural development in these areas should be expanded.

The main mechanism by which the government had sought to promote competition under the existing incomes policy was the development of consumer cooperatives. Given evidence that the majority of goods were priced lower in the cooperatives than in other retail outlets, the commission recommended that consumer cooperatives continue to receive support. However, the general thrust of its recommendations on competition was that the government should remove the existing barriers to entry in a variety of rural markets. These recommendations are considered in section 7.1.2.

What is most important about the commission's findings in this area, is its conclusion that intervention in the price mechanism to deliver support to low income rural households was fundamentally flawed. In addition to the system of price control, it was observed that there existed a range of subsidies which had the same basic intention. Indeed, we have drawn attention to some of the subsidies available under the agricultural development programmes, ARAP and ALDEP; and we have pointed out that these subsidies had the primary function of delivering income support to specific groups in the rural economy. The commission found that there existed a wide range of subsidies providing indirect support to the low paid, including subsidies on housing, foodstuffs, land and water. It argued that such subsidies necessarily involved allocative inefficiency – since subsidized prices do not reflect the true scarcity of the commodities concerned and so encourage their overutilization – and recommended that price intervention be replaced by direct income support for those in need. It argued that if the government wished to support groups such as the remote area dwellers, it should do so directly, and not by the introduction of generalised price controls which had distortionary effects across the whole economy. In addition, it argued that if it was desirable to deliver income support, then that support should be closely targeted.

7.1.2 Industrial licensing and rural diversification

While the commission took the view that competition could provide consumers with better protection against exploitative pricing that the existing system of price controls, it recognised that this would involve reducing the biases against competition inherent in other areas of policy. It noted, for example, that the existing system of licensing had been widely used to inhibit competition. In terms of the *Trade and Liquor Act (1986)*, no one was allowed to undertake any of the scheduled trades or businesses without a licence issued by either the National Licensing Authority (responsible for the issuance of wholesale, import and export, hotel liquor, agent, auctioneer, external representative, drillers and travel agents licences) or a Local Licensing Authority (responsible for the issuance of all other licences). The Licensing Authorities were required to publish all applications and to consider any objections to those applications; to verify that applications did not contravene zoning or planning regulations; that the applicant had no more than three other licences, and was not an unrehabilitated insolvent, a minor, or convicted of an offence involving dishonesty. In addition, the Licensing Authorities were required to determine whether an application was 'in the public interest' – a requirement which provided enormous scope for inhibiting competition. On top of this, they were required to ensure that licences are only issued to Batswana where the activity was 'reserved'.[1]

Although the commission's recommendations in this area were primarily concerned with the promotion of competition, they effectively also addressed the question of diversification. To promote competition, it was argued that the existing system of licensing should be revised so as to prevent licences being used to grant monopolies, to relieve Licensing Authorities of the obligation to make commercial judgements about applications, to make it impossible for existing licence-holders to object to the granting of a licence to a business rival, to separate the granting of licences from the protection of the public interest, and to eliminate delays in the granting of licences. In respect of Batswana Preference, the commission did not oppose the reservation of the activities since most of the activities covered were small-scale and subject to competition, but it recommended that the enabling legislation be amended to permit activities to be reserved only in cases where reservation would not inhibit competition.

It was noted that in cases where there were no zoning regulations, which included much of the rural economy, the existing system had shown itself to be conservative in respect of the type of land use admitted, and prone to the creation of monopolies. It was argued that while the long-term solution lay in the introduction of zoning regulations that would make approvals automatic, in the short and medium term the Ministry of Local Government and Lands should reconsider the procedures by which land is allocated with a view to reducing delays in the allocation of land for non-traditional activities.

7.1.3 Minimum wage policy and rural wage income

Under the existing incomes policy, a number of sectors in the economy had been subject to minimum wage laws designed both to protect vulnerable employees from monopsonistic exploitation and to assure an equitable rural-urban distribution of income. The baseline against which urban minimum wages were notionally set under this policy was average rural income. However, as the HIES had shown, the gap between urban and rural incomes in Botswana has been a widening one, and by 1988 it was argued that since there was no longer any discernible link between urban minimum wages and average rural income, the latter should be replaced by the Poverty Datum Line as the yardstick against which minimum wages were set (Scoville and Nyamadzabo, 1988). The same report argued that the current level of minimum wages was acceptable, in that it appeared not to have led to any significant effects on either employment or output, although part of the explanation for this was that minimum wage laws were not enforced for smaller enterprises in the rural areas. The report recommended that for those industries where minimum wages did have a significant effect, such as the small-scale retail (particularly rural retail) trade, the rate should be reduced.

Although the minimum wage applied (at least in principle) to a number of activities in the rural economy, it did not apply to agriculture. Indeed, a survey of the agricultural sector showed that a very high proportion of wage earners in that sector received an income substantially below the minimum wage in those sectors covered by the Act (Gyekye and Mazonde, 1989). Whereas the 1989 monthly cash income of an unskilled worker earning the lowest of the statutory minimum rates was estimated to be P132.00, the average cash and in kind income of a sample of 455 employees in the agricultural sector was P90.86. Moreover, over 30 per cent of the sample of agricultural workers were shown to receive a cash income of less than P30.00, the sum allocated to councils to cover the basic needs of destitutes.

The commission considered a number of aspects of the minimum wage, including its effects on employment, output and investment, the appropriate level of the minimum wage, whether there should be special youth rates, how payments-in-kind should be treated in assessing compliance with the minimum wage, and what effect current wage differentials had on urban–ruralmigration and rural development. It accepted that the original standard for the minimum wage, average farm income, was no longer viable, and supported the Scoville and Nyamadzabo recommendation that it be replaced by a PDL that was sustainable in terms of productivity levels and prospects in the Botswana economy. Since this would formally delink urban and rural incomes, however, the commission also considered whether the minimum wage should be extended to cover the agricultural sector. It concluded that all wage employees in Botswana should be covered by a minimum wage, but that the minimum wage should not be set such as to cause significant disemployment of any category of employees. The commission further rejected the idea that ability to pay should determine the minimum wage to be applied in any given industry, and recommended that all industries operating in the same location should face the same minimum wage, based on the cost of the PDL in that location. In addition, the commission recommended that payment-in-kind should be included as an integral part of the minimum wage: that is, all in-kind payments should be quantified and costed in the employment contract, and should be taken into account for purposes of establishing compliance with the minimum wage.

While the commission's recommendations on prices were generally accepted, and while its recommendations on licenses were approved with the exception of recommendation that exclusive licenses be abolished, all substantial recommendations in respect of the minimum wage except for those relating to the use of the PDL and the inclusion of in-kind payments were rejected. The implications of this are considered later.

7.2   THE BOTSWANA NATIONAL CONSERVATION STRATEGY

The National Conservation Strategy prepared for Botswana (BNCS) is designed to offer an environmental perspective on the development planning process. The aim is to develop an integrated approach to the management of the natural resource base, with a view to protecting the opportunities available to the future generations who will have to depend on the same resource base. For the most part the ecological systems on which the majority of Batswana depend have only a limited margin of resilience to natural variations in climate and other external events, and there is increasing evidence that this margin is narrowing as a consequence of the private behaviour of individual resource users. The more the natural environment is degraded, the more the margin of resilience of its ecosystems is reduced. What makes this important is that if ecosystems do lose resilience to the point where they collapse before the natural variations of climate, the changes that take place in the options available to future generations may well be irreversible. The BNCS was devised as a means of protecting against irreversible loss of opportunity by guiding current behaviour along sustainable lines.

The concerns of the BNCS may not differ substantially from conservation strategies developed elsewhere, but are more urgent precisely because of the narrowness of the margins of resilience in Botswana. The extraordinary growth performance of the last two decades has not been able to protect against the degradation of the non-mineral resource base, which means that output is ever more sensitive to climatic variation. It will take an increasingly minor reduction in rainfall to induce a major collapse in agricultural output. The major recommendations of the BNCS are for the diversification of economic activity – away from the minerals and livestock sectors – through the development of a structure of incentives that encourages resource users to explore options other than the traditional ones of livestock and, to a lesser extent, arable agriculture. The strategy emphasises that conservation of the resource base will only be realized if it is in the private as well as the social interest, and that this implies a change in the set of signals currently guiding private activity.

At the same time the BNCS suggests few specific avenues for diversification. This is for two reasons. The first is a sense that the role of government has been excessively *dirigiste* in the past – indeed, that this is a large part of the environmental problem. Hence it is expected that opportunities for diversification will be identified by private resource users as the current biases in the system of incentives are eliminated. The second reason is the fact that apart from the present rather imperfect series on rangeland quality, there is no data-base that the government can call on to measure the environmental implications of specific activities. The following section addresses the two issues raised by the BNCS: diversification and the data-base.

7.2.1 Diversification in the BNCS

The starting point of the BNCS is that the development programme should be sustainable over time, and that sustainability requires diversification away from the mineral sector. This raises a number of questions about the role of agriculture. It is recognized that in certain areas of the country neither arable agriculture nor livestock may offer either an intertemporally efficient or sustainable use of the resources. Indeed, a high rate of agricultural growth will almost certainly not be environmentally sustainable except through the larger commercial operations. The BNCS accordingly recommends a more broadly based environmentally sensitive strategy of resource use. It accepts that some agricultural growth and so some increase in rural incomes may be possible with the adoption of simple improvements in farm management as demonstrated by various farming systems projects. But it also accepts that future sustainable growth of the rural economy will depend on the expansion of off-farm activities rather than on-farm activities.

There is already considerable diversification of sources of rural income, as the HIES and other surveys have shown. Abel *et al.* (1987) found that in the drought years the main source of rural cash income was wage remittances. The second source of income was informal non-farm employment (from casual labour or from building, trading, beer brewing, handicraft activities, etc.). Livestock income ranked only third, and arable income last. Moreover, the latter was not only a minor source of income, it was a highly unreliable source. While it might produce up to 25 per cent of the income of progressive farmers in good years, it was a universally loss-making activity in bad years.

The BNCS suggests diversification through the expansion of the second income source identified by Abel *et al.* This is argued to be important not only in the more remote areas, but in all areas of rural Botswana. The BNCS, like the commission on the Incomes Policy, acknowledges that the extension of the Labour Based Relief Programme represents a move in this direction, but argues that there is considerable scope for supporting individual diversification initiatives through, for example, a more imaginative use of the FAP. It also recognizes that, as experience with grapple and mokola palm has shown, the commercialization of gathering can lead very rapidly to overutilization of the resource unless there are either controls on the level of activity or charges sufficient to cover the costs of the backstop technology including domestication of the plant.

The point was made earlier that the BNCS has few specific recommendations to make so far as diversification of the rural economy is concerned. Nevertheless, it does canvas a number of options. These include both the development of the hunting and gathering activities that are a major part of the traditional Kalahari economy, and the domestication of various resources that have, in the past, been harvested only in the wild. Examples given of the sort of resources that might be harvested more intensively in the wild include a number of dryland veld products such as fuelwood, construction timber, a variety of roots, tubers, fruit, edible leaves, fungi, shoots, grasses, mokola palm leaves, grapple tubers and mophane worms. Markets currently exist for the last three, but most of the others are still largely produced for the direct use of the households concerned. Examples of the sort of resources that might be domesticated include fisheries and game.

Little progress has yet been made in the commercialization of fisheries in Botswana, and the BNCS does recommend investigation of the fishing industry based on the surface water resources of the Okavango delta and the Chobe system. It points out that both fish and crocodile farming have recently been proved commercially viable in Botswana (on a small scale) and in neighbouring territories. Considerably more progress has been made in respect of other wildlife. There already exists a Wildlife Conservation Policy based on the creation of buffer zones between the national parks and game reserves, and the rangeland used by pastoralists (Republic of Botswana, 1991). These Wildlife Management Areas (WMAs) are ultimately expected to account for some 8 per cent of the land area of Botswana (see Appendix 7). Unlike the parks and reserves, where observation is the only legal basis for the economic exploitation of the resource, the WMAs will admit a range of activities. The goal of the policy is to obtain as high a sustainable return on wildlife as possible. Wildlife will be recognized as the primary resource in these areas, and other activities will be allowed only if they do not prejudice the primary resource.

The Wildlife Conservation Policy is designed to increase utilization of wildlife resources in order to generate income and employment opportunities in rural Botswana. The policy is predicated on the assumption that the national park, game reserve, and WMA land will yield highest net return if allocated to wildlife-based activities. It is argued to be more efficient to use this land for the rearing of wildlife, than for the rearing of livestock. There are two strands to the argument. First, wild animals are physically better adapted to the conditions in these areas than livestock, and so more productive (in terms of liveweight gains) than livestock. Second, wildlife utilization opens up the prospect of much greater rural diversification than livestock. For example, the husbanding of drought-tolerant and sedentary grazing species, such as Gemsbok, may be more profitable than husbanding livestock in certain areas of the country (Nchunga, 1988). The greater potential for diversification in wildlife is argued to lie in the fact that wildlife have value not only in consumption, but also in hunting and observation. Game ranches which admit both hunting, observation and the supply of animal products are well developed features of neighbouring rural economies, and it is argued that they could become much more prominent features of the Botswana economy.

The BNCS makes the point that the current structure of incentives offered by the government is not oriented towards the commercialization of wildlife. Moreover, it recognizes that a necessary condition for the diversification of the rural economy, whether into wildlife utilization or other areas, is some diminution of the powerful incentive to augment cattle herds. This incentive currently operates irrespective of the costs imposed on other users of the range now and in the future. To be sure, there are few data currently available on the short or long run environmental effects of changing price incentives. Indeed, the linkages between producer prices, short run agricultural supply responses, and the user costs of agriculture has yet to be identified. This means that policy analysts are necessarily blind to the environmental implications of different price structures. It is possible to provide guidance as to the lower bounds on the opportunity cost of natural resource use, but under current accounting conventions and given existing environmental statistics, many of the most important policy questions cannot yet be answered. It is not possible to determine at what prices it is optimal to deplete arable or grazing land, and what the user cost of depletion is. But nor, it turns out, is there any requirement that the cost of depletion be registered in the national accounts. For this reason the BNCS places considerable emphasis on the importance of generating an adequate data base.

7.2.2 Environmental statistics and natural resource accounting[2]

The only systematic data currently available to macroeconomic decision-makers in Botswana, as elsewhere, are those contained in the system of national accounts (SNA). In Botswana's case these are augmented by a set of social accounting matrices SAMs) derived from those accounts, and recently revised (see Republic of Botswana, 1990d). The SAMs set the conventional national accounting details into a framework which shows the interaction between production, consumption, and capital accumulation. However, neither the SAMs nor the accounts on which they are based record changes in stocks of natural resources or natural capital. The SNA treatment of the depletion, degradation or depreciation of environmental assets offers no guide at all to user cost (the cost of future opportunities foregone). This is clearly more of a problem in some countries than in others. The SNA convention on depletion turns out to be most misleading to the least well-off resource-based economies of the South where no allowance is made for the depletion of mineral stocks, changes in wildlife or fish populations, soil loss, or alterations in vegetation.

It should be added, though, that even if the existing accounts do not contain adequate information on the resource base, Botswana is significantly better off in terms of its data-base than most countries in Sub-Saharan Africa. In general, though there is indirect evidence that pressure on renewable resources and the assimilative capacity of the environment is a binding constraint on economic growth, there are virtually no statistics of the impacts of resource-based activities. In Botswana's case, the SAMs do identify flows deriving from various resource-based activities including traditional and commercial agriculture, hunting, forestry, mining, various (marketed) veld products, water, electricity, and housing. But not all inputs and outputs are treated the same. Values are imputed for resources that are tradable under the existing structure of property rights, but not for those which are not tradable. So, for example, the accounts include estimates of the value of wood used by households, but not water. This means that most natural resources used for commercial gain are implicitly assigned a zero price.

In order to provide macroeconomic policy makers with the data necessary to incorporate environmental concerns into macroeconomic policy in a systematic way, the BNCS recommended the development of natural resource accounts (NRA) of the stocks and flows of those environmental assets on which the economy depends. This section presents the results of preliminary work on the development of a set of accounts for Botswana (see Perrings *et al.*, 1989; and Gilbert, 1990).

The starting point for this work is a sense of what information is necessary to identify the sustainability of either current patterns of resource use, or current policies. The concept of sustainability has been defined in a number of ways, but two principles are central. The first is that the present generation should avoid activities which impose irreversible costs on future generations in terms of access to the resource base through, for example, the loss of biological diversity (World Commission on Environment and Development, 1987; Pearce, 1987; Goodland and Ledoc, 1987). The second, which is very closely related to the first, is that present generations should leave future generations a stock of natural and produced assets such that future generations do not face a declining set of opportunities (Howe, 1979; Repetto, 1986; Turner, 1988; Pearce and Turner, 1990). Both principles require that we have some sense of the changes in the value of the stock of natural or environmental assets as a consequence of present activity. This is what a set of natural resource accounts should show.

What is recommended for Botswana is a step-by-step construction of a new set of accounts, commencing with a description in physical terms of changes in the stocks and flows in the key resource-based sectors, livestock and arable agriculture. There will be two types of accounts: 'resource user accounts' measuring flows of natural resources into the economy and of wastes and other materials into the environment, and 'stock accounts' measuring stocks of environmental assets. Both accounts will distinguish between non-renewable and renewable resources: renewable resources including abiotic flow resources such as solar and wind energy; abiotic stocks such as water and soil nutrients regenerated via biogeochemical cycles; species populations and communities regenerated through reproduction; and ecosystems (complex resources) regenerated through interaction between their biotic and abiotic components.

Resource users include both economic agents and what may be termed environmental users: that is forestry, fisheries, agriculture etc and the ecosystems of which the resources used in those sectors are an integral part. Four broad economic sectors are defined:

- extractive resource sectors which use resources in their natural form and convert them into raw materials;
- non-extractive resource sectors which do not generate a product for intermediate or final consumption;
- resource dependent sectors which process the raw materials supplied by extractive resource sectors; and
- other sectors.

The relationship between these broad sectors and the economic sectors identified in the existing accounts in Botswana is shown in Table 7.1.

It is expected that resource user accounts will be prepared for each sector providing data on stocks (inventoried stocks or net changes from inventoried stocks of environmental assets); primary inputs; intermediate inputs; capital investment; output (in physical and monetary terms); net income (in monetary units); disposition of output and environmental impacts including waste production (expressed in physical units); changes to land resources; and changes to ecosystems. Table 7.2 offers an example of such a resource user account for the livestock sector in Botswana. In addition to the resource user accounts the NRA should contain stock accounts. Indeed, since the SNA offer no data on changes in stocks of environmental assets, the stock accounts are a key component of the NRA. These accounts provide the basic information on stock dynamics.

The physical indicators used in these accounts include both population/stock measures of species, abiotic cycling resources, and non-renewable resources; and environmental stress measures of complex resources or ecosystems. A stock account prepared for the same sector is shown in Table 7.3.

While population indicators of this sort do abstract from the dynamics of the ecosystems on which the population depends, they represent necessary steps towards the construction of accounts including the dynamics of ecosystems or 'complex resources'. As of now complex stock accounts have not been developed for any of the major ecosystems of Botswana, but the first priority would seem to be to get reliable measures of population stocks. For example, while surveys of some wildlife species have been conducted, and although

Table 7.1 Resource user accounts: sectoral classification

Sector type	Resource	Economic sector
Extractive resource sectors	Minerals	Mining, quarrying and prospecting
	Water	Agriculture, mining
	Arable land	Traditional and commercial arable agriculture
	Rangeland	Traditional and commercial livestock farming
	Forest resources	Forestry, agriculture
	Wildlife	Subsistence hunting, non-resident hunting, game farming, tourism, fisheries
	Landscape	Tourism
	Veldproducts	Non-farm traditional activities including medicine, food, clothing, construction
Resource dependent sectors	As above	Power generation and distribution, water reticulation, meat processing, hides and skins, food manufacture, wood products, crafts, tourism, trade, construction
Non-extractive resource sectors	Assimilative capacity of the environment	Waste disposal, pest control
Cultural resource sectors	Cultural 'heritage'	Tourism

data on hunting licenses and recorded kills are available, limitations of the wildlife sample surveys, and the difficulty of estimating losses due to poaching mean that the construction of wildlife balances is not currently possible. The result is that construction of stock accounts at the national level is possible for some resource stocks, but severely constrained for others. Construction of accounts at the district level is

130

Table 7.2 Resource user account for the livestock sector, 1979/80–1985/86.

	Unit	Traditional 1979–80	Traditional 1985–86	Commercial 1979–80	Commercial 1985–86	Total 1979–80	Total 1985–86
INPUTS:							
STOCKS							
levels	'000 LSU¹	2,989	3,187	421	382.1	3,410	3,569
PRIMARY INPUTS							
own account production	no. of farms²	—	73,900	—	530	—	74,430
value of own account production	'000 Pula	—	25,579	—	0	—	25,579
wages etc	'000 Pula	—	0	—	3,627	—	3,627
INTERMEDIATE INPUTS³	'000 Pula	—	27,095	—	24,900	—	51,995
INVESTMENT³							
net D in stocks	'000	-225	-262	-63	-62	-288	-324
	Pula		-26,800		2,000		-24,800
fixed assets	'000 Pula		4,300		2,600		6,900
depreciation	'000 Pula		3,200		2,100		4,300
OUTPUTS:							
GROSS OUTPUT							
output	'000 beasts	280	329	106	167	386	496
stock	% offtake	9.4	10.3	25.2	43.7	11.3	13.9
value	'000 Pula		84,600		26,700		111,300
NET INCOME⁴	'000 Pula		28,700		800		29,500
DISPOSITION OF OUTPUT							
intermediate	'000 LSU⁵	230	225	99	151	329	376
households	'000 LSU⁵	58	104	7	16	65	120

Table 7.2 cont.

	Traditional		Commercial		Total	
	1979–80	1985–86	1979–80	1985–86	1979–80	1985–86
ENVIRONMENTAL IMPACT						
D land indicator	0	–1	0	–1	0	–1
D ecosystem indicator	0	–1	0	–1	0	–1
downstream effects[6] indicator	0	–1	0	–1	0	–1

Note: 1 Cattle, goats and sheep only; expressed as total number of Livestock Units (LSUs).
2 No. of farms = sum of following categories: cattle only; cattle and smallstock; cattle, crops and smallstock; crops and smallstock; smallstock only; and other.
3 Totals for traditional and commercial agriculture from MFDP; coefficient applied on basis of ratios of gross outputs.
4 Data supplied by national account section of MFDP.
5 Intermediate consumption equals all sales of cattle, sheep and goats. Household consumption equals home slaughter.
6 Negative effect on wildlife populations, and therefore possibly on wildlife use sector.

Source: Perrings *et al.* (1989).

Table 7.3 Stock account for the livestock sector, 1979—80 and 1985—86.

	Traditional		Commercial		Total	
	1979–80	*1985–86*	*1979–80*	*1985–86*	*1979–80*	*1985–86*
CATTLE						
S_0	2,377.0	2,112.0	440.0	370.4	2,817.0	2,482.4
N	244.0 (10.3)	13.2 (0.6)	77.0 (17.5)	62.3 (16.8)	321.0 (11.4)	75.5 (3.0)
Births	582.0 (24.5)	467.2 (22.1)	95.0 (21.6)	95.5 (25.8)	677.0 (24.0)	562.7 (22.7)
Deaths	338.0 (14.2)	454.0 (21.5)	18.0 (4.1)	33.2 (9.0)	356.0 (12.6)	487.2 (19.6)
I	40.6 (1.7)	41.4 (2.0)	41.0 (9.3)	100.6 (27.2)	81.6 (2.9)	142.0 (5.7)
C	206.6 (8.7)	212.2 (10.0)	102.0 (23.2)	155.5 (42.0)	308.6 (11.0)	367.7 (14.8)
Intermediate	190.1 (8.0)	176.8 (8.4)	97.0 (22.0)	144.1 (38.9)	287.1 (10.2)	320.9 (12.9)
Final	16.5 (0.7)	35.4 (1.7)	5.0 (1.1)	11.4 (3.1	21.5 (0.8)	46.8 (1.9)
S_1	2,455.0	1,954.4	456.0	377.8	2,911.0	2,332.2
DS	78.0 (3.3)	157.6 (−7.5)	16.0 (3.6)	7.4 (2.0)	94.0 (3.3)	150.2 (−6.1)
DS_1	422.6 (17.8)		62.2 (14.1)		484.8 (17.2)	
GOATS						
S_0	604.0	1,082.8	12.0	30.8	616.0	1,113.6
N	64.6 (10.7)	294.6 (27.2)	2.7 (22.5)	9.1 (29.5)	67.3 (10.9)	303.7 (27.3)
Births	281.0 (46.5)	530.1 (49.0)	5.5 (45.8)	15.1 (49.0)	283.8 (46.1)	241.5 (21.7)

	Traditional		Commercial		Total	
	1979–80	1985–86	1979–80	1985–86	1979–80	1985–86
Deaths	216.4 (35.8)	235.5 (21.7)	2.8 (23.3)	6.0 (19.5)	219.2 (35.6)	241.5 (21.7)
I	12.1 (2.0)	23.1 (2.1)	0.7 (5.8)	2.5 (8.1)	12.8 (2.1)	25.6 (2.3)
C	56.7 (9.4)	104.7 (9.7)	1.9 (15.8)	6.6 (21.4)	58.6 (9.5)	111.3 (10.0)
Intermediate	31.7 (5.2)	42.5 (3.9)	1.5 (12.5)	3.9 (12.7)	33.2 (5.4)	46.4 (4.2)
Final	25.0 (4.1)	62.2 (5.7)	0.4 (3.3)	2.7 (8.8)	25.4 (4.1)	64.9 (5.8)
S_1	624.0	1,295.8	13.5	35.8	637.5	1,331.6
DS	20.0 (3.3)	213.0 (19.7)	1.5 (12.5)	5.0 (16.2)	21.5 (3.5)	218.0 (19.6)
DS^*	691.8 (114.5)		23.8 (198.3)	715.6 (116.2)		

Note: * Denotes the change in stocks over the period 1979–1986.
The stock accounts are balanced for single resource stocks through the identity:
$$S_0 + N + I = C + S_1$$
where S_0 = stock at beginning of time period;
$\quad\;\; N$ = net natural increase;
$\quad\;\; I$ = net imports;
$\quad\;\; C$ = extraction by resource user; and
$\quad\;\; S_1$ = stock at end of time period.
The net change in stocks, DS, is given by $DS = S_1 - S_0 = C - N - I$

Source: Perrings *et al.* (1989).

more feasible, and may be desirable where there is some correspon-
dence between the political and ecological 'boundaries'.

It is worth emphasizing that the estimation of stock accounts in
physical terms is intended to be an intermediate step in the valuation of
stocks so as to permit analysis both of the efficiency of the economic
use of each individual resource, and of changes in the value of the
natural capital stock of Botswana over time. The rationale for the
preparation of accounts lies in the fact that a wide range of
environmental goods and services of crucial importance to the
sustainability of economic activity are not being adequately priced in
the market. Because the existing national accounts are based on the
market valuation of goods and services, they are incomplete. This
makes it impossible for macroeconomic policy makers to assess the
impact of policy changes on what Perrings *et al.* (1988) referred to as
the 'natural balance' – the balance between economic and environmental exchanges.

Nonetheless, given the immediacy of environmental problems
associated with the depletion of non-renewable resources and the
depletion/enhancement of renewable natural resources, there is
considerable advantage in the construction now of accounts for
measuring the stocks of those natural resources which are Botswana's
capital for further development (the stock accounts); and accounts
which measure the flows of natural resources into the economy and
wastes and other materials into the environment (the resource user
accounts). Although it is only through the valuation of environmental
resources that their importance to the economy may be determined, the
preparation of the physical accounts will both identify environmental
resources for which imputed values are needed, and allow analysis of
the effects of economic activity under a range of imputed values for
those resources. If there is doubt about the right shadow prices for
environmental resources, there is advantage in the construction of
accounts that permit analysis of the outcome under different pricing
assumptions.

This is, of course, just as true of those resources for which there
currently exist market prices. The full social cost of using natural
resources such as water, forest or rangeland includes not only the direct
costs of extraction or harvesting, but also the external costs imposed on
other users both now and in the future. In general, market prices will
reflect neither the user costs nor the external costs of resource use. This
means that the full social cost of resource use tends to be greater than
the market price of inputs directly required for their extraction or

harvesting. Indeed, it is precisely because market prices determine the actual rate of resource use that resources are overutilized. If it is possible to value natural resources properly, then it will be much easier to construct environmentally sustainable development policies.

7.2.3 The economic implications of the BNCS

The major economic implications of the BNCS were reported in Perrings *et al.* (1988). Three sets of implications were distinguished: those bearing the structure of incentives facing resource users, those bearing on the appraisal of particular investment projects, and those bearing on the general question of macroeconomic and sectoral planning. On the first of these, it was argued that a number of adjustments were needed if the gap between the social and private cost of resource use was to be narrowed. The recommendations were highly specific, dealing with well-defined areas of policy and market failure.

In respect of property rights and their enabling institutions it was argued that consideration should be given to offering communities the exclusive use of defined areas of rangeland and the means to police that right; that the dual grazing rights referred to above should be eliminated; that current laws to ensure the conservation of agricultural resources should be enforced; and that the District Conservation Committees and the Land Boards should be strengthened to enable them to do this.

In respect of the price system, it was argued that administered output and input prices should be adjusted to bring social and private profit in natural resource-based activities closer together; that the input subsidies offered under ARAP and ALDEP should be reviewed for their impact on resource use, and should be abolished where it could be shown that they had undesirable environmental effects (such as the stumpage subsidy); and that consideration should be given to fixing charges at a community level for grazing land, water and timber.

In respect of the tax system, it was argued that it should be examined with a view to removing the disincentives to invest in non-agricultural productive activities; that consideration should be given to replacing the tax investment incentives in the livestock sector with FAP grants, and associated with this, that the FAP should be extended to include non-traditional investments, projects with a longer gestation period than five years, and that it should be linked with overdraft facilities.

On the second set of implications, those bearing on the appraisal of particular investment projects, the report recommended several changes to current appraisal practice with a view to ensuring that environmentally-sensitive projects would not be undertaken without assessment of the true economic benefits and costs involved. These included recommendations that projects should be appraised on the basis of full economic cost and benefit streams; that activity in renewable resource-based projects should be restricted to levels that did not run down the stock of natural capital employed in the project, or should include the cost of regeneration or rehabilitation of the resource; and that projects generating largely unmeasurable future benefits, such as environmental education, should have output levels fixed as a matter of policy and be appraised for cost effectiveness relative to similar existing or proposed projects.

It was further argued that in order to generate the data needed to assess projects in this way, all major natural resource-based projects should be legally required to fund an independent Environmental Impact Assessment (EIA); and that any projects with environmental effects should be routinely monitored for as long as the effects are felt, either by government or by community organizations. In addition, local community organizations such as the Land Boards and District Conservations Committees should have a stronger input into the appraisal of public and private sector projects expected to have external environmental effects, and should be empowered to investigate the external effects of such projects.

On the third set of implications, those bearing on the general question of macroeconomic and sectoral planning, the report recommended several changes designed to ensure that account would be taken of the intersectoral and intertemporal effects of natural resource-based activities. These changes included the recommendation that planning should not have a sectoral focus, but should instead identify development programmes for each of a number of ecologically distinct regions in which Land Use Planning Units and other local organizations would have a role. Aside from this it was recommended that the economic projections on which the development plans are based should be made more sensitive to the intersectoral and intertemporal effects of different levels of activity in each sector; that consideration should be given to extending the I–O model to include flows of 'ecological' or environmental inputs and outputs to economic processes; that the database for the economy should be widened to include natural capital.

Moreover, since a necessary condition for the sustainable development of Botswana is the diversification of the economy, change is recommended in two key areas of policy. First, it is argued that the infrastructural development needed to make diversification within both rural and urban sectors of the economy privately viable should be accorded high priority. Second, it is argued that regulatory intervention, such as industrial licensing and immigration/residence requirements, should be reviewed in order to minimize the impediments to investment in non-traditional sectors of the economy.

8 Incentives for Sustainable Development

We noted earlier that Botswana had been selected as a case study through which to investigate the problem of incentives for the sustainable use of human and natural resources in dryland areas because of features that make it at once typical and atypical of the countries of Sub-Saharan Africa. The sensitivity of the government of Botswana to the dangers inherent in the structure of incentives that emerged through the 1980s, its willingness to consider options in the face of strong vested interests, and the initiatives it has already taken to construct a sustainable strategy for development are unusual in Sub-Saharan Africa. At the same time, a number of the characteristics of the rural economy in Botswana are typical of many other dryland areas in Sub-Saharan Africa. Not only is the structure of the rural economy similar, but so too are rural institutions, property rights, markets, and the diversity of rural income sources. Moreover, the incentives that have been identified as one source of environmental degradation in rural Botswana during the drought years are similar to those confronting rural resource users elsewhere in the region. The insights into the problem gained from this case study are accordingly relevant to the wider region, although the effectiveness of the system of transfers may mean that rural incomes in Botswana did not fall to the extent they did else where in the region. To draw out the implications of the case study for the general problem, this chapter first reviews the sustainability of resource allocation under the set of incentives that is now emerging in Botswana, and then considers the broader relevance of changes that have taken place in Botswana.

8.1 INCENTIVES FOR THE ECOLOGICAL SUSTAINABILITY OF AGRICULTURE

The development of a set of incentives that will be consistent with the ecologically sustainable use of agricultural resources involves a wide range of adjustments, involving the reform of a number of different areas of policy. The Botswana experience makes it clear that there is no single reform that will 'work': a point worth underlining because of the considerable weight currently being given to market liberalization and the privatization of natural assets as a solution to environmental degradation in many different institutional settings. Natural resources in Botswana are not now allocated through competitive, frictionless and complete markets, in conditions of perfect information and factor mobility. Nor are these conditions attainable. The existence of fundamental uncertainty, combined with the fact that many of the most important environmental assets, such as biodiversity, are in the nature of public goods, means that a market solution to the environmental problem is not feasible. This is not to say that incentives cannot be improved by deepening and widening markets for natural resources: they can. But it does imply that the creation of markets is not a sufficient condition for the sustainability of natural resource use.

Market reform is one aspect of the reforms being undertaken in Botswana to promote the sustainable use of resources, but there are other aspects that are no less important. It is, for example, quite clear that the poverty of present generations of resource users can so bias the weight given to present consumption that the interests of future generations are 'optimally' ignored. Poverty works against the sustainability of resource use whether or not markets exist in which to allocate those resources. The alleviation of rural poverty is therefore a crucial component of the strategy of sustainable development evolving in Botswana, although it is not at all clear that a number of important lessons of the drought years have in fact been learned.

The problem of environmental degradation has been defined in this book in terms of a structure of incentives that makes it privately rational for resource users to place more pressure on the resource base than it can absorb without suffering long lasting and perhaps irreversible damage. A number of causes of this structure have been identified, most of which have been recognized in the recent policy reviews and many have been addressed in the policy reforms. The major sources of distortion in the signals confronting resource users have been the agricultural output and input pricing policies, and the agricultural tax regime, that evolved during the 1980s. Although the overt purpose of these policies was to stimulate the development of the agricultural sector, it has been argued that they were primarily vehicles for effecting transfers to cattle-owners and farmers. Since they acted to depress both input and output prices (in some cases) they drove a wedge between the private and social costs of resource use, so encouraging the systematic overutilization of Botswana's agricultural resource base.

8.1.1 The domestic resource cost of agriculture

Some indication of the distortions involved is illustrated in the domestic resource cost (DRC) exercises carried out in the course of the 1989 agricultural sector review (Edwards *et al.*, 1989). The data from two farm surveys, one in 1984/5 and another in 1987/8, were analysed to determine the DRC of crop production under the influence of the agricultural development programmes ARAP and ALDEP in both a drought year and a 'good rainfall' year, the DRC being defined as:

$$DRC = \frac{\text{labour costs} + \text{domestic capital costs}}{\text{revenue} - \text{tradable input costs}}$$

A domestic resource cost exercise shows the ratio of the cost of domestic factors of production in some economic activity (assumed to be non-tradable and priced at their domestic opportunity cost) to the net revenue of that activity (defined to be equal to the difference between revenue and the cost of all tradable inputs at border prices). It provides a rough measure of the economic profitability of the activity given a certain set of world prices, and given the exchange rate. To the extent that border prices may be taken to approximate the social opportunity cost of tradable resources, it shows whether it is efficient to undertake the activity. We have noted that the degradation of resources in the agricultural sector represents an inefficient allocation of resources, and that the persistence of various agricultural subsidies exacerbates the problem by widening the gap between the private and social costs of resource use. The DRC exercise provides one approximation of the seriousness of the misallocation of resources that is encouraged by these subsidies. As we shall see, the values chosen for both the denominator and the numerator may not be good approximations of the social opportunity cost of the resources involved. But it is still worth looking at the results of the exercise.

In 1984/5, a drought year, the exercise showed that distortions on the output price side were minimal. For three of the four crops examined (maize, beans and millet) producer prices coincided with the border price. Only sorghum was priced below the border price.

Whereas average revenue at actual prices was P180, average revenue at border prices was P185.86. However, the position was very different on the input side. The average value of subsidies on non-labour costs was estimated to be P222.73. The effect of these subsidies was such that on a private cost analysis the net return per man day was not only positive for all crops, it was higher than the return to labour invested in the most highly valued alternative activity (wage labour). On the other hand, an economic cost analysis showed that the economic net return per man day was negative for all crops except millet, and was negative overall. Since the difference between total revenue at border prices and non-labour tradable inputs excluding subsidies was negative, so too was the DRC ratio. Even if labour had been zero priced, the economic profits of crop production were negative in that year.

In 1987/8, a good rainfall year, the pattern was similar. Once again sorghum was priced below the border price, and once again a private cost analysis showed a positive net return per man day that exceeded the opportunity cost of agricultural labour, largely due to subsidies on non-labour costs valued, on average, at P418.73. The difference between 1987/8 and 1984/5 was that, on an economic analysis, the net return per man day in the earlier year was positive, but below the opportunity cost of agricultural labour. The DRC ratio was likewise positive for all crops, but since it was also greater than unity it showed that the production of all crops was economically inefficient.

The point was made earlier that the values chosen for the exercise may not have been very good approximations of social opportunity cost. There are two sources of bias. The first lies in the fact that non-labour domestic 'capital' was assigned a zero price. This implies that land, water, graze, browse, timber and other products of the communally owned resource base were assumed to have zero opportunity cost. The assumption is not at all unusual for the type of analysis conducted, but it is misleading. Indeed, a great deal of global resource degradation is due to the fact that analysis of the economic efficiency of resource-based activities has depended on essentially the same assumption. In effect, it is an assumption that the natural resources in question are non-scarce, and it is unhelpful. The structure of property rights which authorizes individual users of a resource to ignore the costs of the depreciation or degradation of that resource distorts the price set in the same way as ARAP and ALDEP, and this should be recognized in an analysis of the economic costs and benefits of the activity. It is not true that the depreciation of the resource base is costless. A second source of bias in the DRC exercise is the assumption that border prices define the social opportunity cost of tradable resources. Since the same distortions tend to exist in the international markets in which the prices of these resources are struck, border prices will tend to underestimate the social opportunity cost of tradable resources. That is, it is more reasonable to regard border prices as defining only the lower bound of the social opportunity cost of tradable resources. What this implies is that the DRCs estimated in the agricultural sector review will underestimate the social opportunity cost of both domestic resources and tradables. Since one is the numerator and the other the denominator, it is not obvious what this means for the overall bias in the estimate. But it is likely that the estimates would worsen if 'true' measures of social opportunity cost were employed.

8.1.2 Incentive reform

The reforms initiated through the reviews of the agricultural sector and the incomes policy show that the government of Botswana is aware that explicit subsidies on tradable inputs have had distortionary effects. However, it is not as clear that it has appreciated the extent of those effects. Following the agricultural sector review the government announced a new agricultural policy which recognized that foodgrain self-sufficiency is not achievable at acceptable cost given the physical and climatic conditions obtaining in the country. Instead, the future goal of policy is defined to be food security, rather than food self-sufficiency, with strategic grain reserves replacing the past emphasis on the expansion of grain output. As a by-product of this shift in policy many of the subsidies designed to lead to an expansion of grain production will be reduced.

In respect of the livestock sector, there is some evidence that the government does appreciate the allocative effects of the implicit subsidies granted via the system of communal property rights in rangeland.[1] The new policy allows for the introduction of rangeland fences. This is a highly significant and far reaching reform, since it admits exclusive rights over rangeland (argued in the BNCS to be a necessary condition for the elimination of overgrazing), and facilitates the introduction of the 'user-pays' principle – that those who have the use of a resource should be liable for the full economic cost (the social cost) associated with that use. Since the report has identified the overutilization of resources with a gap between private and social cost, application of the user-pays principle would be sufficient to protect rangeland against overgrazing.

Notice that application of the user pays principle does not necessarily imply the creation of markets. It may, for example, be satisfied by a system of community charges for the use of community resources (grazing land, arable land, water, fuel and construction timber and so on) and community services. NDP7 does show a very clear movement in this general direction. Pricing policy will, for example, include the following targets:

- the use of import parity prices for agricultural products;
- the reduction of subsidies on urban housing;
- utility tariffs to reflect marginal social costs;
- government services to be supplied on a cost recovery basis (consistent with social justice); and
- rural water pricing to be related to opportunity cost ('taking full account of income and affordability').

It is not yet clear, however, how far these principles will affect community level charges. Grazing fees have in fact been recommended in the past in Botswana, but have always been rejected on the grounds that ownership patterns are so difficult to determine that one would not know who to charge. Certainly, if an inventory of ownership could be drawn up this objection would disappear, but it is not in fact important to determine ownership. Whoever has immediate responsibility for cattle may be made liable. Since acceptance of the principle is crucial to the development of incentives that will assure the sustainable use of rangeland, it is important that this trend in policy reform be extended to the community level.

What appears to stand in the way of the adoption of a user pays principle in respect of resources used in the rural economy is the 'affordability' criterion. Just as government policy on water pricing is qualified by the limits of 'affordability', so too is policy on the recovery of the costs in respect of a wide range of other rural goods and services. The subsidies offered under the agricultural development programmes were designed to make resources affordable to people whose income had dropped with the drought, and although it is now recognized that this had undesirable effects on patterns of resource use, there is no sign that the use of input specific subsidies for this purpose has been abandoned. Indeed, the agricultural sector review specifically recommended the continued use of input subsidies as a means of helping farmers who market only a small proportion of their output. Moreover, a list of their recommended subsidies includes all the areas in which the distortionary effects of the existing policies had been most marked: an early ploughing subsidy, a second land preparation subsidy, a fencing subsidy, a water storage subsidy, a seed subsidy plus capital equipment subsidies (Edwards *et al.*, 1989). Once again, because these subsidies will be tied to an increasingly narrow range of activities, farmers will be locked into particular patterns of resource allocation, and prevented from exploring options that might represent socially more efficient use of the resource base.

The sustainability of rural employment generation is discussed in Chapter 9, but it is important to stress that from an ecological perspective the sustainable use of agricultural resources will not be served by continuing to subsidize agricultural inputs (without regard for the impact this has on the agricultural product). Recent findings on the environmental implications of different incentive structures in the livestock sector show that the producer price to be an effective lever on stocking densities. However, the positive effect of an increase in producer prices may be readily offset by increases in the net benefits of livestock holdings or inventory (Perrings, 1993). Indeed, wherever offtake prices are increased by less than the increase in the net benefit of inventory the result will be higher, not lower, on stocking densities. Both ALDEP and ARAP offered significant draft power/ploughing subsidies which very substantially increased the net benefits of inventory relative to offtake, but it is not at all clear that this source of bias will be removed in the new agricultural policy. In principle, the policy should include three elements: the pricing of agricultural 'inputs' at marginal social cost (implying the elimination of subsidies); the introduction of a livestock tax or grazing fee equal to the marginal external cost of grazing); and the pricing of offtake at marginal social opportunity cost. In respect of the livestock sector, the pricing of livestock 'inputs' at marginal social cost and the introduction of a livestock tax or grazing fee equal to the marginal external cost of grazing would reduce the net benefit of livestock holdings, while the pricing of offtake at marginal social opportunity cost would increase the net benefit of offtake.

In addition, the policy should address the difficulties created by the preservation of existing property rights in natural resources. The point has already been made that one reason for the low rate of domestic rural credit expansion has been the inability of borrowers to use land as collateral. In the absence of markets for land, traditional sector borrowers have been unable to secure loans from the commercial bank and have had to deal with a number of special agencies, of which the National Development Bank and the Small Business Fund it administers are the most important. As the World Bank's review of the financial sector (World Bank, 1989) made clear, however, the use of the latter as a vehicle for transfers, and the adoption of rates of interest that do not reflect the opportunity cost of capital, have both been sources of bias that have exacerbated the problem of overutilization of resources.

There are other initiatives designed to ease the problem of rural credit, including the Small Business Unit of Barclays Bank, Tswelelo, the USAID Loan Guarantee Scheme, the Integrated Field services unit of the Ministry of Commerce and Industry, and the small scale enterprise component of the Financial Assistance Policy. The last of these has both rural credit and employment generation as its aims, and has perhaps the greatest potential of the existing institutions as a vehicle for providing credit for non-traditional rural activities. At the same time it currently suffers from a number of weaknesses, including a very rigid and unimaginative screening process which discourages investment in untried activities. The general point here is that access to the capital needed to stimulate expansion of the rural economy into non-traditional areas is hampered by the nature of land rights in a way that forces policy makers to rely on second best options, and up to now none of these second best options have satisfactorily dealt with the collateral problem. The only assets on which rural dwellers can raise capital from commercial institutions are livestock (more particularly cattle) and human capital (as the avenue to wage or salary income). The first of these merely exaggerates the net benefits of inventory relative to offtake, and so encourages overstocking. At the same time, the most valuable assets to which Batswana have rights of access, the natural resource base, are unavailable for conversion from one use to another.

It should be noted that there are a number of options other than the granting of freehold rights to land which would get around this difficulty. One particularly promising example would be the conversion of use rights from inalienable to alienable rights. Individual Batswana hold use rights that are currently inalienable. There may be significant gains in terms of efficiency and the operation of capital markets if such use rights became tradable, even if only within a restricted market. In many places the transition from inalienable to alienable use rights has occurred quite naturally. In Botswana, the emergence of restricted markets in water rights as a result of borehole policy is an example. The new policy on fencing rangeland may create pressure for another such market in grazing rights. The formalization of rights of this sort may be the best way to address the collateral problem.

It is not only the ecological sustainability of agricultural production that is at issue here. It is highly unlikely that the goal of employment and income generation in rural Botswana can be met without changing the role of the traditional agricultural sector as medium for the delivery of rural welfare payments. The important lesson of the drought years is that the embodiment of welfare payments to the rural poor in the grants and subsidies of the agricultural development programmes had undesirable allocative effects that threaten the wellbeing of both present and future generations of Batswana. It is essential that policies which have had these effects be rescinded – not reformed and that the problem of how else to deliver welfare payments to the rural poor be addressed directly. The best way of supporting the rural poor is to expand – not contract – the opportunities open to them, and to ensure that their choices are made on the basis of the real costs and benefits of the available options, and not in terms of an illusory web of subsidies.

8.2   IMPLICATIONS FOR THE DEVELOPMENT OF DRYLANDS

While this book has leaned heavily on a particular case study, the marked similarities in the resource degradation problems in the agricultural sector of Botswana and other semi-arid countries in Sub-Saharan Africa suggests that many of its findings will be relevant in other situations. The observation that intervention in Botswana during the drought years has created a set of incentives which has encouraged resource degradation could be made of a number of other countries in Sub-Saharan Africa. So too could the inferences drawn from this observation: that it is important to identify the impact of intervention on the gap between the private and social cost of resource utilization before introducing policies which change the set of incentives. The implications of this for the database on which economic policy is based similarly apply to all countries. Environmental statistics should not only be added to the range of data gathered by the Central Statistical Office, but should be integrated into the planning process through natural resource accounts. The proper evaluation of environmentally sensitive projects should include the estimation of private non-monetary costs and benefits. It is generally true that the database for the sustainable management of renewable resources will be greater than that currently used for economic planning.

Considerable work has now been done on the estimation of the true costs of the overutilization of renewable resources in the developing countries, and the analysis of the causal connections between particular policies and patterns of resource use. In particular, work by the World Resources Institute and the World Bank (Repetto, 1986; Warford, 1987; Davis and Schirmer (eds), 1987; Falloux and Mukendi (eds), 1988) has examined the effect of a range of policies on the relative prices of natural resources. Many of the findings of this book confirm their general results.

8.2.1 'Variable' and 'user enabling' incentives

Conway and Barbier (1990) distinguish two classes of incentive: 'variable' incentives and 'user enabling' incentives. Variable incentives are taken include the standard microeconomic incentives – taxes, subsidies, user charges – used to bring the private and social costs of resource use into line with one another. User enabling incentives, on the other hand, address the institutional environment within which resources are allocated. To see how each class of incentive is argued to operate, consider the recommended liberalization of agricultural markets reported in Chapter 2. This is an example of a policy recommendation directed at variable incentives. Liberalization affects traded goods and services, and works on the relative prices of those goods and services. The problem of the misallocation of resources may, however, persist despite price reform wherever the resources in question are non-traded or subject to open access to common property. Institutional changes designed to remove these barriers to adjustment are 'user enabling' incentives. Such user enabling incentives may involve the allocation of individual tenure, or the introduction of new and more secure forms of usufructual tenure, or the strengthening of institutions charged with regulating the level of activity (such as grazing associations) or any combination of these things.

We have identified problems with both variable and user enabling incentives in the Botswana case. Moreover, although the recent policy reforms promise to go some way to removing disincentives to the sustainable use of the resource base of both types, there are a number of areas in which there remains some way to go. In addition, however, we have placed considerable weight on the impact of the distribution of income and assets on producer responses to the institutional conditions and relative prices facing resource users. It has been argued that while an appropriate set of variable and user enabling incentives may be a necessary condition for the sustainable use of resources, it is not sufficient. Poverty so distorts the decisions of resource users that even if private and social costs were aligned, and even if there were no institutional barriers to adjustment, it may still be optimal to degrade the resource base to the point where the welfare of future generations is irreparably harmed. That is, poverty may lock resource users into unsustainable patterns of resource use even more securely than institutions.

The idea behind the allocation of property rights is that these are a precondition for the emergence of markets in the resources concerned, and so for the internalization of the environmental externalities associated with the existing communal tenure arrangements. However, this begs a very important question. From an efficiency perspective, the allocation of property rights may be sufficient to internalize environmental externalities irrespective of equity considerations (at least in the small numbers, low cost of negotiations case). But if the distribution of income is as important in the allocation of natural resources in rural Sub-Saharan Africa as I have suggested earlier, then resources may be allocated efficiently, but still not sustainably. In the case of both tradable and non-tradable resources it is generally assumed that the set of relative prices associated with the existing system of administered pricing has been a major factor in the choice of technology (Markandya, 1991). By implication, the choice of 'traditional' input and output combinations is driven by the relative prices of traditional versus non-traditional inputs and outputs. This is undoubtedly a part of the story, but it is only part. The choice of technique is also influenced both by the degree of risk-aversion and the time preference of resource users. Since both of these factors are partly a function of income, it turns out that choice of technology is also driven by income.

To be sure, the income of resource users is affected by relative resource prices, and this is one motivation behind the recommended liberalization of agricultural markets, but income also depends on both the distribution of assets in society (endowments) and the system of transfers. Ignoring transfers for the moment, if endowments are such that resource users are impoverished, then traditional techniques may still be optimal even if these are inconsistent with the ecologically sustainable use of resources. A collapse in the income of agricultural producers (for whatever reason) may provoke an increase in the level of intensity with which the land is exploited, irrespective of the costs in terms of reduced future productivity. In the extreme case, where the ecological system is globally unstable, such behaviour can be fatal but still optimal.

The connection between rural income and the degradation of the rural resource base have been frequently explored and it has been shown that, in the absence of appropriate policies, rural poverty and rural resource degradation feed off one another. The right policy mix in any given economy will therefore be one that ensures that producers respond to relative prices which approximate the marginal social costs of resource use, and that resource users' decisions are not distorted by the exigencies of poverty. It follows that an appropriate valuation of resources and distributional equity are both essential ingredients in any strategy for the sustainable use of the resource base. There is, however, little evidence that policy-makers have changed their perception of the role of rural resources, natural as well as human, in the development process. In almost every case the rural economy continues to be 'mined' in the interests of industrialization despite the growing volume of evidence as to the high cost of ignoring the environmental repercussions of existing development strategies. In this respect, Botswana offers a partial exception to an unfortunate rule. The government of Botswana has committed itself to the goal of sustainable development through diversification of the economy. Nevertheless, as we have shown, there remain several areas of policy that have yet to meet the challenge offered by that goal.

8.2.2 Risk and uncertainty

The adoption of an environmental perspective on development highlights the importance of risk and uncertainty in the decision process. Risk, in this context, refers to the existence of a known number of outcomes for any decision, to each of which it is possible to attach a measure of probability. To take an obvious example, agricultural output is a function of the level of rainfall, and the highly variable rainfall in most of the semi-arid regions introduces the possibility that the yield from planting a certain area, in any given year, will lie anywhere between a minimum at or close to zero, defined as 'total failure', and a maximum, defined as 'bumper harvest'. Since it is possible to compute the probability that rainfall will be at the level associated with each yield, it is also possible to compute the probability that actual agricultural output will differ from expected (planned) output by any proportion consistent with the range of yields from total failure to bumper harvest. It is widely accepted that risk analysis is appropriate in such circumstances. In terms of the macroeconomic planning process, this suggests, at the very least, the value of contingent planning.

Uncertainty, on the other hand, arises when it is not possible to predict the set of outcomes of an action, nor to ascribe a probability to each outcome in the set. In other words, uncertainty arises when there is genuine ignorance about the future effects of present decisions. This makes uncertainty a particular feature of innovative activities. Change in the utilization of the natural resource base in the developing countries accordingly introduces uncertainty wherever the effects of the change on the resource base are not known. All that is known with certainty in the semi-arid regions, is that the ecosystems are in a delicate balance, and are easily dislodged from that balance. But it is not known how a given innovation will change the ecosystem. To be sure, the experience of the Sahel and the Horn of Africa in the last two decades is providing us with some very painful evidence of the effects of specific agricultural innovations. But most innovative natural resource-based activities in such regions generate real uncertainty, and this suggests the value of flexibility of response.

At the microeconomic level, the very conservative attitude to risk-taking and uncertainty of most rural households has militated against the sort of innovative activity that is a prerequisite for diversification. This attitude is, in large part, a product of the very small margin for error in most rural household strategies. Where a wrong decision in terms of the type of seed planted can mean the difference between survival and non-survival, the temptation to err on the side of safety is very strong. The low level of the endowments of most rural resource users is sufficient to make the risks of diversification unacceptable. This underlines the importance of distributional issues and the system of transfers in any strategy for the sustainable development of the resource base. The use of tied transfers as a means of stimulating technological change in Sub-Saharan Africa is well established. Indeed, the destumping, herbicide, pesticide, fertilizer, seed, and draft power grants and subsidies that have been blamed for much of the recent land degradation in the region are examples of such tied transfers, and have been extensively investigated for their effects on technology choice. But transfers may also have a crucial role to play in influencing risk-taking behaviour. This issue has so far been neglected in the literature on incentives, but deserves closer analysis. The general point is that where the extreme risk-aversion of impoverished resource users has prevented the innovation that would enable them to realize the specialization gains from exploiting a non-traditional area of comparative advantage, then there ought to exist a set of transfers which will enable them to accept the greater uncertainty of change.

At the macroeconomic level, the existence of risk and uncertainty underlines the importance of flexibility of responses. Development plans can provide, at most, broad guidelines for the evolution of public expenditure, but should not bind policy-makers to paths of action irrespective of outcome. Nor should they preclude remedial expenditures required where actual outcomes are different from expected outcomes. If planning involves risk, it should be made contingent to allow for adjustments as and when these are needed. If planning involves uncertainty, the scenarios involved should be made explicit, and the policy-makers given the flexibility to respond to unforseen outcomes. To illustrate the point using the Botswana case, the conservatism of the government's economic strategy (the very high levels of import cover in the foreign exchange reserves, for example) is one response to risk. The diversification of the economy is another. However, the expenditure programmes contained in the development plans are not contingent, and flexibility of response is allowed only in the existence of separate contingency funds. Similar comments might be made of the planning process in most other countries of Sub-Saharan Africa. Since so little is currently known about the environmental effects of economic activities, particularly of innovative activities, it is important to retain the institutional flexibility to respond to changing information on the environment.

9   Population, Employment and the Environment

In Botswana, as elsewhere in Sub-Saharan Africa, environmental degradation and population growth have gone hand in hand. While a positive correlation between high rates of population growth and environmental degradation does not imply a well-defined causal relationship – there is evidence that population growth may be as much an effect as a cause of resource degradation – it is clear that the relationship is neither ecologically nor economically sustainable. The increasing pressure of population growth on an already stressed environment implies a progressively greater ecological sensitivity to shocks, just as the decreasing productivity of natural resources in conditions of high population growth implies an increasing risk of famine. It takes less and less extreme events to trigger a complete collapse in the rural economies of the region. In this final chapter we return to the question of population growth and the scope for developing a strategy of ecologically sustainable development in conditions of population growth.

There are three aspects of the question. The first concerns the relationship between population growth and carrying capacity in the rural economy. The concept of the carrying capacity of the range has been used frequently in this book. Section 9.1 extends this to consider the human carrying capacity of the ecological systems underpinning the rural economy. The second aspect of the question concerns the driving forces behind population growth. It was argued in the Introduction that while current population growth rates in the countries of the Sudano-Sahelian region are not consistent with the ecological sustainability of resource use in the region, there is no reason to believe that a Malthusian adjustment in the form of widespread famine would re-establish a stable equilibrium population. Deepening rural poverty increases the risks of morbidity and mortality among the existing population. It also creates a powerful incentive to expand that population, to compensate both for the risk of infant mortality and the risk of income failure. This implies that private decisions affecting the rate of population growth are guided by the economic environment in the same way as other private decisions – affecting the growth of livestock or the area under cultivation, for example. Population growth is not independent of the incentives offered by the relative costs and benefits of family size. Section 9.2 discusses the problem of population incentives. The third aspect of the question, addressed in section 9.3, relates to the scope for population absorption through ecologically and economically sustainable employment generation. This is the question underlying much of what has gone before. If current resource management techniques are not sustainable, what options do policy-makers face? Indeed, this is likely to be the fundamental policy question in all Sub-Saharan African countries over the next decade.

9.1 POPULATION AND CARRYING CAPACITY

From first ecological principles we know that ecological sustainability does not imply a unique equilibrium level of human population, or a unique rate of human population growth. Ecological sustainability requires that ecological systems retain their resilience and this does not imply a unique balance between human and other populations. Against this is the fact that the resilience of ecosystems depends on the level of stress they have to bear, and the level of stress depends on human population density. Increasing human population under a given technology and a given structure of production implies increasing levels of stress, which may imply loss of resilience. The related concepts of 'carrying' and 'assimilative' capacity are measures of the sustainable level of stress. If either the carrying capacity or the assimilative capacity of some ecosystem is exceeded, then that ecosystem will experience a loss of resilience, which implies an increasing level of susceptibility to damage in the face of exogenous shocks. It follows that for any ecosystem, continued population growth will, other things being equal, eventually exceed the carrying and assimilative capacities of that ecosystem, so increasing its vulnerability to shocks, and the risk of collapse.

Population biologists define human carrying capacity to be the number of people who can be maintained without degrading the capacity of the system in question to support future generations. They argue that on this basis global carrying capacity has already been exceeded (Ehrlich *et al.*, 1992b). The fact that some 200 million people have starved to death worldwide in the last three decades may reflect the maldistribution of income and food resources more than it does the inability of the world's farmers to feed the present level of population. But they argue that much of the increased global capacity in terms of food production has involved the degradation of key environmental resources, and so has already compromised the ability of those resources to support future generations.

One important point here is that carrying capacity is a function of technology, and may be increased or decreased by technological change. Since carrying capacity has been defined to mean sustainable carrying capacity, this implies that technological change can generate a permanent change in the population that may be supported by the resource base. To this point, the literature on carrying capacity has been dominated by a strong strain of optimism. In an extensive study of the food carrying capacity of more than one hundred countries in the mid-1980s, the FAO (1986) generated estimates of sustainable population under three different technology scenarios. The first, a 'low-level' technology scenario, involved no use of fertilizers, pesticides or herbicides, no long-term conservation measures and traditional crops. The second, an 'intermediate-level' technology, involved use of basic fertilizers, herbicides and pesticides, plus some long-term conservation measures and some improved crop varieties. The third, a 'high-level' technology, involved extensive use of fertilizers and biocides, improved crop varieties and mixes, and conservation measures. On this basis the study then calculated both the potential calorie output and, using World Health Organization recommended calorie intakes, the maximum sustainable population associated with each level of technology. This level of population was then compared with the population level expected in the year 2000 to give a sense of how closely population is pressing up against the limits in different regions. For Africa the results were surprisingly optimistic. If only low-level technologies were used it was estimated that by 2000 the continent could support 160 per cent of the expected population, and that this figure rose to 580 per cent if intermediate-level technologies were used, and 1650 per cent if high-level technologies were used.

Ehrlich *et al.* (1992b) argue that there is no scientific basis for such optimism, and that in numerous cases an apparent increase in current carrying capacity as a result of technological change has masked a decline in longer-term carrying capacity. The adoption of 'green revolution' technologies in agriculture (the intermediate- and high-level technologies of the FAO study) is a case in point. Given the various ecological side-effects of the increasing dependence of farmers on pesticides, herbicides and artificial fertilizers, they argue that it is not at all clear that the increase in the number of people of the present generation who can be maintained by those technologies is sustainable. The extensive use of fertilizers, biocides and irrigation over a number of years has resulted in falling yields, groundwater pollution and depletion, the irreversible alteration of hydrological cycles, increasing susceptibility to pests and an increase in the range of pests. There are certainly examples of technological change which has resulted in a permanent increase in the carrying capacity of a particular set of natural resources, and in a region such as Sub-Saharan Africa. Where green revolution technologies have had little impact there may indeed be scope for expansion of food carrying capacity, but the point is that this cannot be taken for granted.

In Botswana, as elsewhere in Sub-Saharan Africa, agriculture is dominated by low-level technologies. The reaction to food deficits caused by increasing population pressure in the early 1980s was the introduction of policies to expand agricultural output to achieve food self-sufficiency (cf. Rukuni and Eicher (eds), 1987). Although the drive to food self-sufficiency did involve some intermediate-level technology, for the most part it rested on the intensification of production under existing technologies – largely for institutional reasons. These policies have since been argued to be one of the proximate causes of resource degradation in the region, precisely because they encouraged an expansion in output in the short to medium term without regard for longer-term environmental consequences (Perrings *et al.*, 1989). And, more recently, the focus has switched to the promotion of food security through income security, which directs attention away from food production and towards the conditions necessary to assure a level and distribution of income that will guarantee the means to acquire food. In other words, it is understood that in terms of food production, the carrying capacity of natural resources of Botswana may be less than the current population under existing technologies.

The change in focus from food self-sufficiency to food security, however, switches the emphasis from carrying capacity narrowly defined in terms of food production, to carrying capacity defined in terms of a wider set of options. The argument that carrying capacity will be increased by widening the set of options open to resource users is equivalent to the argument that relaxation of a binding constraint on resource utilization will be welfare-improving. But the use of the concept of carrying capacity does sharpen the point being made about the rate of population growth. If, at a given rate of population growth:

- it is not possible to expand food production under existing (traditional) technology without damaging the long term sustainability of the resource base;
- employment outside the traditional agricultural sector is growing at a lower rate than the labour force; and
- the traditional agricultural sector provides employment of the last resort

then that rate of population growth is not sustainable. It implies a reduction in the capacity of the resource base to meet the needs of future generations.

Based on data from the 1981 census, one would expect the 1991 census to show the formal sector employment gap to be widening in Botswana – despite very strong growth in formal sector manufacturing, construction and services. Since any shortfall in formal sector employment growth translates as additional employment in traditional agriculture, if an expansion in agricultural output is indeed unsustainable, there is reason to be concerned. On the evidence of the last decade, expansion of agricultural employment has indeed been associated with the degradation of the agricultural resource base, and agricultural incomes have been maintained only through an extensive system of public and private transfers. An important caveat is that the carrying capacity of agricultural resources has been reduced as a result of drought during this period, and might be expected to increase substantially during the wet phase of the rainfall cycle. If it does, this will provide a breathing space, but at the cost of steadily increasing levels of stress on the resource base, and vulnerability to exogenous shocks.

This puts the diversification arguments of the Botswana National Conservation Strategy in perspective. Diversification is a shorthand for the widening of the choice set facing resource users, and it is quite intuitive that in the conditions just cited it is a necessary condition for the sustainability of resource use. I shall return to this point in section 9.3. What is important here is that with population growth rates around 3.4 per cent, and with little scope under existing institutional conditions for expanding the food carrying capacity of the traditional agricultural sector, that sector can only continue to be the employer of last resort at the cost of the degradation of key agricultural resources.

9.2 POPULATION, EMPLOYMENT AND THE INCENTIVE STRUCTURE

There is, as Pearce (1991) puts it, 'a special problem of population growth in Sub-Saharan Africa'. Although population growth rates in all other regions of the world are declining, population growth rates in Sub-Saharan Africa are still rising. Thirty years ago the average annual population growth rate in the continent was around 2.5 per cent. Ten years ago it was around 3 per cent. In the 1985–1990 period, it is estimated that two countries, Kenya and Côte d'Ivoire, had population growth rates in excess of 4 per cent, and a further nine, including Botswana, had growth rates in excess of 3.4 per cent (WRI, 1990). This is partly due to declining mortality rates, but it also reflects the fact that average fertility rates have fallen only slowly and, in a large number of cases, have actually increased. Not surprisingly, such high rates of population growth have had a major impact on the labour force. Indeed, Botswana is one of eight countries in the continent to have experienced average annual growth rates of the labour force over three per cent during the decade 1980–1990.

The question addressed here is what is driving the fertility side of the equation? What is the structure of incentives that has encouraged the very high rates of fertility observed in Botswana and elsewhere in the continent? Statistically, there is a very strong correlation between rates of fertility and a number of demographic–economic variables. Fertility rates are, for example, negatively correlated with both income and some index of human capital development such as literacy rates, and positively correlated with the proportion of the population engaged in agriculture. That is, fertility rates are highest among illiterate agricultural households with low levels of income. The question is why this should be so.

The answer to this question is complicated by the nature of the household in Sub-Saharan Africa. In Botswana, for example, many households have both urban and rural components. The rural component, or the part of the household at the villages, the lands or the cattleposts, will typically contain a high proportion of the household's economically inactive members: both the very young and the very old. Moreover, as was remarked in Chapter 6, the income of the household will typically derive from a mix of sources: wage income, the sale of agricultural goods and services, private and public transfers and the direct consumption of own production. Although individual household members may earn income through a range of activities, they tend to do agricultural work for at least part of their lives. While there are households which fit the statistical stereotype, they are not as common as might be supposed from census data that defines a household in terms of the number of people living at a particular location, rather than the number of people contributing to or drawing from a common income pool. The 1985/6 Botswana household income and expenditure survey, using this definition of the household, showed that rural households were larger than urban households and had a higher proportion of children to adults (Table 9.1). It is not possible to identify what proportion of those under 15 years of age in the rural households were the children of people listed as members of urban households, but is likely to have been significant.

With these caveats in mind, the following sub-sections consider the elements in the implicit cost–benefit analysis associated with different fertility rates. My starting point is the presumption that fertility decisions are rational, given the constraints within which households make such decisions. So, for example, the negative correlation between fertility rates and some index of human capital development does not imply that fertility rates amongst agricultural communities are high because of a lack of formal education. Anthropological studies of Kalahari communities with no access to formal education have shown very different fertility rates depending on the economic circumstances of the household. Lee (1972), for example, showed that among Kung San people who maintained a high degree of mobility in the course of hunting and gathering activities, the interval between births was

Table 9.1   Household composition: Botswana, 1985/6

	Urban households	Rural households	All households
Aged < 15	1.67	2.79	2.49
Household size	4.02	5.33	4.98
Adults/children	1.40	0.91	1.00

Source: Republic of Botswana (1988), *Household Income and Expenditure Survey: 1985/6* (Gaborone: CSO), table 4.

around four years. This period was much longer than among households 'settled' at cattle posts. The explanation for the difference lies in the fact that the children of the former group of households were not only nursed, but also carried by their mothers during foraging, for more than three years. Additional births during that period would directly threaten the survival prospects of such children. The same restrictions did not apply to the more settled households. This is not to deny research findings which have suggested the importance of the informational content of education, but to assert that irrespective of whether women are educated or not, observed differences in fertility rates have a rational foundation. The role of education in fertility rates is not that it lifts some veil of ignorance about optimal number of births, but that it changes the optimal number of births by changing the structure of incentives.

9.2.1 Fertility and income risks

The point has been made in Chapter 6 that Botswana has no formal system of social security under which those without adequate means of support by reason of age, unemployment or disability are automatically assured of government assistance. Assistance to the needy is supplied on an ad hoc basis, although such ad hoc arrangements can be very extensive. During the drought years of the last decade, assistance in one form or another has been extended to approximately 60 per cent of the rural population. In principle, though, support for those who are economically inactive for any reason is the responsibility of the household, and the first and most potent explanation for fertility rates in rural Botswana – as elsewhere in Sub-Saharan Africa – is the security of income of the aged. The larger the pool of economically active members of a household relative to those incapacitated through age or illness, the greater the income security of the latter. In the absence both of a formal system of social security and of the annuity markets that enable individuals to provide their own retirement income, children offer the only means of support in old age. Indeed, there are now a large number of studies confirming the incentive effects of social security systems on fertility rates. In Mexico, to give only one example, it has been shown that the provision of pensions for the aged is indeed a substitute for children (Nugent and Gillaspy, 1983).

The optimal number of children from this perspective is related to the expected income stream deriving from each birth, and this varies with both expected survival rates and expected earnings. The calculation to be undertaken is of the following sort: how many births are needed to ensure that there is a surviving child or children earning sufficient income to meet the needs of the parents when they 'retire' (cf. Cain, 1981, 1983; Dasgupta, 1992, 1993). The relation between fertility and survival rates is the easier to identify. In Sub-Saharan Africa there is a positive correlation between rates of change in infant and child mortality and fertility, implying that the optimal number of births does fall as the rate of infant and child mortality decreases. Indeed, the impact of environmental degradation on infant mortality is one reason to believe in a positive feedback effect between environmental degradation and population growth. The relation between fertility and the expected stream of earnings of children is less easy to handle. Although the generally negative correlation between fertility rates and income supports the notion that higher expected earnings implies a lower optimal number of births per household, the problem is complicated by the fact that income security is also associated with security of access to assets – farmland in particular. This too is influenced by the number of births.

In Botswana, as Table 9.2 shows, there is prima facie evidence that declining rates of infant and child mortality have put downward pressure on fertility rates. But the work has not yet been done to identify the impact of changes in the structure and level of income. In particular, it is not yet clear what the significance is of changes in the contribution of agricultural income. What is clear, however, is that children are still an important part of the calculus with respect to the

Table 9.2   Fertility, mortality and nutrition

	Year	
	1965–70	*1985–90*
Fertility rate	6.9	6.3
Life expectancy at birth	48.8	56.5
Infant mortality[1]	110	67
Child mortality[2]	160	92

Note: 1.   Infant deaths per 1000 live births
         2.   Deaths of children < 5 years old per 1000 live births

Source: World Resources Institute (1990), *World Resources 1990–1991* (Oxford: Oxford University Press) tables 16.2 and 16.3.

security of income in old age, and that this continues to put generally upward pressure on fertility rates.

9.2.2   Fertility and agricultural labour

The next important explanation of rural fertility rates concerns the role of children as producers. It is generally recognised that people become economically active at a much younger age in rural communities in Sub-Saharan Africa than in many other regions, and this too has been advanced as a factor in high fertility rates. The general hypothesis of demographic transition theory (Caldwell, 1976) is that the transition from high to low fertility rates is a function of the direction of the intergenerational flow of resources. So long as the intergenerational flow of resources is from the young to the old, fertility rates will be high. It is only when the intergenerational flow of resources reverses – where children are the net beneficiaries of the flow of resources – that fertility rates drop. It turns out that the argument may be closely related to the explanations of rural resource degradation.

The general pattern of rural employment is one in which young people perform a number of productive tasks, including gathering firewood, dung, grass and other veld products, caring for siblings and assisting in domestic work, assisting with harvesting, and, most importantly, tending livestock. In Botswana, some indication of the proportion of young people who are economically active in this sense is given by the data on the percentage of each age cohort which is not either at school or in some form of formal paid employment (Table 9.3).

Table 9.3   Economic activity of young persons: Botswana, 1985/6

Age cohort	Percentage of each age cohort								
	Males			Females			Total		
	School	Paid empl't	Other	School	Paid empl't	Other	School	Paid empl't	Other
5–9	31.2	0.0	68.8	31.9	0.0	68.1	31.5	0.0	68.5
10–14	67.4	3.4	29.2	81.4	0.8	17.8	74.3	2.1	23.6
15–19	36.7	21.2	42.1	29.7	16.8	53.5	33.2	19.1	47.7

Source: Republic of Botswana (1988), *Household Income and Expenditure Survey: 1985/6* (Gaborone: CSO), tables 5c,d,f.

The striking feature of the table is the difference in school attendance between males and females in the age cohorts 10–14, and 15–19. For a very significant proportion of young males in rural households, schooling either stops altogether or is deferred at an age when they are deemed sufficiently responsible to tend livestock at the cattleposts. The labour generated in this way is generally remunerated in kind at very low rates, implying either that the opportunity cost of such labour – the foregone discounted increment in the stream of earnings due to schooling – is also very low, or that there exists a high degree of domestic monopsonistic exploitation. Both implications may be true to a certain extent. The other side of the remuneration coin, is that the productivity of such labour is also low, and this reflects directly on the degradation of the natural assets base. To give only two examples, the impoverishment of the range requires extensive grazing practices which are only viable if herding is remunerated at a very low rate. Similarly, the depletion of fuelwood in the vicinity of villages implies that increasingly greater distances have to be travelled to obtain supplies which, again, is only viable if the costs of collection are low. In other words, the greater the degradation of natural resources, the greater the incentive to reduce the costs of exploiting those resources through the use of child labour.

9.2.3   Fertility: education and other factors

Other factors behind the high rates of fertility observed in Sub-Saharan Africa include a set of cultural and religious biases. Aside from the frequently discussed restrictions imposed by the Catholic Church on its adherents in terms of the acceptability of particular birth control methods, it has been argued that most traditional religions in Sub-Saharan Africa are closely associated with the concept of reproduction of lineage, and that this has been a disincentive to declining fertility (cf. Caldwell and Caldwell, 1987). In this connection, education of women is sometimes seen as providing an alternative cultural perspective on the problem. This implies that literacy is a proxy for exposure to alternative value systems which may place different weights on fertility, or the role of women in society (cf. Pearce, 1991). In terms of the discussion in the last two sections, however, education in general has a number of more readily identifiable incentive effects.

If private returns to education are positive – if it pays individuals to invest time in schooling – then one implication is it that it will be privately inefficient to invest time in non-educational economic activity during the first fifteen years of life. It will not pay to undertake the sort of work described in the last section. If this is the case, it reduces the incentive to have children for their role as low cost producers. In addition, a positive private return on education implies that the expected stream of earnings per birth is augmented by education, and this reduces the incentive to have children for the second reason discussed above, that of providing income security in old age. Since a positive private return on education presupposes that education will augment expected income, it follows that for an agricultural household education must either increase expected agricultural productivity, or provide access to more high-paying employment outside the agricultural sector. Since the expected increase in income from non-agricultural work is a function of employment options, the expected return on education will be negatively correlated with the rate of unemployment and positively correlated with the degree of labour mobility. It follows that high rates of unemployment and restrictions on the mobility of labour will both act, indirectly, as a spur to fertility.

Recent studies of the rate of return to education in Africa show that a remarkable change has taken place since the mid-1960s when the rate of return on primary education was shown to be both very high, and well in excess of the rate of return to secondary education. By the mid-1980s, high levels of unemployment meant that the expected value of the increase in earnings due to primary education had fallen dramatically. In Kenya, for example, a World Bank study showed not only that the rate of return on primary education was falling (the marginal rate of return was below the average rate of return), but that the differential between primary and secondary education had been eliminated (World Bank, 1988). Nor is there any reason to believe that this trend has been reversed since then. The implication is that the incentive offered by education to decrease rural fertility rates has been steadily weakened since the mid-1960s, and that this is both part cause and part effect of high fertility rates.

9.2.4 Population externality

So far, this chapter has considered the private costs and benefits of births only. However, as in the case of environmental degradation, the reason for the existence of a population 'problem' is that the private decisions of individual households necessarily ignore the wider costs of population expansion. That is, there are a set of external costs to population growth which are omitted in the household calculus.

Consider what these might be. The private costs of an additional birth may be summarized as the private costs of developing the various capacities of the child required if it is to contribute the services to the household described above. These costs are ordinarily thought of as the child's consumption requirements plus the cost of whatever investments are made in its education. The private costs of the child's consumption, in turn, comprise the private costs of purchasing or producing consumer goods, both being important in rural households.

Now the central point of this book is that for various reasons the private cost of food production in Botswana is strictly less than its social cost. The fact that many natural resources in the agricultural sector lie in the public domain and are open to all, together with the existence of a set of public subsidies on resource use, means that individuals are encouraged to use these resources beyond socially optimal levels. This is the source of the environmental externalities of agricultural production. The same set of implicit subsidies on environmental resources may be argued to lead to birth rates above the socially optimal level. This is the source of population externality.

To be specific about the nature of the population externality, if the privately optimal fertility rate exceeds the socially optimal fertility rate, the result will be 'overcrowding' of the resource base. Overcrowding is, of course, a strictly relative concept. It implies only that the population density will exceed the carrying capacity of the resource base, and is therefore subject to all the caveats about carrying capacity mentioned in section 9.1. In some cases overcrowding will indeed imply high population densities, and in such cases the population externality will include increased epidemiological risks – the greater propensity for the spread of viruses, for example Dasgupta (1992). What is really at issue in the overcrowding, however, is that population densities will exceed those at which the productive potential of the resource base can be sustained. That is, the most important of the costs of excessive population growth that are being ignored in the decisions of present households will be borne by future generations. Indeed, intergenerational costs would seem to be at the core of the problem of population externality (cf. Ehrlich *et al.*, 1992a). Decisions that are taken on the basis of the current private costs and benefits of births risk leaving future generations with a legacy of resources of permanently reduced productive potential.

Fertility rates that exceed the socially optimal rate have a number of insidious and self-perpetuating implications. Since the number of people coming on to the job market exceed the number of new jobs being created, it implies rising levels of both open unemployment and participation in the agricultural sector. Rising unemployment reduces the expected private return on education. Rising levels of participation in agriculture increases the pressure on the resource base, and in the absence of technological change, raises the probability of the degradation of agricultural resources, and so the reduction of average agricultural productivity. This in turn increases the downward pressure on agricultural costs. Lower expected private returns to education and lower levels of productivity in agriculture in turn feed back into the fertility decisions of households. In other words, high fertility rates are part of a vicious circle of population growth, environmental degradation and poverty.

9.3 POPULATION GROWTH AND EMPLOYMENT GENERATION

The implication of the FAO report on population, carrying capacity and food production referred to earlier is that if a vicious circle of this sort does exist, it is because producers are locked into a technology level at which the current population levels exceed the carrying capacity of the resource base. There is undoubtedly a good deal of truth in this. Indeed, in this book, we have offered numerous instances of the way in which institutional and other conditions have locked agricultural producers into unsustainable patterns of resource use. At the same time we have shown that many of the recommendations coming out of the government of Botswana's own reappraisal of its strategies recognize the importance of reducing the barriers to adjustment in agricultural technology. But technology is only part of the problem, and policies designed to promote flexibility in the choice of technology will do little to alter the private costs and benefits of births. The problem of population externality should be addressed from both sides. That is, it is necessary both to promote population absorption, through employment generation, and to restrict population growth to socially optimal levels by correcting the current imbalance between the private and social costs of births.

9.3.1 Diversification and employment generation

It is estimated that the average annual growth in the labour force in Sub-Saharan Africa will be 2.7 per cent between 1985 and 2000, and will be over 3 per cent for many of the countries in the dryland areas of the Sahel, the Horn of Africa, East and Southern Africa – including Botswana. In the longer term, the international mobility of resource users is likely to be most effective means of assuring the ecological sustainability of resource use not only in Sub-Saharan Africa, but globally. Indeed, unless there is free mobility across national boundaries, Malthusian crisis may be the only means of reducing intolerable levels of stress on the environment in the very low income countries. For the present, however, mobility between national labour markets remains highly restricted, and there is little indication of any impending change. Entry and exit to most national labour markets remains strictly controlled, and such liberalization as has taken place – within the European labour market, for example – has paradoxically raised the barriers to entry from regions like Sub-Saharan Africa. The prospects for agricultural producers choosing to exit agricultural markets in the region tend to be limited to either the domestic formal and informal labour markets, or to a very restricted set of foreign markets, such as the market for mine and farm labour in South Africa.

This implies that domestic policy initiatives are going to have to carry the burden of reducing stress on the resource base, whilst simultaneously generating sufficient new employment opportunities to cover the expansion of the domestic labour force due to population growth. In respect of the domestic formal sector markets, the scope for absorbing increases of this magnitude is limited. The industrial sector was estimated to be able to provide only 2.5 per cent of new employment in Sub-Saharan Africa in the late 1980s (van Ginneken, 1988), and the rate of increase in manufacturing employment remains well below that in Latin America and Asia (van Ginneken and van der Hoeven, 1989). The service sector has been growing at a faster rate, but it too remains small. This implies that in the absence of further structural change the majority of new entrants to the labour force may be expected to be absorbed by the informal sector or to be locked into the agricultural sector of the national economies. Yet on all the available evidence, the agricultural sector will not be able to absorb the projected increase in the labour force in the region without massively diminishing returns.

Part of the problem is that prospects are limited not only by the impact of domestic policies, but by international trends as well. The scope for improvement in the terms of trade of agricultural products is limited. There is a strong trend towards the liberalization of international financial markets, and it is possible to identify a much weaker trend towards the liberalization of product markets. But agricultural markets remain highly protected, and subject to a considerable price intervention. Indeed, since the mid-1980s, the United States and the EEC have both increased the level of export subsidies on agricultural products, while maintaining farm income and domestic price support schemes. At the same time, protective measures against agricultural products from the low income countries have increased (Conway and Barbier, 1990).

In addition, per capita production of agricultural products and food products alone is currently declining, reflecting both the use of increasingly marginal lands and the degradation of existing arable and range lands. There is certainly some potential for increasing both productivity and employment in the agricultural sector. Indeed, its has been argued that there exists considerable scope for productivity improvements in agriculture, even on the most marginal land. Conway and Barbier (1990), for example, cite a number of examples to show that while levels of productivity on marginal lands in Sub-Saharan Africa will always be below that of 'favoured' lands elsewhere, they can be significantly greater than levels of productivity now being attained. Given the use of the right farming-system techniques, along with adequate research and extension, plus an appropriate set of economic incentives, they argue that it is possible to achieve sustainable results in the 'most difficult agricultural conditions'. Nevertheless, it is clear that the agricultural sector alone will be unable to expand at a rate equal to the rate of increase of the labour force into the indefinite future.

In Botswana, the size and urgency of the problem was illustrated in Chapter 4 through an estimate of the formal sector employment gap. Definitive information on the present size of the formal sector employment gap will become available with the full results of the 1991 census. But if it is still growing, as was suggested in Chapter 4, diversification of the rural economy as a means of employment generation is going to be critical. Long-term growth of agricultural output is not expected to exceed 0.5 per cent, so the agricultural sector itself will be unable to absorb the new entrants to the labour force. It was suggested earlier that this implies that most new jobs will have to be found in the non-agricultural parts of the informal sector.

An important component of an ecologically sustainable development strategy should be the removal of those barriers to adjustment in the economic system which have locked resource users into environmentally damaging practices. The general arguments for the appropriate pricing of agricultural and other resources and the rationalization of property rights are based on the assumption that the economic system will adjust to environmental imbalances if permitted to do so, and that adjustment is likely to involve diversification of the rural economy away from traditional agriculture. The question is whether there exists a set of incentives that will both stimulate the diversification of the rural economy, and yet protect the renewable resource base from being 'mined' in the process. While the policy reforms in Botswana do place considerable weight on diversification, it is argued below that they still contain contradictory elements which, so long as they remain, threaten the sustainability of resource use.

What is required of any structure of incentives if it is to be consistent with the sustainable development of the resource base is the following: a set of relative prices that will reflect the social opportunity cost of resource use (weighting the environmental effects of economic activity appropriately); an institutional structure that will not prevent the reallocation of resources from one use to another on the basis of those relative prices; and a distribution of assets and income that will enable resource users to take decisions based on a longer view of the costs and benefits of different options. One difficulty here, as Markandya (1991) has recently pointed out, is that it is not yet clear what the distributional or employment implications of different incentive structures is. He describes research on the cross price elasticities of demand for labour and the range of inputs targeted for their effect on the environment as 'sporadic', and claims that the traditional partial equilibrium analysis of environmentally innovative activities is inadequate to identify the longer term feedback effects on employment. It is not at all obvious, for example, that labour intensive technology is more environmentally sound or more sustainable than capital intensive technology. What this means is that the revision of the system of incentives, whether through the liberalization of markets or institutions, is necessarily in the nature of an experiment in which the potential economic benefits and costs are largely unknown. The application of a precautionary principle in these circumstances suggests a conservative approach, informed so far as possible by analysis of the general equilibrium longer term implications of change. This militates against sudden and dramatic swings in policy, but it is not a justification for leaving intact policies that have been shown to be directly or indirectly environmentally damaging.

The promotion of rural diversification is, accordingly, a principle theme of Botswana's NDP7. This requires both the removal of current institutional impediments to the reallocation of agricultural resources into non-farm activities, and the creation of an environment conducive to investment in non-traditional resource-based activities such as tourism, wildlife, fisheries (in the appropriate areas), veld products and farm-service activities. To this end, both the BNCS and the review of the incomes policies identified various regulatory restrictions that have inhibited diversification, and recommended that these be removed wherever possible. Some of these recommendations have been accepted, but there remain a number of bureaucratic impediments to the launching of innovative activities in the rural economy.

9.3.2 Public sector employment generation: environmentally-compensating projects

The creation of an economic environment conducive to diversification implies the creation of incentives favouring private investment in off-farm activity. While this will remain the main source of additional employment in Botswana in the foreseeable future, and so an important part of an employment generation strategy, it is worth recalling that during the second half of the 1980s public sector employment grew faster than any other category. Indeed, this is one reason for Harvey's recently stated concern that the government has lost control over public spending (Harvey, 1992). There is, however, one area in which rural public expenditure and employment might be expanded, and that is in the area of environmentally compensating projects. The principle of environmentally compensating projects is very straightforward. Define the basic condition for the acceptability of the ith project in an n project investment programme:

$$0 \leq \sum_{0}^{T} [b_{it} - c_{it} - e_{it}](1 + rt)^{-t}$$

where b_{it} denotes a non-negative vector of benefits; c_{it} denotes a non-negative vector of economic costs; and e_{it} denotes a non-negative vector of environmental costs, all from project i at time t. Sustainability requires that the programme involves no net environmental costs (Barbier, Markandya and Pearce, 1990). That is, sustainability requires that

$$\sum_1^n e_{it} \le 0 \text{ for } t = 0, \ldots, T$$

This condition may be satisfied by including in the programme environmentally compensating projects. So, if the *j*th project is environmentally compensating, then sustainability requires that

$$e_{jt} - \sum_1^n e_{it} \ge 0 \text{ for } t = 0, \ldots, T, \text{ and for all } i \ne j$$

Given that a number of agricultural policies have had environmentally-damaging effects, there is a strong case for the promotion of environmentally-compensating projects in countries such as Botswana. More particularly, there is a strong case for adopting environmentally-compensating projects using technology appropriate to the relative factor prices of the region. In a number of European countries, environmentally compensating projects have been used as counter-cyclical employment measures with considerable success. In Botswana, there is a case for reviving the very successful Labour Based Relief Programme (introduced during the drought) for these purposes.

9.3.3 Population policy

The achievement of full employment in Botswana, as in the rest of Sub-Saharan Africa, is enormously complicated by the high rate of growth of the labour force due to the high fertility rate. Moreover, even if birth rates were halved tomorrow this would continue to be a problem for decades. A critical part of any strategy for the sustainable use of Botswana's resources is therefore the development of a population policy that aims at reducing fertility. This is not an argument for direct intervention in the decisions of households: the inhumane and entirely arbitrary control over private decisions exercised in some countries have very little appeal. But then neither do the sort of Malthusian checks which will come in to play if successive governments do nothing. What is needed is a policy that plots a course between the Scylla of sterilization and abortion and the Charybdis of starvation and disease.

There are two parts to such a policy, one direct, the other indirect. The direct part of a population policy concerns the mechanics of regulating family size to the privately optimal level. Although I have emphasised the private rationality of fertility rates, there obviously remains considerable room for error in attaining optimal family size. Accordingly, the provision of contraceptive information and services is an important part of any population policy. The 'education' of women in this respect falls into the same category. This part of population policy is not, however, my concern here. The indirect part of population policy is. It addresses the incentive structure within which fertility rates are determined, and is concerned to bring the privately and socially optimal fertility rates into line with one another.

In one sense, the second part of population policy involves the same instruments as does environmental policy. Since the private costs of births are depressed by the same factors as the private costs of livestock or arable farming, correction of the environmental externality will go some way to correcting the population externality. The elimination of subsidies on agricultural inputs will also eliminate some of the bias in the costs of child rearing. Of course there are other sources of bias in the cost of child rearing. In Botswana, the provision of school meals is a case in point. However, addressing the private cost of access to public environmental resources would go a long way to correcting the problem.

A number of proposals to change the private costs of child rearing so as to reflect social costs already exist. Ehrlich *et al.* (1992a), for example, point out that the tax system in the United States effectively subsidizes child-rearing, and they argue for a progressive tax based on household size. This is analogous to the Chinese system of differential charges for access to public services based on household size. While there is a case both for pricing public services at cost and for eliminating such biases in the tax system, it is difficult to justify differential charges in cases where the costs are actually the same. It would seem better to raise the cost of child-rearing in general to socially optimal levels, and then to leave the choice as to how many children to have to individual households. If one household chooses to devote a greater proportion of its collective resources to child-rearing than another, and if it pays the full social cost for the resources involved, there is nothing wrong with this. There is, on the other hand, something very wrong if the state arbitrarily rations the right to have children among households – whether the distribution of such rights is egalitarian or not. Such an approach is neither efficient nor equitable.

In addition to removing the wedge between the private and social costs of child rearing, a population policy should address the motives – the driving forces – behind high fertility rates. Two prime motives have been suggested in the case of Sub-Saharan Africa: the role of children in insuring against the risk of loss of income in old age, and the role of children as producers. The first motive exists because there are no other sources of social security to meet the needs of individuals disabled by either illness or age. In none of the countries of Sub-Saharan Africa is there an effective public system of income support for people in this category. Nor are there effective insurance or financial markets where individuals might invest in annuities or other financial assets to the same purpose. This is partly a problem of supply (the existing financial and insurance institutions tend to be very conservative in their approach to new markets), but it also reflects a lack of demand. Indeed, so long as rural households derive such a large part of their income from either own-production or in-kind transfers, such markets are unlikely to develop, and savings will continue to take the form of real assets – livestock, land or children. In Botswana in the mid-1980s, two-thirds of all rural households received half or more of their income in-kind (Republic of Botswana, 1988), and a much higher proportion of all savings was in the form of real assets.

If a population policy is to address the motives behind high rates of fertility, therefore, it follows that one plank of such a policy should be the development of an alternative and accessible means of guaranteeing the security of income of rural Batswana. Moreover, since there is no reason to expect this to develop out of existing markets, there is a case for developing a partially funded social security system as long-range insurance against the costs of continuing excessive population growth. It is unlikely that such a dedicated social security system would be a greater drain on public resources than the ad hoc welfare system that has operated in the guise of agricultural development assistance, and it would contribute signally to the freeing up of agricultural resources. This is not, of course, the only option open to governments interested in addressing the problem of income security, but it may well be the most transparent to households contemplating the optimal number of children.

The other motive to be addressed is the role of children as producers, and in this case there are three issues. The first two have already been discussed, if only indirectly, and concern the costs of child rearing: the costs of both child maintenance and education and training. Since the costs of child maintenance are also, in this case, the costs of household labour, the implicit subsidies on rural resources referred to elsewhere in this book encourage higher levels of employment of child labour within the household than is socially optimal. The effect is to stimulate higher rates of fertility than are socially optimal. As before, the solution lies in the appropriate pricing of rural resources.

The second issue concerns the costs of human capital development, and raises the issue of education and whether or not schooling should be compulsory. The point has already been made that the private returns to primary education in much of Sub-Saharan Africa have been declining for the last decade at least. That is, the private incentive to invest time in primary education has been weakening. It has been suggested that this has also encouraged the employment of child labour within the household, with similar implications for fertility. If, as seems likely on the basis of all the available evidence, the social return exceeds the private return on primary education, the level of school attendance based on private decisions will be less than the level of school attendance from a social perspective. Indeed, this is the economic rational for making school attendance compulsory, or at least for changing the costs and benefits taken into account in the private calculus. In principle, compulsory education changes the private cost–benefit ratio of education by raising the private cost of non-attendance. That is, it changes the net benefits of employment of people of school age, but this is the case only if households are actually penalized financially for not sending children to school. It seems clear that in much of Sub-Saharan Africa the incentive effects of compulsory education are considerably diluted by non-enforcement, and by the fact that penalties are not imposed. This may be because the most likely offenders are households relatively least able to bear the penalties. But if one stratum of society is exempted from the social costs of their behaviour because it is relatively 'poor', it will be locked into the very cycle of high fertility rates, environmental degradation and poverty which is the original cause of our concern. It is better by far to address the income needs of such households directly through a social security system.

A separate but related issue concerns the terms on which labour – child labour included – is absorbed into the (broadly-defined) informal sector. The point has already been made that this sector is the largely unprotected residuum of the national labour market. It is, moreover, a very large residuum. In Botswana, more people find employment in the informal sector than in the formal sector, and a growing proportion of new entrants to the labour force are active in the informal sector not on their own account, but as wage earners – whether the wage is in cash or kind. The terms on which they are employed are entirely unregulated, and are not subject to enforceable contracts. Any protection offered to this segment of the labour force tends to be ad hoc. During the drought, for example, support was provided to those who lost jobs in both the formal and the informal sectors by the labour component of the drought relief programme. Those employed in the agricultural sector who suffered reduced incomes were targeted through the assistance given to farmers, and those in off-farm employment in the informal sector were assisted on an ad hoc basis through food aid.

In a highly fragmented, imperfectly competitive market this system offers little guarantee against the exploitation of labour, and so against the impoverishment which is a large part of the cause of both environmental and population externalities. Studies of two areas of informal sector employment, domestic service (Boyd and Mugabe, 1989) and traditional agriculture (Gyekye and Mazonde, 1989), have shown how prevalent exploitation in this sector is. Average rates of cash and in-kind remuneration in unskilled labour in the traditional agricultural sector were less than half the lowest minimum wage (see also Scoville and Nyamadzabo, 1988). At the same time, the studies showed a very high variance in remuneration in both agricultural employment and domestic service with remuneration for many employees falling well below the value of destitute rations.

In the light of this evidence, the commission appointed to review the incomes policy had recommended the extension of minimum wage requirements to cover these two sectors: to formalize the informal labour market. The commission was aware of the importance of establishing wage minima at levels that would not result in significant disemployment in a sector that remains the major source of employment for Batswana, but considered that it was essential to offer at least some protection to members of the labour force without assets of their own (particularly livestock) who received compensation below the value of their contribution to output. As was remarked in Chapter 7, the commission's recommendations were rejected by the government on the grounds that they were 'unenforceable, and thus impracticable' (Republic of Botswana, 1990c). It should be made very clear that amongst the costs of this decision are two of the trends that most threaten the sustainability of Botswana's development programme: continued high rates of population growth and the overutilization of the resource base. It was noted earlier in this book that the use made of the resources to which all Batswana have rights of access is strongly influenced by their level of income. The depression of wages in the monopsonized pockets of a fragmented labour market will involve costs to society, whether in terms of ad hoc relief, foregone development of skills, excessive pressure on the natural resources to which the poor do have access, or rising fertility rates.

10 Concluding Remarks

It seems clear that the driving forces behind the degradation of environmental resources in Botswana in the last decade, as in much of Sub-Saharan Africa, are social rather than environmental. There is some evidence that secular climatic trends, such as global warming, will affect the resilience of the ecological systems that underpin Botswana's natural resource base. It is also manifest that the recent years of drought have had a major impact on water resources, soil moisture content, erosion and vegetation. But the greatest source of damage to these resources has been a set of social processes. These include:

- the weakening of social control over access to the resource base, as rural institutions and property rights are redefined in the development process;
- the distortion of the private costs of resource use as a result of the extensive system of agricultural subsidies and the use of the agricultural development programme as a system of income support;
- a distribution of income that leaves a proportion of the rural population little affected by the income generated in the formal sector;
- the development of a labour market strategy which deliberately assigns to the informal sector in general, and to traditional agriculture in particular, the role of employer of last resort; and above all
- a rate of population growth that has led to a widening formal sector employment gap.

These processes have taken place at the same time as Botswana has been enjoying unprecedented rates of economic growth, and this has undoubtedly weakened their environmental impact. But as the long post-independence mineral boom comes to an end, it is important to understand that these processes have the potential to cause irreversible damage on an increasingly fragile environment.

In another context, I have argued that the ecological sustainability of economic activity depends on the interaction of two environments: an economic environment and a natural environment. If relative prices dictate optimal herd densities greater than the maximum sustainable herd density, for example, both the herd and the range will be more prone to collapse in the face of climatic shocks than if relative prices dictate optimal herd densities less than the maximum sustainable herd density. In short, by determining the optimal level of stress on ecological systems, the economic environment determines the resilience of those systems in the face of climatic shocks. Policies which change the economic environment change the sustainability of resource-based economic activities (Perrings, 1993).

The important point is that these social processes all influence the economic environment – the incentive system – within which individuals allocate resources, and an incentive system which leads to environmentally damaging decisions generally turns out to be neither efficient nor equitable. If private decisions ignore social costs, the resulting allocation of resources is inefficient. Where those same private decisions worsen either the intragenerational or intergenerational distribution of assets and income, that allocation is also inequitable. For both reasons, this report has argued that a strategy for sustainable development must address the structure of incentives.

Much can be achieved by the elimination of distortionary subsidies – which would have the double advantage of reducing public expenditure. At the same time, however, a case has been made for the expansion of public expenditure in a number of areas:

- a systematic and targetted treatment of income support to (rural) individuals disadvantaged by age or disability;
- infrastructural development to facilitate rural diversification;
- the introduction of environmentally compensating public sector projects (along the lines of the Labour Based Relief Programme);
- the development of an environmental data base and a natural resource accounting system.

While the last three categories of expenditure would certainly involve an extension of existing programmes, the first partly implies a change in the form in which rural development expenditures are currently delivered in order (a) to remove the 'traps' built in to the existing system which lock individuals into unsustainable patterns of resource use, and (b) to align private and social costs so as to internalize externalities. Both (a) and (b) imply more than 'getting the prices right', although that is obviously a large part of it. The solution to the population externality, for example, involves changing not only the private costs of environmental resources, but also the private return on education, the expected stream of household income, the 'rights' of child labour and even the values of rural households. It would be misleading to suggest either that such a change would pay quick dividends, or that it would be costless, but the central argument of this report is that the government of Botswana, and governments throughout Sub-Saharan Africa, are going to have to find both the will and the resources to address the problem either sooner or later.

Appendix 1
Botswana: Economic Profile

	unit	Year								
		1983	1984	1985	1986	1987	1988	1989	1990	1991
Macroeconomic indicators										
Population	k(000)	1012	1049	1088	1128	1169	1212	1256	1301	1347
GDP per capita	P	1287	1583	2054	2312	2794	4116	4050	4536	
Real GDP growth	% p.a.	20	8.1	8	10.1	9	13.6	5.7	6.7	
GDP at market prices	Pm	1302	1661	2235	2608	3266	4988	5901	6577	
GDP at constant (1980) prices	US$m	1185	1424	1507	1693	1773				
Consumer price inflation	% p.a.	8.3	6.5	10.4	10.8	8.1	10.4	11.3	12	
GDP deflator (change)	% p.a.	3.4	18	24.7	7.5	17.8	29.3			
Formal sector employment	k(000)	100.6	110	116	130.1	150.2	169.8	175.7		
Foreign trade and payments										
Exports (FOB)	Pm	696	857	1385	1613	2664	2686	3667	3262	
Imports (cif)	Pm	804	895	1096	133	1572	2129	2557	2988	
Current account	Pm	2.1	13.6	251	325	1155	798	779	256	
Foreign reserves	US$m			784	1197	2013	2257	2803	3345	
Public foreign debt	Pm	199	232	373	409	438	558	739	796	
Government finances										
Revenue	Pm	563	803	1133	1548	1825	2556	2751	3296	3183
Expenditure	Pm	460	615	719	1001	1312	1788	2219	2706	3318
Expenditure (% GDP)	%	35.3	37.0	32.2	38.4	40.2	35.8	37.6	41.1	

	unit	1983	1984	1985	1986	1987	1988	1989	1990	1991
					Year					
Budget surplus	Pm	103	188	414	547	513	768	532	590	−135
Budget surplus (% GDP	%	7.9	11.3	18.5	21.0	15.7	15.4	9.0	9.0	
Mineral revenue (% revenue	%	34.4	46.9	51.3	54.6	56.7	59	58	58.8	46.2
SACU receipts (% revenue)	%	27.9	19.4	13.2	12.4	12.8	11.4	12.8	14.4	25
Monetary indicators										
Discount rate	%	10.5	9	9	9	8.5	6.5	6.5	8.5	
Prime rate	%	13	11.5	11.5	10	10	7.5	8	9	12
Money supply (M3) increas	% p.a.	31.3	13.6	47.5	14.3	65.9	20.5	47.4	−14	
Commercial bank assets	Pm	288.4	398.8	465.9	469.1	601.2	828.9	1082	1354	
Excess liquidity (%)	%	53.7	62.4	65.6	49.8	58.6	61.5	52.7	45.5	

Sources: Republic of Botswana, *Statistical Bulletins, 1984–1990*; Barclays Botswana, *Economic Reviews, 1990–1991*.

Appendix 2
Botswana and Sub-Saharan Africa: A Socioeconomic Comparison

Demographic comparison	year	Botswana	Sub-Saharan Africa	Industrial countries
population	1988	1.2	470	1200
rural population %	1988	78	70	28
growth rate	1960–88	3.3	2.8	0.8
fertility rate	1988	6.2	6.5	1.9
crude birth rate	1988	47	46	15
crude death rate	1988	12	16	10
Income				
GNP per capita (US$)	1987	1050	440	10760
Real GDP per capita (PPPUS$)	1987	2496	990	14260
Urban population below poverty line	1974–1987	40	34	
Rural population below poverty line	1974–1987	55	61	
Welfare				
Urban population with access to services (%)				
health		100	72	
water		84	74	
sanitation		93		
Rural population with access to services (%)				
health		85	38	
water		46	24	
sanitation		28	17	
Gender gaps (females % males)				
Life expectancy		110.8	107	110.4
Literacy	1985	95	61	
Primary enrolment	1986–88	105	77	100
Secondary enrolment	1986–88	106	58	104
Labour force	1988	55	62	71
Food security				
Food production pc index (1979–81 = 100)	1985–87	75	93	101
Daily calorie supply pc	1986	2200	2160	3390
Food import dependency ratio	1984–8	5.1	6.3	16

Sources: Republic of Botswana, *Statistical Bulletins*, 1984–1990; Barclays Botswana, *Economic Reviews*, 1990–1991.

Appendix 3
Regression Results:
Expenditure against Income
Sources (Level Data)

WHOLE SAMPLE
Response: ESAVE
Summary of Fit
Rsquare   0.8573582
Root Mean Square Error   69.44482
Mean of Response   56.62333
Observations (or Sum Wgts)   126

Effect Test

Source	Nparm	DF	Sum of Squares	F Ratio	Prob > F
SEXHD	1	1	2175.0	0.4510	0.5033
HHVILL	3	3	243039.6	16.7987	0.0000
Poly(ITRANSF,3)	3	3	74918.9	5.1783	0.0022
Poly(IGIFTS,3)	3	3	27394.0	1.8935	0.1351
Poly(IRENTS,3)	3	3	204897.8	14.1624	0.0000
Poly(IWAGES,3)	3	3	1689316.8	116.7643	0.0000
Poly(ISALE,3)	3	3	605071.3	41.8221	0.0000

Whole-Model Test
Analysis of Variance

Source	DF	Sum of Squares	Mean Square	F Ratio
Model	19	3072565.8	161714	33.5326
Error	106	511193.8	4823	Prob > F
C Total	125	3583759.6		0.0000

Response: ECAP

Summary of Fit
Rsquare   0.9745487
Root Mean Square Error   60.77976
Mean of Response   103.6993
Observations (or Sum Wgts)   126

Effect Test

Source	Nparm	DF	Sum of Squares	F Ratio	Prob > F
HHVILL	3	3	8686	0.7837	0.5056
Poly(ITRANSF,3)	3	3	8609	0.7768	0.5095

184

Poly(IGIFTS,3)	3	3	2561	0.2311	0.8745
Poly(IRENTS,3)	3	3	429601	38.7638	0.0000
Poly(IWAGES,3)	3	3	140004	12.6329	0.0000
Poly(ISALE,3)	3	3	10676992	963.4066	0.0000
SEXHD	1	1	1965	0.5319	0.4674

Whole-Model Test
Analysis of Variance

Source	DF	Sum of Squares	Mean Square	F Ratio
Model	19	14994004	789158	213.6220
Error	106	391583	3694	Prob > F
C Total	125	15385587		0.0000

QUARTILE 1

Response: ESAVE

Summary of Fit

Rsquare	0.7619108
Root Mean Square Error	19.97694
Mean of Response	−5.22064
Observations (or Sum Wgts)	31

Effect Test

Source	Nparm	DF	Sum of Squares	F Ratio	Prob > F
SEXHD	1	1	57.2752	0.1435	0.7109
HHVILL	3	3	3408.4966	2.8470	0.0786
Poly(ITRANSF,3)	3	3	898.0489	0.7501	0.5415
Poly(IGIFTS,3)	3	3	199.3042	0.1665	0.9171
Poly(IRENTS,3)	3	1	61.1008	0.1531	0.7019
Poly(IWAGES,3)	3	3	1157.8699	0.9671	0.4377
Poly(ISALE,3)	3	3	3664.6666	3.0609	0.0660

Whole-Model Test
Analysis of Variance

Source	DF	Sum of Squares	Mean Square	F Ratio
Model	17	16602.217	976.601	2.4471
Error	13	5188.018	399.078	Prob > F
C Total	30	21790.235		0.0538

Response: ECAP

Summary of Fit

Rsquare	.5994773
Root Mean Square Error	9.301695
Mean of Response	8.433871
Observations (or Sum Wgts)	31

Effect Test

Source	Nparm	DF	Sum of Squares	F Ratio	Prob > F
SEXHD	1	1	3.67503	0.0425	0.8399
HHVILL	3	3	206.67324	0.7962	0.5176
Poly(ITRANSF,3)	3	3	673.60125	2.5951	0.0971
Poly(IGIFTS,3)	3	3	382.12451	1.4722	0.2680

Source	Nparm	DF	Sum of Squares	F Ratio	Prob > F
Poly(IRENTS,3)	3	1	30.51068	0.3526	0.5628
Poly(IWAGES,3)	3	3	37.99037	0.1464	0.9302
Poly(ISALE,3)	3	3	60.00061	0.2312	0.8730

Whole-Model Test
Analysis of Variance

Source	DF	Sum of Squares	Mean Square	F Ratio
Model	17	1683.5009	99.0295	1.1446
Error	13	1124.7801	86.5215	Prob > F
C Total	30	2808.2809		0.4088

QUARTILE 2

Response: ESAVE

Summary of Fit

Rsquare	0.7801616
Root Mean Square Error	30.29856
Mean of Response	13.88843
Observations (or Sum Wgts)	32

Effect Test

Source	Nparm	DF	Sum of Squares	F Ratio	Prob > F
SEXHD	1	1	89.5077	0.0975	0.7602
HHVILL	3	3	9293.3357	3.3745	0.0545
Poly(ITRANSF,3)	3	3	4440.8686	1.6125	0.2383
Poly(IGIFTS,3)	3	3	1528.8793	0.5551	0.6545
Poly(IRENTS,3)	3	3	2517.5931	0.9142	0.4632
Poly(IWAGES,3)	3	3	1685.4114	0.6120	0.6201
Poly(ISALE,3)	3	3	5141.7779	1.8670	0.1890

Whole-Model Test
Analysis of Variance

Source	DF	Sum of Squares	Mean Square	F Ratio
Model	19	39093.674	2057.56	2.2413
Error	12	11016.034	918.00	Prob > F
C Total	31	50109.708		0.0776

Response: ECAP

Summary of Fit

Rsquare	0.8205986
Root Mean Square Error	17.20566
Mean of Response	18.76312
Observations (or Sum Wgts)	32

Effect Test

Source	Nparm	DF	Sum of Squares	F Ratio	Prob > F
SEXHD	1	1	4.0454	0.0137	0.9089
HHVILL	3	3	936.4179	1.0544	0.4044
Poly(ITRANSF,3)	3	3	4674.4843	5.2634	0.0151
Poly(IGIFTS,3)	3	3	3362.1487	3.7858	0.0403
Poly(IRENTS,3)	3	3	1416.3904	1.5948	0.2423

Poly(IWAGES,3)	3	3	3879.7783	4.3686	0.0268
Poly(ISALE,3)	3	3	5809.2647	6.5412	0.0072

Whole-Model Test
Analysis of Variance

Source	DF	Sum of Squares	Mean Square	F Ratio
Model	19	16249.093	855.215	2.8889
Error	12	3552.418	296.035	Prob > F
C Total	31	19801.510		0.0322

QUARTILE 3

Response: ESAVE

Summary of Fit

Rsquare	0.9107732
Root Mean Square Error	30.90357
Mean of Response	84.70281
Observations (or Sum Wgts)	32

Effect Test

Source	Nparm	DF	Sum of Squares	F Ratio	Prob > F
SEXHD	1	1	40.886	0.0428	0.8396
HHVILL	3	3	3746.579	1.3077	0.3172
Poly(ITRANSF,3)	3	3	14812.874	5.1701	0.0160
Poly(IGIFTS,3)	3	3	4242.597	1.4808	0.2694
Poly(IRENTS,3)	3	3	12691.249	4.4296	0.0258
Poly(IWAGES,3)	3	3	15796.813	5.5135	0.0129
Poly(ISALE,3)	3	3	16521.505	5.7665	0.0111

Whole-Model Test
Analysis of Variance

Source	DF	Sum of Squares	Mean Square	F Ratio
Model	19	116980.63	6156.88	6.4468
Error	12	11460.37	955.03	Prob > F
C Total	31	128441.00		0.0010

Response: ECAP

Summary of Fit

Rsquare	0.6719291
Root Mean Square Error	19.25341
Mean of Response	25.155
Observations (or Sum Wgts)	32

Effect Test

Source	Nparm	DF	Sum of Squares	F Ratio	Prob > F
SEXHD	1	1	1132.7132	3.0557	0.1060
HHVILL	3	3	34.6132	0.0311	0.9922
Poly(ITRANSF,3)	3	3	792.2305	0.7124	0.5631
Poly(IGIFTS,3)	3	3	3318.7847	2.9843	0.0737
Poly(IRENTS,3)	3	3	1914.8173	1.7218	0.2156
Poly(IWAGES,3)	3	3	437.0865	0.3930	0.7603
Poly(ISALE,3)	3	3	3288.2999	2.9569	0.0753

Whole-Model Test
Analysis of Variance

Source	DF	Sum of Squares	Mean Square	F Ratio
Model	19	9110.717	479.511	1.2936
Error	12	4448.327	370.694	Prob > F
C Total	31	13559.044		0.3297

QUARTILE 4

Response: ESAVE

Summary of Fit

Rsquare	0.9442671
Root Mean Square Error	117.9902
Mean of Response	133.5954
Observations (or Sum Wgts)	31

Effect Test

Source	Nparm	DF	Sum of Squares	F Ratio	Prob > F
SEXHD	1	1	1934.7	0.1390	0.7158
HHVILL	2	2	244531.6	8.7824	0.0045
Poly(ITRANSF,3)	3	3	109774.1	2.6284	0.0981
Poly(IGIFTS,3)	3	3	8060.0	0.1930	0.8991
Poly(IRENTS,3)	3	3	146193.2	3.5004	0.0496
Poly(IWAGES,3)	3	3	1015092.3	24.3048	0.0000
Poly(ISALE,3)	3	3	522727.2	12.5159	0.0005

Whole-Model Test
Analysis of Variance

Source	DF	Sum of Squares	Mean Square	F Ratio
Model	18	2830456.0	157248	11.2952
Error	12	167060.3	13922	Prob > F
C Total	30	2997516.3		0.0001

Response: ECAP

Summary of Fit

Rsquare	0.9837073
Root Mean Square Error	130.1649
Mean of Response	367.7190
Observations (or Sum Wgts)	31

Effect Test

Source	Nparm	DF	Sum of Squares	F Ratio	Prob > F
SEXHD	1	1	48623.9	2.8699	0.1160
HHVILL	2	2	7466.5	0.2203	0.8054
Poly(ITRANSF,3)	3	3	30300.1	0.5961	0.6295
Poly(IGIFTS,3)	3	3	14822.8	0.2916	0.8307
Poly(IRENTS,3)	3	3	442177.6	8.6994	0.0024
Poly(IWAGES,3)	3	3	191839.2	3.7742	0.0406
Poly(ISALE,3)	3	3	5334566.0	104.9517	0.0000

Whole-Model Test
Analysis of Variance

Source	DF	Sum of Squares	Mean Square	F Ratio
Model	18	12275596	681978	40.2515
Error	12	203315	16943	Prob > F
C Total	30	12478911		0.0000

Appendix 4
Regression Results: Expenditure against Income Sources (Share Data)

WHOLE SAMPLE

Response: ESAVSH

Summary of Fit
Rsquare   0.5040057
Root Mean Square Error   0.3537354
Mean of Response   0.1519518
Observations (or Sum Wgts)   126

Effect Test

Source	Nparm	DF	Sum of Squares	F Ratio	Prob > F
SEXHD	1	1	0.0461064	0.3685	0.5451
HHVILL	3	3	7.4038643	19.7233	0.0000
Poly(ISALESH,3)	3	3	0.0928014	0.2472	0.8632
Poly(IRENTSH,3)	3	3	0.1024902	0.2730	0.8447
Poly(IWAGESH,3)	3	3	0.3728086	0.9931	0.3991
Poly(ITRANSH,3)	3	3	1.0136276	2.7002	0.0494
Poly(IGIFTSH,3)	3	3	0.1056299	0.2814	0.8387

Whole-Model Test
Analysis of Variance

Source	DF	Sum of Squares	Mean Square	F Ratio
Model	19	13.477893	0.709363	5.6691
Error	106	13.263651	0.125129	Prob > F
C Total	125	26.741544		0.0000

Response: ECAPSH

Summary of Fit
Rsquare   0.3606397
Root Mean Square Error   0.2177210
Mean of Response   0.2042960
Observations (or Sum Wgts)   126

190

Effect Test

Source	Nparm	DF	Sum of Squares	F Ratio	Prob > F
SEXHD	1	1	0.02252073	0.4751	0.4922
HHVILL	3	3	0.49429877	3.4759	0.0186
Poly(ISALESH,3)	3	3	0.00226385	0.0159	0.9972
Poly(IRENTSH,3)	3	3	0.20430039	1.4366	0.2363
Poly(IWAGESH,3)	3	3	0.06480839	0.4557	0.7138
Poly(ITRANSH,3)	3	3	0.56041016	3.9408	0.0104
Poly(IGIFTSH,3)	3	3	0.07384651	0.5193	0.6699

Whole-Model Test
Analysis of Variance

Source	DF	Sum of Squares	Mean Square	F Ratio
Model	19	2.8342278	0.149170	03.1469
Error	106	5.0246623	0.047402	Prob > F
C Total	125	7.8588901	0.0001	

QUARTILE 1

Response: ESAVSH

Summary of Fit

Rsquare	0.8144029
Root Mean Square Error	0.3878197
Mean of Response	−0.141767
Observations (or Sum Wgts)	31

Effect Test

Source	Nparm	DF	Sum of Squares	F Ratio	Prob > F
SEXHD	1	1	0.0291572	0.1939	0.6670
HHVILL	3	3	1.0954292	2.4277	0.1121
Poly(ISALESH,3)	3	3	0.9197368	2.0384	0.1582
Poly(IRENTSH,3)	3	1	0.0004737	0.0031	0.9561
Poly(IWAGESH,3)	3	3	0.4506387	0.9987	0.4243
Poly(ITRANSH,3)	3	3	1.9347782	4.2880	0.0261
Poly(IGIFTSH,3)	3	3	1.1060780	2.4513	0.1098

Whole-Model Test
Analysis of Variance

Source	DF	Sum of Squares	Mean Square	F Ratio
Model	17	8.579689	0.504688	3.3555
Error	13	1.955254	0.150404	Prob > F
C Total	30	10.534943		0.0160

Response: ECAPSH

Summary of Fit

Rsquare	0.7972999
Root Mean Square Error	0.2143333
Mean of Response	0.1991901
Observations (or Sum Wgts)	31

Effect Test

Source	Nparm	DF	Sum of Squares	F Ratio	Prob > F
SEXHD	1	1	0.00116370	0.0253	0.8760
HHVILL	3	3	0.11834111	0.8587	0.4869
Poly(ISALESH,3)	3	3	0.08600511	0.6241	0.6120
Poly(IRENTSH,3)	3	1	0.02376923	0.5174	0.4847
Poly(IWAGESH,3)	3	3	0.02985166	0.2166	0.8831
Poly(ITRANSH,3)	3	3	0.90133240	6.5401	0.0062
Poly(IGIFTSH,3)	3	3	0.14219445	1.0318	0.4108

Whole-Model Test
Analysis of Variance

Source	DF	Sum of Squares	Mean Square	F Ratio
Model	17	2.3490417	0.138179	3.0079
Error	13	0.5972044	0.045939	Prob > F
C Total	30	2.9462460		0.0249

QUARTILE 2

Response: ESAVSH

Summary of Fit
Rsquare	0.790525
Root Mean Square Error	0.2730977
Mean of Response	0.1501188
Observations (or Sum Wgts)	32

Effect Test

Source	Nparm	DF	Sum of Squares	F Ratio	Prob > F
SEXHD	1	1	0.0971858	1.3031	0.2759
HHVILL	3	3	1.4106541	6.3047	0.0082
Poly(ISALESH,3)	3	3	0.1848854	0.8263	0.5044
Poly(IRENTSH,3)	3	3	0.2322503	1.0380	0.4108
Poly(IWAGESH,3)	3	3	0.1854748	0.8289	0.5031
Poly(ITRANSH,3)	3	3	0.4574195	2.0444	0.1614
Poly(IGIFTSH,3)	3	3	0.1034923	0.4625	0.7136

Whole-Model Test
Analysis of Variance

Source	DF	Sum of Squares	Mean Square	F Ratio
Model	19	3.3775418	0.177765	2.3835
Error	12	0.8949882	0.074582	Prob > F
C Total	31	4.2725300		0.0634

Response: ECAPSH

Summary of Fit
Rsquare	0.5976483
Root Mean Square Error	0.2147384
Mean of Response	0.1779243
Observations (or Sum Wgts)	32

Effect Test

Source	Nparm	DF	Sum of Squares	F Ratio	Prob > F
SEXHD	1	1	0.04299259	0.9323	0.3533

HHVILL	3	3	0.22977603	1.6610	0.2279
Poly(ISALESH,3)	3	3	0.13006918	0.9402	0.4516
Poly(IRENTSH,3)	3	3	0.12076220	0.8730	0.4821
Poly(IWAGESH,3)	3	3	0.00918187	0.0664	0.9767
Poly(ITRANSH,3)	3	3	0.11239663	0.8125	0.5112
Poly(IGIFTSH,3)	3	3	0.03030486	0.2191	0.8813

Whole-Model Test
Analysis of Variance

Source	DF	Sum of Squares	Mean Square	F Ratio
Model	19	0.8219413	0.043260	0.9381
Error	12	0.5533513	0.046113	Prob > F
C Total	31	1.3752926		0.5637

QUARTILE 3

Response: ESAVSH

Summary of Fit

Rsquare	0.8722145
Root Mean Square Error	0.1593227
Mean of Response	0.4090093
Observations (or Sum Wgts)	32

Effect Test

Source	Nparm	DF	Sum of Squares	F Ratio	Prob > F
SEXHD	1	1	0.01841914	0.7256	0.4110
HHVILL	3	3	0.09265292	1.2167	0.3459
Poly(ISALESH,3)	3	3	0.16712345	2.1946	0.1415
Poly(IRENTSH,3)	3	3	0.03706180	0.4867	0.6979
Poly(IWAGESH,3)	3	3	0.12315479	1.6172	0.2373
Poly(ITRANSH,3)	3	3	0.06718991	0.8823	0.4777
Poly(IGIFTSH,3)	3	3	0.11912387	1.5643	0.2492

Whole-Model Test
Analysis of Variance

Source	DF	Sum of Squares	Mean Square	F Ratio
Model	19	2.0791158	0.109427	4.3109
Error	12	0.3046047	0.025384	Prob > F
C Total	31	2.3837205		0.0064

Response: ECAPSH

Summary of Fit

Rsquare	0.5590339
Root Mean Square Error	0.1320897
Mean of Response	0.1276336
Observations (or Sum Wgts)	32

Effect Test

Source	Nparm	DF	Sum of Squares	F Ratio	Prob > F
SEXHD	1	1	0.00604060	0.3462	0.5672
HHVILL	3	3	0.01442710	0.2756	0.8419
Poly(ISALESH,3)	3	3	0.05553618	1.0610	0.4018
Poly(IRENTSH,3)	3	3	0.02779870	0.5311	0.6695

Poly(IWAGESH,3)	3	3	0.02835446	0.5417	0.6628
Poly(ITRANSH,3)	3	3	0.06009604	1.1481	0.3695
Poly(IGIFTSH,3)	3	3	0.01923706	0.3675	0.7778

Whole-Model Test
Analysis of Variance

Source	DF	Sum of Squares	Mean Square	F Ratio
Model	19	0.26543138	0.013970	0.8007
Error	12	0.20937230	0.017448	Prob > F
C Total	31	0.47480368	0.6780	

QUARTILE 4

Response:　　　ESAVSH

Summary of Fit

Rsquare	0.8024611
Root Mean Square Error	0.2791262
Mean of Response	0.1822138
Observations (or Sum Wgts)	31

Effect Test

Source	Nparm	DF	Sum of Squares	F Ratio	Prob > F
SEXHD	1	1	0.0008733	0.0112	0.9174
HHVILL	2	2	1.1263162	7.2282	0.0087
Poly(ISALESH,3)	3	3	0.0704527	0.3014	0.8238
Poly(IRENTSH,3)	3	3	0.0653322	0.2795	0.8392
Poly(IWAGESH,3)	3	3	0.3083223	1.3191	0.3138
Poly(ITRANSH,3)	3	3	0.1468344	0.6282	0.6106
Poly(IGIFTSH,3)	3	3	0.1528647	0.6540	0.5957

Whole-Model Test
Analysis of Variance

Source	DF	Sum of Squares	Mean Square	F Ratio
Model	18	3.7979923	0.211000	2.7082
Error	12	0.9349376	0.077911	Prob > F
C Total	30	4.7329299		0.0415

Response:　　　ECAPSH

Summary of Fit

Rsquare	0.6970979
Root Mean Square Error	0.2495057
Mean of Response	0.3157598
Observations (or Sum Wgts)	31

Effect Test

Source	Nparm	DF	Sum of Squares	F Ratio	Prob > F
SEXHD	1	1	0.02235556	0.3591	0.5601
HHVILL	2	2	0.00185574	0.0149	0.9852
Poly(ISALESH,3)	3	3	0.08680014	0.4648	0.7122
Poly(IRENTSH,3)	3	3	0.31682725	1.6964	0.2206
Poly(IWAGESH,3)	3	3	0.05188452	0.2778	0.8403
Poly(ITRANSH,3)	3	3	0.03924150	0.2101	0.8875
Poly(IGIFTSH,3)	3	3	0.04811817	0.2576	0.8545

Whole-Model Test
Analysis of Variance

Source	DF	Sum of Squares	Mean Square	F Ratio
Model	18	1.7192294	0.095513	1.5343
Error	12	0.7470373	0.062253	Prob > F
C Total	30	2.4662667		0.2269

Appendix 5
Land Tenure in Botswana

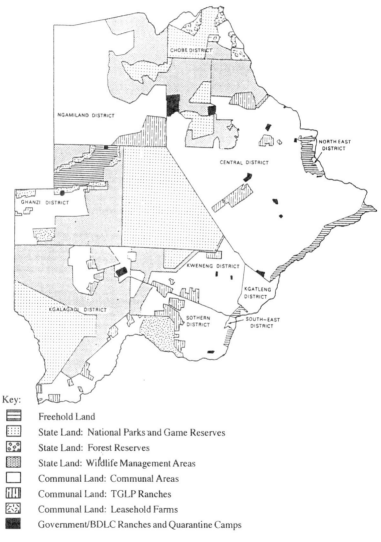

Key:

▤	Freehold Land
▦	State Land: National Parks and Game Reserves
▨	State Land: Forest Reserves
▓	State Land: Wildlife Management Areas
☐	Communal Land: Communal Areas
▥	Communal Land: TGLP Ranches
▩	Communal Land: Leasehold Farms
■	Government/BDLC Ranches and Quarantine Camps

Source: Republic of Botswana, Ministry of Finance and Development
Planning (1991) *National Development Plan 1991–1997 (NDP7)*
(Gaborone, Government Printer).

Appendix 6
Vegetation in Botswana

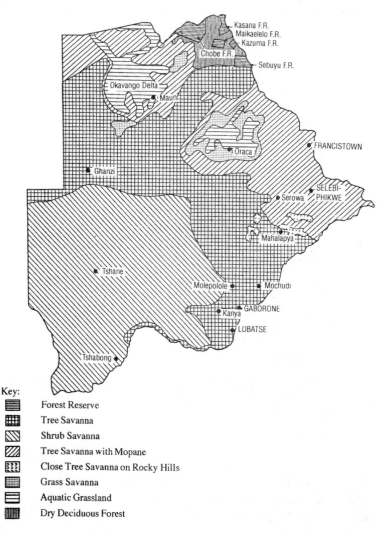

Key:

▤	Forest Reserve
▦	Tree Savanna
▨	Shrub Savanna
▨	Tree Savanna with Mopane
▦	Close Tree Savanna on Rocky Hills
▦	Grass Savanna
☰	Aquatic Grassland
▥	Dry Deciduous Forest

Source: Republic of Botswana, Ministry of Finance and Development Planning (1991) *National Development Plan 1991–1997 (NDP7)* (Gaborone, Government Printer).

Appendix 7
Ministry of Agriculture
Facilities

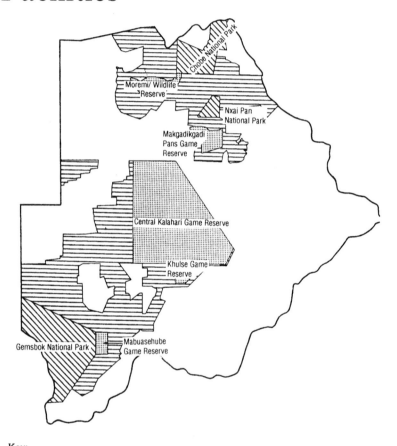

Key:

▨	National Parks
▦	Game Reserves
▤	Wildlife Management Areas

Source: Republic of Botswana, Ministry of Finance and Development
Planning (1991) *National Development Plan 1991–1997 (NDP7)*
(Gaborone, Government Printer).

Notes and References

1 Introduction

1. The term drylands comprises both arid lands with insufficient rainfall to sustain crop production but capable of supporting pastoralism (< 250 mm rainfall per annum), and semi-arid lands capable of supporting some drought-resistant crops (< 600 mm rainfall per annum). In Africa this includes not only the Sahara and Kalahari deserts, but also all of the Sudano-Sahelian region and much of East, Central and Southern Africa.
2. From 92 to 91 per cent.
3. Sudan at 65 per cent and Ghana at 59 per cent. The percentage of the labour force in Zambia in agriculture was reported to be 37.9 per cent in 1985-7 (UNDP, 1990]).
4. No data are available for Burkina Faso, Mauritania, Mozambique, Senegal, Uganda, Tanzania and Zambia in this period, all of which have very high levels of rural poverty.
5. The human development index [HDI] is equal to one minus an average deprivation index, which is a simple average of three indicators: life expectancy, literacy, and GDP. On a scale in which Japan has an HDI of 0.996, twenty countries have an HDI of less than 0.3. All but three of these are in Sub-Saharan Africa. The eight most deprived countries in terms of this index are: Niger, Mali, Burkina Faso, Sierra Leone, Chad, Guinea, Somalia and Mauritania.
6. See Appendix 2 for a statistical summary of some of the socioeconomic similarities between Botswana and the rest of Sub-Saharan Africa.

2 Secular Trends and Environmental Degradation in Sub-Saharan Africa

1. It does not necessarily follow that if the relative sizes of the populations of different species changes, a system will lose resilience. An important qualification to this is that an ecosystem will tend to be more resilient, the greater the 'interconnectedness' of species within the system (interconnectedness being a measure of the interactions between species populations). The greater the interdependence of species in an ecosystem, and the more species it involves, the greater its potential resilience. Hence biodiversity loss, which implies a reduction in the 'interconnectedness' of an ecosystem, does imply a reduction in system resilience.
2. The first group of plants are known as C4 plants, since the first product in the growth sequence has 4 carbon atoms; the second group are known as C3 plants. The latter respond much more positively to increased concentrations of CO_2. See for example Akita and Moss (1973).

3. Where, for example, the out-migration of labour results in environmental maintenance tasks being neglected, land degradation and a declining population may go together. Evidence from elsewhere supports the general proposition that population changes can work both ways. In the dryland environments of Mexico, for example, Garcia-Barrios and Garcia-Barrios (1990) argue that emigration is one of the main factors in the weakening of institutions charged with regulating access to resources held in communal property.

3 Environmental Management in Sub-Saharan Africa

1. While the short- and long-run supply elasticities for cocoa, coffee and sisal were reported to be significantly different, the short- and long-run elasticities for cotton, groundnuts, palm kernels, and palm oil were reported to be identical.
2. The trend was started by a colonial policy to combat the drought of the early 1960s, when exclusive rights to the water issuing from new boreholes were allocated to larger cattle owners – typically those with traditional positions of authority – giving them 'de facto exclusive rights to extensive areas of new grazing land'. Despite the fact that this violated customary law with respect to both grazing land and natural resources (aquifers), the policy was maintained for at least a decade after independence. The result was that poorer herdsmen were moved on to progressively more marginal land, and by 1976 Colclough and Fallon estimated that 39 per cent of all rural households owned no cattle at all, while the distribution of cattle amongst the remaining 61 per cent of households was highly unequal (Colclough and Fallon, 1983, pp. 144–5).

4 Botswana: Economy and Environment

1. What is interesting about this is that per capita income is also rising: a combination of trends that is highly unusual. The most likely explanation is that fertility is rising only in the rural areas where average income has declined during the drought.
2. The most important product, by value, is boneless beef, followed by wet blue hides, corned beef, offal and other products.
3. Though not universally so. In the 1970s and early 1980s beef from Botswana was banned in EEC markets because of an outbreak of foot and mouth disease and this remains a continuing threat.

6 Income and Asset Distribution

1. Migrant worker remittances in 1985 were estimated at P27.5m.
2. These provide a graphical illustration of the impact on the squared residuals (error) in the model tested of removing the regressor from the model. The distance from each point to the horizontal line shows the error

that occurs if the parameters on the regressor are set equal to zero (the effect is removed from the model). The slope of the line of fit in the leverage plots is equal to the parameter estimate for the regressor. The line of fit is shown, in each case, with 5 per cent confidence curves. If the confidence region contains the horizontal line the effect is not significant. If the confidence region crosses the horizontal line it is.

7 Policy Reform

1. Commercial activities reserved for Batswana included: hawking and vending; butcheries and fresh produce suppliers; dairies; small general trading; petrol filling stations; bottle stores; bars; taxi services; security guard services; chibuku bars; village restaurants; general traders (excluding chain stores and franchise operations); and simple specialty operations. Industrial activities reserved for Batswana included; school furniture manufacture; uniform manufacture; manufacture of cement bricks and baked bricks; sorghum milling; (ordinary) baking; burglar bar manufacture; fencing; road work; road maintenance; reserve and drainage; culvert construction; transport and plant hire; bush clearing and scrubbing; stockpiling of materials; carting gravel and chips; bridge painting and road marking.
2. This section draws on Perrings *et al.* (1989), Gilbert (1990) and Markandya and Perrings (1991).

8 Incentives for Sustainable Development

1. Argued in the BNCS to be a necessary condition for the elimination of overgrazing.

Bibliography

ABEL, N.O.J., FLINT, M.E., HUNTER, N.D., CHANDLER, D., and MAKA, G. (1987) *Cattle Keeping, Ecological Change and Communal Management in Ngwaketse* (Gaborone: Integrated Farming Pilot Project).

ABEL, N.O.J. (1990) *Destocking communal pastures in Southern Africa: is it worth it?*, Paper prepared for the Technical meeting on Savannah Development and Pasture Production, Commonwealth Secretariat and the Overseas Development Institute, Woburn, November.

ADDISON, A. and DEMERY, L. (1989) 'The economics of rural poverty alleviation', in S. Commander (ed.) *Structural Adjustment and Agriculture: Theory and Practice in Africa and Latin America* (London: ODI) pp. 71–89.

AKITA, S. and MOSS, D.N. (1973) 'Photosynthetic responses to CO_2 and light by maize and wheat leaves adjusted for constant stomatal apertures', *Crop Science*, 13, pp. 234–7.

ALAUDDIN, M. and TISDELL, C. (1991) *The Green Revolution and Economic Development: The Process and its Impact in Bangladesh* (London: Macmillan).

ALLAN, W. (1965) *The African Husbandman* (Edinburgh: Oliver and Boyd).

ARNTZEN, J.W. and VEENENDAAL, E.M. (1986) *A Profile of Environment and Development in Botswana*. Report of a study conducted for the Environment–Development Linkages Project by the Institute for Environmental Studies, Free University, Amsterdam, and the National Institute of Development, Research and Documentation, Gaborone, University of Botswana.

ARUP-ATKINS INTERNATIONAL (1988) *Review of Subsidies and Price Incentives in Food Grain Production and Marketing in Botswana*. Report prepared for the Government of Botswana, Gaborone, Arup Atkins.

AULT, D.E. and RUTMAN, G.L. (1979) 'The Development of Individual Rights to Property in Tribal Africa', *Journal of Law and Economics*, 22, 1, pp. 163–182.

BANK OF BOTSWANA (1985–1990) *Annual Reports* (Gaborone: Bank of Botswana).

BANK OF BOTSWANA (1987) *Report on the Rural Economic Survey 1986* (Gaborone: Bank of Botwana).

BARBIER, E.B. (1988) *Sustainable agriculture and the resource poor: policy issues and options*. LEEC Paper 88-02.

BARBIER, E.B. (1989) 'The contribution of environmental and resource economics to an economics of sustainable development', *Development and Change*, 20, pp. 429–459.

BARBIER, E.B., MARKANDYA, A. and PEARCE, D.W. (1990) 'Sustainable agricultural development and project appraisal', *European Review of Agricultural Economics*, 17, pp. 181–196.

BEHNKE, R.H. (1985) 'Measuring the benefits of subsistence versus commercial livestock production in Africa', *Agricultural Systems*, 16, pp. 109–35.

BEHNKE, R.H. (1990) *Open-Range Management and Property Rights in Pastoral Africa: a Case of Spontaneous Range Enclosure in South Darfur* (Sudan and London: Overseas Development Institute).

BEHRMAN, J.R. (1986) 'Shadow Prices and Subsidies in Botswana', *Journal of Development Economics*, 22, pp. 351–92.

BERNUS, E. (1980) 'Desertification in the Eghazer and Azawak Region, Niger' in J.A. Mabbutt and C. Floret (eds), *Case Studies in Desertification* (Paris: UNESCO), pp. 115–46.

BERRY, L. (1984) *Assessment of Desertification in the Sudano-Sahelian Region 1978–1984*. UNEP Governing Council, 12th Session, Nairobi, UNEP.

BEYNON, J.G. (1989) 'Pricism v. structuralism in sub-Saharan African agriculture', *Journal of Agricultural Economics*, 40, 3, pp. 323–35.

BIOT, Y. (1990) *How long can high stocking densities be sustained?*, Paper prepared for the Technical Meeting on Savannah Development and Pasture Production, Commonwealth Secretariat and the Overseas Development Institute, Woburn, November.

BOND, M.E. (1983) *Agricultural responses to prices in sub-Saharan African countries*. IMF Staff Papers, 30.

BOSERUP, E. (1965) *The Conditions of Agricultural Growth* (London: Allen and Unwin).

BOSERUP, E. (1981) *Population and Technological Change: A Study of Long Term Trends* (Oxford: Basil Blackwell).

BOYD, M. and MUGABE, M. (1989) *A Study of the Minimum Wage Possibilities in Agricultural and Domestic Service Sectors of the Botswana Economy. Volume I: Domestic Service Sector Report* (Gaborone, NIR and University of Botswana).

BRUCE, J. (1988) 'A perspective on indigenous land tenure systems and land concentration', in R.E. Downs and S. Reyna (eds), *Land and Society in Contemporary Africa* (Hanover, NH: University Press of New England).

CAIN, M. (1981) 'Risk and insurance: perspectives on fertility and agrarian change in India and Bangladesh', *Population and Development Review*, 7, pp. 435–74.

CAIN, M. (1983) 'Fertility as an adjustment to risk', *Population and Development Review*, 9, pp. 688–702.

CALDWELL, J.C. (1976) 'Towards a Restatement of Demographic Transition Theory', *Population and Development Review*, 2, pp. 321–366.

CALDWELL, J.C. and CALDWELL, P. (1987) 'The cultural context of high fertility in Sub-Saharan Africa', *Population and Development Review*, 13, pp. 409–37.

CHARNEY, J. (1975) 'Dynamics of deserts and drought in the Sahel', *Quarterly Journal of the Royal Meteorological Society*, 101, pp. 193–202.

CLARK, C. (1976) *Mathematical Bioeconomics: The Optimal Management of Renewable Resources* (New York: Wiley).

CLEAVER, K. (1985) *The impact of price and exchange rate policies on agriculture in sub-Saharan Africa*. World Bank Staff Working Paper, 728.

CLEAVER, K. (1988) *The use of price policy to stimulate agricultural growth in sub-Saharan Africa*. Paper presented to the 8th Agricultural Sector Symposium on Trade, Aid, and Policy Reform for Agriculture.

COLCLOUGH, C. and FALLON, P. (1983) 'Rural Poverty in Botswana: Dimensions, Causes, Constraints', in D. Ghai and S. Radwan (eds), *Agrarian Policies and Rural Poverty in Africa* (Geneva: ILO, pp. 129–154).

COMMANDER, S. (ed.) (1989) *Structural Adjustment and Agriculture: Theory and Practice in Africa and Latin America*, (ODI: London).

CONWAY, G.R. and BARBIER, E.B. (1990) *Sustainable Agriculture for Development* (London: Earthscan).

COOKE, H.J. (1985) 'The Kalahari Today: A Case of Conflict Over Resource Use', *The Geographical Journal*, 151, 1, pp. 75–85.

COUSINS, B. (1987) *A survey of Current Grazing Schemes in the Communal Lands of Zimbabwe* (Harare: University of Zimbabwe, Centre for Applied Social Sciences). Mimeo.

DARITY, W.A. (1980) 'The Boserup theory of agricultural growth: a model for anthropological economics', *Journal of Development Economics*, 7, pp. 137–157.

DASGUPTA, P. (1992) 'Population, resources and poverty', *Ambio*, 21, pp. 95–101.

DASGUPTA, P.S. and HEAL, G.M. (1979) *Economic Theory and Exhaustible Resources* (New York: Cambridge University Press).

DAVIS, E.J. and SCHIRMER, I.A. (eds) (1987) *Sustainability Issues in Agricultural Development: Proceedings of the Seventh Agriculture Sector Symposium* (Washington DC: World Bank).

DELGADO, G.L. and MELLOR, J.W. (1984) 'A structural view of policy issues in African agricultural development', *American Journal of Agricultural Economics*, 66, 5, pp. 665–670.

DI CASTRI, F. (1987) 'The Evolution of Terrestrial Ecosystems', in O. Ravera (ed.), *Ecological Assessment of Environmental Degradation, Pollution and Recovery* (Amsterdam: Elsevier).

DIXON, J.A., JAMES, D.E. and SHERMAN, P.B. (1989) *The Economics of Dryland Management* (London: Earthscan).

DORNER, P. (1972) *Land Reform and Economic Development* (Harmondsworth: Penguin).

DREGNE, H.E. (1983) *Desertification of Arid Lands* (New York: Harwood).

DREWNOWSKI, J. (1977) 'Poverty: its meaning and measurement', *Development and Change*, 8, pp. 183–208.

DYSON-HUDSON, N. (1984) 'Adaptive resource use by African pastoralists', in Di Castri *et al.*, (eds), *Ecological Practice* (Paris: UNESCO).

ECKHOLM, E.P. (1976) *Losing Ground: Environmental Stress and World Food Prospects* (New York: Norton).

EDWARDS, E.O. AMANI, H. FRANKENBERGER, T.R. and JANSEN, D. (1989) *Agricultural Sector Assessment: A Strategy for the Future Development of Agriculture in Botswana* (Gaborone: Ministry of Agriculture).

EHRLICH, P.R. DAILY, G.C. and GOULDER, L.H. (1992) *Population growth, economic growth and market economies*. Stanford University, mimeo.

EHRLICH, P.R. EHRLICH, A.H. DAILY, G.C. (1992) *Population, ecosystem services and the human food supply*. Stanford University, Morrison Institute for Population and Resource Studies, Working Paper 0044.

FALLOUX, F. and MUKENDI, A. (eds) (1988) *Desertification Control and Renewable Resource Management in the Sahelian and Sudanian Zones of West Africa*. Technical Paper 70 (Washington DC: World Bank).

FEDER, G. and NORONHA, R. (1987) 'Land rights systems and agricultural development in sub-Saharan Africa', *World Bank Research Observer*, 2, 2.

FEI, J.C.H. and RANIS, G. (1978) 'Agrarianism, Dualism, and Economic Development', in S.P. Singh (ed.), *Underdevelopment to Developing Economies* (Oxford: OUP) pp. 1–42.

FIDZANI, N.H. (1985) *A Critical Evaluation of the Botswana Livestock Industry's Pricing Policy* (Washington DC: World Bank).

FOOD AND AGRICULTURAL ORGANIZATION (1985) *The State of Food and Agriculture 1984* (Rome: FAO).

FOOD AND AGRICULTURAL ORGANIZATION (1986) *Land, Food and People* (Rome: FAO).

FOWKES, J.D. (1985) *The Contribution of the Tourist Industry to the Economy of Botswana* (Gaborone: Kalahari Conservation Society).

GAMMAGE, S. (1990) *Report on Environmental Economics in the Developing World* (Washington DC: USAID).

GARCIA-BARRIOS, R. and GARCIA-BARRIOS, L. (1990) 'Environmental and technological degradation in peasant agriculture: a consequence of development in Mexico', *World Development*, 18, 11, pp. 1569–85.

GHAI, D. and RADWAN, S. (eds) (1983) *Agrarian Policies and Rural Poverty in Africa* (Geneva: ILO).

GHAI, D. and SMITH, L.D. (1987) *Agricultural Prices, Policy and Equity in sub-Saharan Africa* (Boulder, Colorado: Lynne Rienner).

GILBERT, A.J. (1990) *Natural resource accounts: theory, logistics and application to Botswana*. Paper presented to the ISEE conference, Washington DC, May 1990.

GITHINJI, M. and PERRINGS, C. (1993) 'Social and Economic Sustainability in the Use of Biotic Resources in Sub-Saharan Africa', *Ambio*, 27, pp. 110–16.

GOODLAND, R. and LEDOC, G. (1987) 'Neoclassical economics and principles of sustainable development', *Ecological Modelling*, 38.

GRAINGER, A. (1990) *The Threatening Desert – Controlling Desertification* (London: Earthscan).

GREEN, R.H. (1989) 'Articulating stabilization programmes and structural adjustment' in S. Commander (ed.), *Structural Adjustment and Agriculture: Theory and Practice in Africa and Latin America* (London: ODI) pp. 35–54.

GROUZIS, M. (1990) *Dynamics of Sahelian Ecological Systems: The Case of Oursi Pond, Burkino Faso*. Paper presented at the Technical Meeting on Savanna Development and Pasture Production, Woburn, November 1990.

GYEKYE, A. and MAZONDE, I.N. (1989) *A Study of the Minimum Wage Possibilities in Agricultural and Domestic Service Sectors of the Botswana Economy. Volume II: Agricultural Sector Report* (Gaborone: NIR and University of Botswana).

HARDIN, G. (1968) 'The Tragedy of the Commons', *Science*, 162, pp. 1243–124.

HARE, F.K. (1977) 'Climate and Desertification', in *UN Conference on Desertification, Desertification: Its Causes and Consequences* (Oxford, Pergamon Press), pp. 63–168.

HARRISON, P. (1987) *The Greening of Africa* (London: Paladin Grafton Books).

HARVEY, C. and LEWIS, S. (1990) *Policy Choice and Development Performance in Botswana* (London: Macmillan).

HARVEY, C. (1992) *Botswana: Is the economic miracle over?* IDS Discussion Paper 298 (Brighton: IDS).

HARVEY, C. (ed.) (1988) *Agricultural Pricing Policy in Africa: Four Country Case Studies* (London: Macmillan).

HERSKOVITS, M.J. (1940) *The Economic Life of Primitive Peoples* (New York: Alfred Knopf).

HOBEN, A. (1973) *Land Tenure Among the Amhara of Ethiopia* (Chicago: University of Chicago Press).

HOLLING, C.S. (1973) 'Resilience and Stability of Ecological Systems', *Annual Review of Ecological Systems*, 4, pp. 1–24.

HOLLING, C.S. (1986) 'The Resilience of Terrestrial Ecosystems: Local Surprise and Global Change'. In W.C. Clark and R.E. Munn (eds) *Sustainable Development of the Biosphere* (Cambridge: Cambridge University Press).

HOWARD, R. (1980) 'Formation and Stratification of the Peasantry in Colonial Ghana', *Journal of Peasant Studies*, 8, 1, pp. 61–80.

HOWE, C. (1979) *Natural Resource Economics* (New York: Wiley).

INTERGOVERNMENTAL PANEL OF CLIMATE CHANGE (1990) *Scientific Assessment of Climate Change* (Geneva and Nairobi: World Meteorological Organization and United Nations Environment Programme).

JAMAL, V. (1983) 'Nomads and Farmers: Incomes and Poverty in Rural Somalia', in D. Ghai and S. Radwan (eds), *Agrarian Policies and Rural Poverty in Africa* (Geneva: ILO) pp. 281–311.

JAMES, R.W. (1971) *Land Tenure and Policy in Tanzania* (Toronto: University of Toronto Press).

JEFFERIS, K. (1991) 'The Economy in 1990', *Barclays Botswana Economic Review*, 2, 1, pp. 1–18.

JOHNSON, O.E.G. (1989) 'The agricultural sector in IMF stand-by arrangements', in S. Commander (ed.), *Structural Adjustment and Agriculture: Theory and Practice in Africa and Latin America* (London: ODI) pp. 19–34.

JUNANKAR, P.N. (1989) 'The response of peasant farmers to price incentives: the use and misuse of profit functions', *Journal of Development Studies*, 25, 2, pp. 169–182.

KATES, R.W., JOHNSON, D.L. and HARING, K.J. (1977) 'Population, society and desertification', in *United Nations Conference on Desertificiation, Desertification: Its Causes and Consequences* (Oxford: Pergamon Press) pp. 261–318.

KONCZACKI, Z.A. (1978) *The Economics of Pastoralism: A Case Study of Sub-Saharan Africa* (London: Frank Cass).

LEE, R.D. (1972) 'Population growth and the beginnings of sedentary life among the !Kung Bushmen', in Spooner, B. (ed.) *Population Growth: Anthropological Implications* (Cambridge, MA: MIT Press).

LEIBENSTEIN, H. (1957) *Economic Backwardness and Economic Growth* (New York: Wiley).

LIPTON, M. (1968) 'The Theory of the Optimizing Peasant', *Journal of Development Studies*, pp. 327–51.

LIPTON, M. (1987) 'Limits of price policy for agriculture: which way for the World Bank', *Development Policy Review*, 5, 2.

LIVINGSTONE, I. (1981) 'Supply responses of peasant producers: the effect of own-account consumption on the supply of marketed output', in *Development Economics and Policy: Readings* (London: George Allen and Unwin) pp. 272–276.

LOVE, R., BABIKANYISA, V. and MREMA, M. (1989) *An Assessment of the Impact of Macroeconomic Policy Adjustment on the Performance of the Agricultural Sector in Botswana* (Gaborone: University of Botswana).

MARKANDYA, A. (1991) *Technology, Environment and Employment: A Survey*. World Employment Programme Working Paper (Geneva: ILO).

MARKANDYA, A. and PERRINGS, C. (1991) *Accounting for Ecologically Sustainable Development* (Rome: FAO).

McGOWAN INTERNATIONAL AND COOPERS & LYBRAND (1987) *National Land Management and Livestock Project: Incentive/ Disincentives Study. Volume 1. Final Report prepared for the Ministry of Local Government and Lands, Botswana.*

MERRON, G. (1987) 'Netting results', *Marung*, 6, 28, pp. 9–13.

MIFSUD, F.R. (1967) *Customary Land Law in Africa* (Rome: FAO).

MIGOT-ADHOLLA, S., HAZELL, P., BLAREL, B. and PLACE, F. (1991) 'Indigenous land rights in Sub-Saharan Africa: a constraint on productivity?', *The World Bank Economic Review*, 5, 1, pp. 155–175.

MILLAR, C. (1987) 'Exploitation of Botswana's Forest Reserves: A Cause for Concern?', *Forestry Association of Botswana Journal*, pp. 33–41.

MOSLEY, P. and SMITH, L. (1989) 'Structural adjustment and agricultural performance in sub-Saharan Africa 1980–1987', *Journal of International Development*, 1, 3, pp. 321–355.

MUGGERIDGE, E. (1988) *BNCS Technical Report: Forestry* (Gaborone: Ministry of Local Government And Lands).

NASH, M. (1967) 'The social context of economic choice in a small society', in G. Dalton (ed), *Tribal and Peasant Economies* (Austin: University of Texas Press).

NCHUNGA, M. (1988) *BNCS Technical Report: Wildlife* (Gaborone: Ministry of Lands and Local Government).

NORMAN, D.W. (1977) 'Economic Rationality of Traditional Hausa Dryland Farmers in the North of Nigeria', in R.D. Stevens (ed.) *Tradition and Dynamics in Small-Farm Agriculture* (Ames, Iowa: Iowa State University Press).

NUGENT, J. and GILLASPY, T. (1983) 'Old age pension and fertility in rural areas of less developed countries: some evidence from Mexico', *Economic Development and Cultural Change*, 31, pp. 809–29.

PARRY, M. (1990) *Climate Change and World Agriculture* (London: Earthscan).

PEARCE, D.W. (1987) *Economic Values and the Natural Environment: The 1987 Denman Lecture* (Cambridge: Granta Publications).

PEARCE, D.W. (1991) 'Population growth', in D.W. Pearce (ed.), *Blueprint 2* (London: Earthscan) pp. 109–37.

PEARCE, D.W. and TURNER, R.K. (1990) *Economics of Natural Resources and the Environment* (London: Harvester-Wheatsheaf).

PEARCE, D.W., BARBIER, E.B. and MARKANDYA, A. (1988) *Environmental Economics and Decision-making in Sub-Saharan Africa.* LEEC Paper 88–01 (London: IIED).

PEARCE, D.W., BARBIER, E.B. and MARKANDYA, A. (1990) *Sustainable Development: Economics and Environment in the Third World* (London: Earthscan).

PERRINGS, C. (1985) 'The Natural Economy Revisited', *Economic Development and Cultural Change*, 33, 4, pp. 829–50.

PERRINGS, C. (1989a) 'An Optimal Path to Extinction? Poverty and Resource Degradation in the Open Agrarian Economy', *Journal of Development Economics*, 30, pp. 1–24.

PERRINGS, C. (1989b) 'Debt and Resource Degradation in Low Income Countries: The Adjustment Problem and the Perverse Effects of Poverty in Sub-Saharan Africa', in H. Singer and S. Sharma (eds), *Economic Development and World Debt* (London: Macmillan), pp. 321–34.

PERRINGS, C. (1993) *Pastoral strategies in Sub-Saharan Africa: The economic and ecological sustainability of dryland range management.* Environment Working Paper 57, Washington DC, World Bank.

PERRINGS, C., GILBERT, A.J., PEARCE, D.W. and HARRISON, A. (1989) *Natural Resource Accounts for Botswana: Environmental Accounting forna Natural Resource-Based Economy.* LEEC Paper 89–11 (London: IIED).

PERRINGS, C., GYEKYE, A., LOVE, R., BOYD, M. and OSAFO-GYIMAH, K. (1990) *Income and Employment Generation in Rural Botswana: Second Report* (Gaborone: University of Botswana).

PERRINGS, C., PEARCE, D.W., OPSHOOR, J.B., ARTSZEN, J.W. and GILBERT, A.J. (1988) *Economics for Sustainable Development: Botswana – A Case Study* (Gland: IUCN).

PIELOU, E.C. (1975) *Ecological Diversity* (New York: Wiley).

PINGALI, P.L., BIGOT, Y. and BINSWANGER, H.B. (1985) *Agricultural Mechanization and the Evolution of Farming Systems in Sub Saharan Africa* (Washington DC: World Bank).

PRYOR, F.L. and MAURER, S.B. (1982) 'On induced economic change in precapitalist societies', *Journal of Development Economics*, 10, pp. 325–53.

RAO, J.M. (1986) 'Agriculture in Recent Development Theory', *Journal of Development Economics*, 22, pp. 41–86.

RAO, J.M. (1989) 'Agricultural supply response: a survey', *Agricultural Economics*, 3, 1, pp. 1–22.

REBER, H.H. and BORKOTT, H. (1983) 'Soil as a Renewable Resource: New Literature on Ecological Value, Regenerating Capacity, and Tolerance Limits of the Community of Organisms in Agricultural Soils', *Natural Resources and Development*, 17, pp. 29–42.

REPETTO, R. (1986) *World Enough and Time* (New Haven: Yale University Press).
REPETTO, R. (1989) 'Economic incentives for sustainable production', in G. Schramme and J.J. Warford (eds), *Environmental Management and Economic Development* (Baltimore: Johns Hopkins for the World Bank) pp. 69–86.
REPETTO, R. and HOLMES, J. (1983) 'The role of population in resource depletion in developing countries', *Population and Development Review*, 9, 4, pp. 609–32.
REPUBLIC OF BOTSWANA (1982) *Migration in Botswana: Patterns, Causes and Consequences. Final Report of the National Migration Study* (Gaborone: MFDP, CSO).
REPUBLIC OF BOTSWANA (1985–88) *Farm Management Survey Results* (Gaborone: Ministry of Agriculture).
REPUBLIC OF BOTSWANA (1985–1990) *Botswana Agricultural Statistics* (Gaborone: CSO).
REPUBLIC OF BOTSWANA (1985) *National Development Plan 1985–91 (NDP6)* (Gaborone: Government Printer).
REPUBLIC OF BOTSWANA (1986–89) *Labour Statistics* (Gaborone: CSO).
REPUBLIC OF BOTSWANA (1987) *Population Projections 1981–2011* (Gaborone: CSO).
REPUBLIC OF BOTSWANA (1988) *Household Income and Expenditure Survey: 1985/86* (Gaborone: CSO).
REPUBLIC OF BOTSWANA (1989) *The Botswana National Conservation Strategy* (Gaborone: Ministry of Local Government and Lands, Department of Town and Regional Planning).
REPUBLIC OF BOTSWANA (1990a) *Report of the Presidential Commission on the Review of the Incomes Policy* (Gaborone: Government Printer).
REPUBLIC OF BOTSWANA (1990b) *National Development Plan 7: Final Macro Outline* (Gaborone: Ministry of Finance and Development Planning).
REPUBLIC OF BOTSWANA (1990c) *The Revised National Policy on Incomes, Employment, Prices and Profits, Government Paper No. 1* (Gaborone: Government Printer).
REPUBLIC OF BOTSWANA (1990d) *Social Accounting Matrix 1985/86* (Gaborone: CSO).
REPUBLIC OF BOTSWANA (1991) *A Poverty Datum Line for Botswana November 1989* (Gaborone: CSO).
REPUBLIC OF BOTSWANA, MINISTRY OF FINANCE AND DEVELOPMENT PLANNING (1991) *National Development Plan 1991–1997 (NDP7)* (Gaborone: Government Printer).
ROHRBACH, D. (1988) *Agricultural Marketing and Support Services.* Diagnostic paper prepared for the Agricultural Sector Assessment (Gaborone: Ministry of Agriculture).
RUDDLE, K. and MANSHARD, W. (1981) *Renewable Natural Resources and the Environment: Pressing Problems in the Developing World* (Dublin: Tycooly International for United Nations University).
RUKUNI, M. and EICHER, C.K. (eds) (1987) *Food Security for Southern Africa* (Harare: Department of Agricultural Economics, University of Zimbabwe).

SAHLINS, M. (1974) *Stonge Age Economics* (London: Tavistock Press).

SCHAEFFER, D.J., HERRRICKS, E., and KERSTER, H. (1988) 'Ecosystem Health: I. Measuring Ecosystem Health', *Environmental Management*, 12 (4), pp. 445–55.

SCHULTZ, T.W. (1964) *Transforming Traditional Agriculture* (New Haven: Yale University Press).

SCOONES, I. (1990) *Why are there so many animals? Cattle population dynamics in the communal areas of Zimbabwe*, Paper prepared for the Technical Meeting on Savannah Development and Pasture Production, Commonwealth Secretariat and the Overseas Development Institute, Woburn, November.

SCOVILLE, J.G. and NYAMADZABO, T. (1988) *Report on the Impact of Minimum Wages in Botswana* (Gaborone: Ministry of Finance and Development Planning).

SEN, A. (1981) *Poverty and Famines: An Essay on Entitlement and Deprivation* (Oxford: Oxford University Press).

SNIJDERS, T.A.B. (1986) 'Interstation correlation and non-stationarity of Burkino Faso rainfall', *Journal of Climate and Applied Meteorology*, 25, pp. 524–31.

SPEECE, M. (1989) 'Market performance of agricultural commodities in semi-arid South Kordofan, Sudan, *Geoforum*, 20, 4, pp. 409–24.

SWEET, J. (1987) *The communal grazing cell experience in Botswana* (Gaborone: MOA, Department of Agricultural Research).

TURNER, R.K. (1988) 'Sustainability, conservation and pollution control: an overview', in R.K. Turner (ed.), *Sustainable Environmental Management: Principles and Practice* (London: Belhaven Press).

UNITED NATIONS (1986) *World Economic Survey 1986: Current Trends and Policies in the World Economy* (New York: UN).

UNITED NATIONS CONFERENCE ON DESERTIFICATION (1977) *Desertification: Its Causes and Consequences* (Oxford: Pergamon Press).

UNITED NATIONS DEVELOPMENT PROGRAM (1990) *Human Development Report 1990* (Oxford: OUP).

VAN DER POEL, J. (1980) *Rainfall Erosivity and its Use for Soil Loss Estimation* (MOA: Department of Agricultural Services).

VAN GINNEKAN, W. (1988) *Trends in Employment and Labour Incomes* (Geneva: ILO).

VAN GINNEKAN, W. and VAN DER HOEVEN, R. (1989) 'Industrialization, employment and earnings', *International Labour Review*, 128, 5, pp. 571–99.

VIAK (1985) *Eastern Botswana Regional Water Study* (3 vols) (Stockholm: VIAK).

WADE, R. (1987) 'The Management of Common Property Resources: Finding a Cooperative Solution', *World Bank Research Observer*, 2, pp. 219–35.

WALKER, B.H. and NOY-MEIR, I. (1982) 'Aspects of the stability and resilience of savanna ecosystems', in B.J. Huntley and B.H. Walker (eds), *Ecology of Tropical Savannas* (Berlin: Springer-Verlag).

WARFORD, J. (1987) *Environment and Development* (Washington DC: World Bank/IMF Development Committee).

WARFORD, J. (1989) 'Environmental management and economic policy in developing countries', in G. Schramme and J.J. Warford (eds), *Environmental Management and Economic Development* (Baltimore: Johns Hopkins for the World Bank) pp. 7–22.

WESTOBY, M., WALKER, B. and NOY-MEIR, I. (1989) 'Opportunistic management for rangelands not at equilibrium', *Journal of Range Management*, 42, 4, pp. 266–74.

WORLD BANK (1986) *Sudan Forestry Sector Review* (Washington DC: World Bank).

WORLD BANK (1987) *World Development Report 1987* (Oxford: OUP for the World Bank).

WORLD BANK (1988) *Education in Sub-Saharan Africa* (Washington DC: World Bank).

WORLD BANK (1989) *Botswana: Financial Policies for Diversified Growth* (Washington DC: World Bank).

WORLD BANK (1990) *World Development Report 1990* (Oxford: OUP for the World Bank).

WORLD COMMISSION ON ENVIRONMENT AND DEVELOPMENT (1987) *Our Common Future* (London: Oxford University Press).

WORLD RESOURCES INSTITUTE (1990) *World Resources 1990–1991* (Oxford: Oxford University Press).

YOUNIS, A.S. (1987) *Soil Conservation in Developing Countries* (Washington DC: World Bank).

YUDELMAN, M. (1964) *Africans on the Land* (Cambridge, Mass,: Harvard University Press).

Index